CliffsNotes®

AP U.S. History with CD-ROM

3RD EDITION

by

Paul Soifer and Abraham Hoffman

WILEY

Wiley Publishing, Inc.

Publisher's Acknowledgments

Editorial

Project Editor: Stephanie Corby

Acquisitions Editor: Kris Fulkerson

Production

Proofreaders: Betty Kish, Vickie Broyles

Wiley Publishing, Inc. Composition Services

Authors' Acknowledgments

We deeply appreciate the loving support our wives — Maralyn and Susan — and our children — Harris, Felicia, Justine, and Josh and Greg — showed us during the writing of this study guide. They're all 5s in our book.

CliffsNotes® AP U.S. History with CD-ROM, 3rd Edition

Published by
Wiley Publishing, Inc.
111 River Street
Hoboken, NJ 07030-5774
www.wiley.com

Copyright © 2009 Paul Soifer and Abraham Hoffman.

Soifer, Paul.
[CliffsAP United States history]
Cliffsnotes AP U.S. history with CD-ROM / by Paul Soifer and Abraham Hoffman. — 3rd ed.
   p. cm.
Originally published as: CliffsAP United States history. 3rd ed. Foster City, CA : IDG Books Worldwide, c2001.
ISBN-13: 978-0-470-40216-0
ISBN-10: 0-470-40216-4
1. United States—History—Examinations—Study guides. 2. Advanced placement programs (Education) —Examinations—Study guides. I. Hoffman, Abraham.
II. Title. III. Title: Cliffsnotes AP United States history with CD-ROM. IV. Title: AP U.S. history with CD-ROM.
E178.25.S65 2009
973'.076—dc22
                        2008048238

Printed in the United States of America

10 9 8 7 6 5 4 3 2 1

WILEY

Table of Contents

PART III: STUDYING UNITED STATES HISTORY

Reading United States History

An Overview of United States History

PART IV: FOUR FULL-LENGTH PRACTICE TESTS

PART I

INTRODUCTION

Introducing the Advanced Placement U.S. History Examination

The Advanced Placement (AP) Examination in United States History is one of the most popular of the subject examinations administered by the College Board in cooperation with high schools and colleges across the country. Every May more than 150,000 students take the exam. Although the exam is open to all students, most are high school juniors enrolled in a special AP U.S. history class that is similar to a university-level survey course in terms of the depth of coverage and the reading required. Those who score well on the exam can receive advanced standing, credit, or both from the college they plan to attend.

Format of the Exam

The AP U.S. history exam is three hours and five minutes long and consists of eighty multiple-choice and two types of essay questions. The exam questions are intended to measure your factual knowledge of the material usually covered in a university U.S. history survey course. Most questions require that you recall specific information about key events, personalities, or movements in U.S. history. There are five possible answers for each question (A through E), and you indicate the correct one by filling in a small oval space in pencil on a separate answer sheet. At the end of the time period for Section I, the answer sheet and the booklet containing the multiple-choice questions are turned in to the proctor. You have fifty-five minutes for Section I.

Section II, the essay portion of the exam, has three parts. Part A is the Document-Based Question (DBQ). All students write on the same DBQ. The DBQ asks you to write an essay based on your analysis of a group of documents and your understanding of the period of U.S. history referred to in the question. You are expected to analyze the documents, select those that are most relevant to the topic, draw on information not provided in the documents, and argue your interpretation effectively. Section II starts with a fifteen-minute required reading period. You will be instructed to use the time to go over the DBQ and documents, making notes and outlining your answer in the green question booklet; if time permits, you are also encouraged to review the essay choices in Parts B and C. As soon as you finish the DBQ, you can go on to the other essays. The suggested time for the DBQ is forty-five minutes.

The documents used in the DBQ cover a broad range of historical sources: excerpts from written materials such as diaries, letters, speeches, novels, magazine articles, court decisions, and laws as well as graphs, charts, tables, maps, photographs, political cartoons, and even artwork. There are usually seven to ten documents presented, and each is identified and dated.

Parts B and C provide you with a choice of essays. You are required to answer one question in each part, and a total of seventy minutes is allotted to write two essays. The instructions encourage you to spend five minutes planning and thirty minutes writing each essay.

The essay questions in Section II are in a green booklet; you are given a pink booklet in which to answer both the DBQ and the standard essays.

You should be aware that the College Board may change the format of the exam from time to time. In recent years, for example, the number of multiple-choice questions has been reduced and the time allowed for essay writing has been increased. Your AP teacher will inform you of any revisions in the exam format. The overall intent of the exam, however, remains the same — to evaluate your ability to analyze and comprehend U.S. history as taught at the college level.

Subject Matter of the Exam

In theory, the exam covers the period from the earliest settlements to the present; in reality, equal emphasis is not given to each era or theme in American history. The percentage distribution of questions in the multiple-choice section roughly breaks down as follows:

Colonial America to the New Nation (1789)	17%
New Nation to World War I (1914)	50%
World War I (1915) to present	33%

The focus is clearly on the nineteenth and twentieth centuries. Although there may be multiple-choice questions on events after 1975, the DBQ and the standard essays won't focus entirely on contemporary U.S. history. This focus reflects the amount of material that can be reasonably covered in your AP U.S. history class by the time the exam is given in May.

The exam does not completely accept the maxim that history is "past politics." Only about a third of the questions in both the multiple-choice and free-response sections deal with political institutions and public policy. Another third emphasize social and economic history, and the rest pertain to international relations as well as social and cultural movements.

Neither the time periods nor the subject areas covered by the exam are absolute. You will be expected to compare (or contrast) developments in different eras — for example, progressivism and the New Deal — and explore the economic, social, or cultural impact of a political decision.

The College Board now provides you with the time frame the DBQ will cover. On the 2000 exam, the period was from 1875–1925, and on the 2001, it will be from 1920–1970. (The sample DBQ in Practice Test 1 is on the period 1875–1925.) This information is extremely helpful to you in allocating your preparation time, and it emphasizes that the focus of the exam is on the nineteenth and twentieth centuries. It will do little good to complain after the fact that you devoted all your studying to colonial America and the American Revolution, for example, and just skimmed over what you were told the DBQ would cover. The DBQ on the 1999 exam, however, dealt with the colonies on the eve of the American Revolution (1750–1776).

How the Exam Is Scored

The exam is scored on a five-point scale:

5 — extremely well qualified

4 — well qualified

3 — qualified

2 — possibly qualified

1 — no recommendation

A grade of 3 is considered passing. The breakdown of the grades on the 1999 exam was as follows:

Grade	Percentage Earning Grade
5	8.89.4%
4	19.819.6%
3	21.921.8%
2	36.335.9%
1	13.2%

Source http://www.collegeboard.org/ap/history/html/grade99.html.

As you can see from the grading scale, a score of 3 is considered passing. Colleges and universities participating in the Advanced Placement Program set their own policies with respect to awarding advanced standing and/or credit for AP examinations. You should check with your college counselor or the schools you plan to apply to for their AP policy.

Scoring the Multiple-Choice Section

The multiple-choice section is worth fifty percent of the score. The difficulty of the questions is such that you must answer about sixty percent correctly to "pass" with a grade of 3. A quarter point is taken off for each incorrect answer. The deduction is intended to discourage "wild" guessing. The multiple-choice score is computed by subtracting the number of wrong answers multiplied by one quarter ($\frac{1}{4}$ or .25) from the number of correct answers. While no points are lost if you leave a question blank, skipping too many will not give you enough points for a passing grade. If you can narrow down the possible answer to two or three choices, guessing may be worthwhile.

Grading the Essays

While the multiple-choice answer sheets are fed into a computer and automatically scored, AP readers grade the essays. About half are college professors and the other half come from the ranks of high school AP teachers. No distinction is made between the college professor and the high school teacher; each brings his or her own expertise to the reading table. AP readers don't just sit down and begin reading. They undergo an intensive orientation session and work toward a clear understanding of what scores apply to what levels of quality the essays will have.

AP readers face a formidable task. Each year the number of students taking the AP U.S. history exam increases (now over 150,000), which means that the readers must go through about 450,000 essays in a week's time. Every morning they face a pile of essays that must be read quickly and efficiently. There is no set time limit for reading an essay, but pressure to get through the pile is a fact of life. On average, a reader takes ninety seconds to grade an essay. All the time you put into studying for the test, the hours, weeks, and months you gave to your AP class, are reduced in the end to a few minutes for the free-response section.

All the readers read the DBQ; they are assigned the essays in Part B depending on how many students have answered individual questions. Your standard essays will not be read by the same person who reads your DBQ. Readers are identified only by their own code numbers. This system of confidentiality protects both the student and the readers and insures a maximum degree of objectivity in grading the essays.

Seven readers, including a table leader, work as a team. Before each annual AP session, the table leaders meet and begin reading essays, searching for representative examples of student work at several levels of quality. These essays are photocopied and presented to the AP readers at their orientation. Under the leadership of the table leader, the readers evaluate them, and the evaluations are then compared with the consensus score reached earlier by the table leaders. At the end of the process, all readers understand and agree on the criteria by which the essays are measured.

Readers use a list of standards in scoring the essays. The standards are on a scale from 0 to 9 and grouped from a high range of 8 to 9 to a low of 0 to 1. The following is a typical example of the standards on the 9-point scale that gives you a general idea of what the readers are looking for in the DBQ:

Standards for the DBQ	
Score	*Comments*
8–9	Contains a well-developed thesis. Makes thorough use of most of the documents. Supports thesis with substantial and significant outside information. Is well written and organized. May contain minor errors.
5–7	Contains a thesis. Uses some of the documents. Supports the thesis with some outside information. Limited analysis. Writing and organization are acceptable. Factual errors do not detract from essay.
2–4	Confused or poorly developed thesis. Quotes or briefly cites documents. Contains minimal or scattered outside information. Poorly written and organized. May contain major factual errors.
0–1	No thesis statement. Ignores the documents or has no understanding of them. No outside information. Difficult to understand because of poor writing and organization. Numerous major factual errors.

The table leaders usually supply a list of suggested outside information examples to aid the readers in evaluating the DBQ.

The standard essays are scored by the same system. Each of the essay questions has a list of standards that may call for student awareness of specific content. A 1988 free-response question, for example, called for an analysis of Lincoln's Emancipation Proclamation in light of his statement in 1858 which seemed to accept racial inequality. Students were asked to reconcile Lincoln's positions.

The standards for this question included the following:

Standards for the General Essay	
Score	*Comments*
8–9	Clear argument regarding the issue of reconciliation. Sophisticated understanding of Lincoln's view on race and slavery. Solid understanding of historical context of the 1850s and 1860s; may emphasize one period. Accurate factual evidence. May contain minor errors.
5–7	Addresses issue of reconciliation. Understanding of Lincoln's views on race and slavery. Understanding of the historical context of the 1850s and 1860s; may emphasize one period. Some factual evidence presented but may contain errors.
2–4	Attempts to address issue of reconciliation. Discussion of Lincoln's views and of 1850s–1860s historical context may be uneven. Limited factual evidence. Some major errors.
0–1	No attempt to address issue of reconciliation. No factual evidence, or evidence irrelevant, inaccurate, confused. Inept or inappropriate response to question. Numerous major errors.

Although the grading standards are given in a range, the essays receive a single number score. Section II is worth half of the total score. Forty-five percent of your score in Section II is the DBQ, and the two standard essays count for a total of 55 percent.

Questions Commonly Asked about the AP U.S. History Examination

The Advanced Placement Examination in United States History is often called the toughest test a student will ever take. With that reputation in mind, you naturally want to know as much about the exam as possible. The following are questions students have asked. You'll certainly have others to put to your AP teacher.

Q. What should I bring to the exam?

A. Two Number 2 pencils with good erasers, two medium ballpoint pens with dark blue or black ink, and a watch; leave everything else — notes, study guides, books — at home.

You have to use a Number 2 pencil to fill in the answer sheet for the multiple-choice section. It should not be sharpened to a fine point. A pencil point that is somewhat rounded is easier to use when marking the answer sheet. Number 3 pencils make marks that are too light and may not be picked up by the electronic scanner. Always have a spare pencil if one breaks. Your mark should be made firmly and clearly.

You should also have a high-quality eraser in case you change your mind about an answer. You must erase that choice thoroughly or else the scoring machine may register two answers for one question. This will be marked wrong.

Don't use pencil to write your essays. Invest some money in two good, medium ball-point pens. A cheap ball-point that you've had in your backpack all semester may smear the ink on the paper. The same is true for felt-tip pens that may skip or leave dots of ink on the paper. You want to avoid anything that makes your essays difficult to read.

Make sure you have the school code for your high school. Your AP teacher or your college guidance counselor can provide you with the number.

You should also have a watch. Although the proctor for the exam will keep you informed about the time, it is always helpful to be able to check the time yourself.

Q. Should I guess on the multiple-choice questions?

A. If you draw a complete blank on a question, you have two options: (1) you can put down a wild guess and almost certainly get it wrong or (2) you can go on to the next question. Wild guessing is a bad idea because a quarter point is deducted for each wrong answer. Leaving too many questions blank may not give you enough points to do well on the multiple-choice section. If you can eliminate two or three choices, make an "educated" guess from the remaining answers.

Q. Does penmanship and spelling count?

A. No, as long as things don't get out of control. With so little time allotted for each essay, the readers look for key phrases and content words; they don't worry if an occasional word is misspelled or subject and predicate don't agree. They understand that you're writing under pressure. If your handwriting is really poor, you must make an extra effort to write as legibly as possible. Remember how much time the readers will spend on your essays; it's impossible for them to take five minutes to "decode" what you've written.

Q. Where can I outline my ideas for the essay questions?

A. The best place to write an outline, make notes, or jot down key words and personalities is in the green booklet that contains the DBQ and standard essay questions. The booklet is yours to keep. Your essays go in a separate pink booklet. While you're not penalized for putting an outline in the pink booklet, it's not a good idea. You want your essay to look as clean as possible.

Q. Should I use all the documents in the DBQ?

A. You should use as many documents as you feel confident can be applied to your answer. Attempting to use all the documents, regardless of how well you understand them or how pertinent they are to your essay, may create an essay that seems artificial and strained. At the same time, you should use more than just two or three of the documents provided; your essay will otherwise lack the authority the documentation can give it. Your ability to use the documents authoritatively is an important element that the readers are looking for in the DBQ.

Q. If I finish my essay early, should I go back and add to it?

A. The readers don't have the time to twist the test booklet around to decipher asterisks and arrows pointing to additional material. Last minute revisions, inserted here and there, can create the impression that your essay is poorly organized. Chances are that you've said all you were going to the first time around, and it's not a good idea to put in something new at the end.

Q. What if I start an essay and then change my mind about doing it? Will I be penalized if I start another essay?

A. If this happens, just draw an X through what you've written. The reader will score only the essay you complete. There's a box on the pink booklet for the number of the essays; make sure this corresponds to the essays you've written. The only thing you lose by starting another essay is time. Use the fifteen-minute mandatory reading period between the multiple-choice and free-response sections to go over the essays and choose the ones you feel most confident in handling.

Q. How long should my essays be?

A. Your essays are scored on content, not length. Obviously, you want to write enough to answer the question as effectively as you can within the time limit of the exam. Avoid adding information that may not be particularly relevant to your answer just to show how much you know or to simply increase the number of pages. It's important to remember that an essay measures your powers of organization as well as your knowledge.

The essays require a balanced allotment of time. Don't hurt your score by devoting too much time to any one of the three questions in Part II. You won't be told that the forty-five minutes for the DBQ is up and to go on to the standard essays. Use the sample questions in this book to practice writing essays in the time allotted on the exam.

Q. How much outside reading should I do for the test?

A. Preparing for the exam involves more than going over your textbook and class notes. Your teacher can suggest useful history monographs or articles in journals. The "Reading United States History" section and the annotated bibliographies beginning on page 101 will also be helpful. Always take notes on what you read, and write a brief summary of the books, highlighting the main points and arguments of the authors. If time becomes a problem, go to the reviews of the books in major history journals.

Q. How much review time should my AP class have before the test?

A. The amount of time an individual teacher devotes to review naturally varies. About a month of intensive review is fairly typical, however.

Q. What about cramming?

A. If spending a year in an AP U.S. history class hasn't prepared you, then staying up until two in the morning the night before the test won't help much. Get a good night's sleep.

Q. When are the scores reported and who receives the scores?

A. The exam is graded in June, and the scores are reported by mail to students, their high schools, and any colleges students have designated by mid-July. If you want to get your scores early (July 1) by phone, you can call toll free (888) 308-0013. There is a fee for this service and you will need a valid credit card.

If you don't designate a college at the time you apply to take the exam or want to have your grade report sent to an additional college, you can still have the scores sent. To do this, contact

AP Services
P.O. Box 6671
Princeton, NJ 08541-6671
Phone (609) 771-7300
Fax (609) 530-0482
E-mail apexams@info.collegeboard.org

Q. Can I withhold from colleges or cancel my scores completely?

A. The answer to both questions is yes, but think about it. Keep in mind, that it is very unlikely for schools to penalize you for not doing well on the AP exam. The fact that you have taken an AP class is a strong indication of your willingness to challenge yourself and to take on added academic responsibilities. These are attributes that interest college admissions officers. If you still want to withhold or cancel your scores, contact the College Board's AP Services. There is a fee for withholding scores but no charge for canceling them. In both cases, requests must be received by AP Services by June 15 of the year you take the exam.

General Test-Taking Strategies for the AP U.S. History Examination

Doing well on the AP U.S. History Examination requires a year of intensive study. You have to be highly motivated and willing to commit the time and energy it takes to prepare properly. While there are no easy shortcuts, the following are helpful hints for scoring high on the multiple-choice section and writing effective DBQ and standard essays. Part II provides tips on handling the specific types of multiple-choice questions and essays that come up on the exam. In addition, basic writing strategies that take into account what AP readers are looking for and suggestions for projects that AP students have found helpful are included.

Hints for the Multiple-Choice Questions

The multiple-choice questions on the exam consist of a question or a sentence stem and five possible answers. The cardinal rule is **always read the question or stem and all the five choices before you mark your answer.** If the first few phrases convince you that the answer is obvious, read the entire question anyway. You may run into an EXCEPT, NOT, or LEAST at the end that turns the right answer upside down. EXCEPT, NOT, and LEAST are markers for what has been called the "reverse multiple-choice." For example: "All of the following happened to Lincoln EXCEPT," followed by four things that did happen to Lincoln and one that didn't — the right answer is the one that didn't. You also need to remember that while each question has a correct answer, the other choices may not be wrong. They may be good answers, just not as good as the correct one. If answer **B** sounds right, hold on; answer **C** may be better.

The multiple-choice section tests your analytical skills as well as factual knowledge about U.S. history. There may be questions based on tables, graphs, or charts that ask you to find an answer that correctly interprets the data. You may have to interpret the meaning of a political cartoon, figure out the point of view of the author of a quoted passage, or recognize important facts from a map. How to handle these types of questions is discussed in Part II.

But regardless of the format, it all comes down to one thing: **You must read the entire question and all the answer choices before putting down an answer.** You're allowed to mark up the question booklet. Take advantage of this privilege by underlining dates, names, or concepts in the question that might help you determine the right answer.

After reading the question and the choices, the correct answer may be crystal clear. Not all of the questions have the same difficulty; some are easier than others. If you're stumped, the trick is to weed out as many of the answers as possible. One or more of the answers may be obviously wrong. When two of the five choices indicate opposite extremes, for example, one or both of them may be incorrect. Put a line through any answers you eliminate in the question booklet:

(A)
~~(B)~~
(C)
(D)
~~(E)~~

The right answer should become easier to identify; if it doesn't, you can make an "educated" guess from the remaining choices. **Avoid wild guessing**. When you can't narrow down the answers, go on to the next question and be sure to clearly mark the one you skip so that you can look at it again, time permitting. Make all such marks only in the *test booklet,* never on the answer sheet. Stray pencil marks may be interpreted by the computer as an answer. Remember that leaving too many questions blank won't give you enough points for a good score. When you skip a question, make sure that you fill in the correct space on the answer sheet for the next question.

Another strategy in reading the choices is to look for "extreme" words such as "always," "never," "completely," "entirely," and "definitely." Since few things in history are ever absolute, these words may signal an incorrect answer. If four of the choices have words such as "demanded," "forced," "required," and "insisted" and the fifth choice is "recommended," there's a strong possibility that the moderate word provides the key to a correct answer.

Time is a factor in the multiple-choice section. You have fifty-five minutes to answer eighty questions, which breaks down to just over forty seconds per question. That's an average; you'll probably spend considerably less time on some questions and somewhat more on others. Questions that require you to analyze statistical data or evaluate an excerpt from a historical source obviously take longer than those that ask you to recall factual information. Still, you can't spend two or three minutes agonizing over the right answer. Use the practice multiple-choice questions in this book in a scientific way. Time how long it takes you to read a sentence stem and all five choices. Then allot the time you need to think about the answer, and toss in a couple of seconds for filling in the answer sheet. How much time did it take? If your personal number exceeds forty seconds, you're not working fast enough; if you have time to spare, you can think a bit more about the correct answer.

Doing the DBQ

Every student taking the AP U.S. History Examination answers the same DBQ. This question asks you to write an essay based on a group of documents *and* "outside" information that the documents themselves don't provide. The DBQ instructions are very clear on what is expected; make sure you thoroughly understand them.

The straightforward directions are often misunderstood or completely ignored by students. Ignore the requirement for outside information at your peril. No matter how well your essay is written or how brilliantly you handle the documents, heavy penalties will result if you don't draw on your own knowledge of United States history.

AP exam rules require students to spend fifteen minutes reading over the questions in Section II. Use this time effectively. Read the question *before* reading the documents. Underline key concepts and dates, and jot down facts and ideas that will provide the content and details for your essay. Let's say the DBQ deals with Jacksonian democracy. You might write down "pet banks," Panic of 1837, nullification crisis, Kitchen Cabinet, Maysville Road veto. Again, note-taking is permitted in the green booklet that contains the DBQ and the standard essays.

After reading the question, go on to the documents. Underline important facts or ideas and note the identification of the sources. In the case of the Jacksonian democracy question, some of the points you made about the question appear in the documents. Other details you jotted down about the period may not be expressed in the documents at all. This is precisely the kind of "outside" information that the AP readers want to see incorporated into the essay.

In answering the DBQ, it's important to stay in control of the documents. Use them to support your arguments and integrate as many as logically apply to the question, but don't shape the essay around them. The documents aren't arranged in the booklet in any particular order; they are simply listed as Document A, Document B . . . Students often make the mistake, however, of writing about them as they appear in the booklet. This order prevents you from creating your own outline in which your thesis argument is logically followed by the supporting evidence.

A very common error on the DBQ is to write an essay as a "laundry list," an essay in which each paragraph begins with the phrase "Document A shows" or "Document D tells us." The "laundry list" approach often results in a poor answer that simply provides a description of the documents. A good answer incorporates the source information into the essay. For example, "Chief Justice Taney's opinion in the Charles River Bridge case supports the idea . . . (Document H)." Understanding what an individual document is about is certainly important, but the key to a high score on the DBQ is your *analysis* of its relevance to the question.

Answering the Standard Essay Questions

Parts B and C of Section II each contain two standard essays (numbered 2 through 5), and you write on ONE question from each part. The suggested time for an essay is thirty-five minutes, which includes five minutes for planning your answer. Part B has questions that cover topics through the Civil War, while Part C focuses on the period from Reconstruction to the late twentieth century. The questions may treat political and economic developments as well as social and cultural trends.

Thirty-five minutes is not a great deal of time for developing and writing a coherent answer. Even if you have a clear understanding of the question, knowledge of what to put down for a strong answer, and the ability to express yourself clearly, your essay will probably be no longer than two pages. It becomes all important to write an essay that stresses the *quality* of what you say rather than the quantity. The format of the standard essays also emphasizes skill in organizing your ideas well and getting to the point quickly. You'll have very little time to go off on tangents or include facts that are not directly relevant to your answer.

The essay questions in Parts B and C do take into account the limited time. The questions may include four terms, events, or developments and ask you to analyze or assess the significance of three of these in the context of American history. For example:

Identify THREE of the following and evaluate the impact of each of the THREE on the coming of the American Revolution.

The Stamp Act Congress

The Boston Massacre

The First Continental Congress

Thomas Paine's *Common Sense*

Here, the question itself limits the scope of your answer. Although you may believe that factors other than those listed were important — for example, the Boston Tea Party or the Coercive Acts — incorporating these additional facts into your essay is a waste of time and, more important, doesn't answer the question. By the same token, the question clearly asks you to write on THREE events. Don't try to impress the reader and write on all four. This will just take precious time and will likely detract from your score.

Again, the cardinal rule is to **read all the questions** before deciding which you can write on most effectively. For questions that do not provide you with a list of terms, it is important to underline key points in each question, including dates, personalities and events, and significant concepts, which helps you focus on the parameters of the questions, their natural limits of time and subject. One of the standard essay questions from a previous exam asked how Americans perceived Manifest Destiny, either as a positive movement or as an example of imperialism. Students were asked to discuss this problem within the time frame of American expansion in the 1840s.

Many students ignored the 1840s and wrote about the Spanish-American War, the annexation of Hawaii, the Open Door policy, and even Vietnam. Another question dealt with the failure of the Socialist movement in America to become a viable political force between 1900 and 1940. Again, many essays followed such false trails as the French Revolution, McCarthyism, which was confused with the 1919 Palmer Raids and the Red Scare of the 1920s, and the Soviet invasion of Afghanistan. In both cases, a little effort spent on understanding what the question asked, particularly with respect to the time frame, was important. While an essay that ingeniously works out a connection between Columbus and American socialism in the early twentieth century might be interesting, it will receive a very low score because it ultimately fails to answer the question.

After selecting the essay, take a few minutes to think about what you will write. Organization is critical. Readers look for a clear thesis statement, a logical progression of evidence supporting the thesis, and a clear conclusion. Jot down a brief outline in the back of the green question booklet. It keeps you in control of what you're writing, and you'll be much less likely to go off the track. Then list key concepts, names, dates, and events next to each major topic you plan to cover. These will add detail and persuasiveness to your essay.

It's not unusual to feel a moment of panic as you read the essay questions. Suddenly all the questions seem equally difficult, equally impossible to answer. Take a deep breath; the panic will pass. Underlining key points in the questions, jotting down ideas, and making an outline all will remind you of the strengths you've developed in preparing for the test.

Hints on Writing Technique

In writing both the DBQ and standard essays, it's imperative that you follow the basic organization principles your English teachers have insisted on for years. Your first paragraph is an introduction and includes your thesis statement; the body of the essay presents evidence to support the thesis; the conclusion restates the thesis and provides a closing comment.

Beyond structuring your essay properly, there are other helpful techniques that you can use. One approach is the "give a little, take a lot" method of stating a thesis. In answering a question that asks you to "assess the validity" of a statement, you might concede that other points of view carry some weight. The answer to a question that asks about the causes of an event — the Civil War or the decision to drop the A-bomb on Japan in 1945, for example — should point out that historians disagree on the causes. Acknowledging these opposing interpretations and going on to state why the thesis you've chosen best fits the question enhances your essay. If you're familiar with the names of historians who have written on the subject, so much the better. Readers are impressed if you can show *accurate* and *appropriate* bibliographical knowledge.

One style of writing to avoid at all costs is "overwriting," making impossibly general statements that incorporate flowery verbs and adjectives. "The Jacksonians surged onto the scene"; "In the Progressive Era protest ran rampant"; "The Socialist movement roared into the twentieth century." Similarly, avoid sentences that are self-evident and add nothing to your essay. "Many things happened during 1952." Anders Henrikson collected all the bad writing and factual errors from his students' term papers in "When Life Reeked with Joy" *(Wilson Library Bulletin,* Spring 1983). It's a good article for AP classes to review.

Be wary of using the language of your sources instead of your own vocabulary and writing to impress rather than to inform — a style called the "false voice." One solution is to practice writing essays with an audience in mind, perhaps a friend. You want to inform your friend about what you've found out in your research; you don't need to impress this person with long words you really don't understand because he or she is your friend, but you do want to clearly explain your thesis. Such writing need not be informal. It does avoid, however, the stiffness that occurs when you depend too much on DBQ documents or how you recall information presented by historians in the articles and books you've studied. Perhaps the best person to write for is yourself. Look inside your own thought processes and say to yourself, "I'm writing down what I understand is the story of my topic." Using this approach prevents you from "overwriting," and you won't be writing to impress anyone.

Writing skills are important for success on the AP U.S. History Exam. Although a reader may spend only ninety seconds on an essay, poor organization, "overwriting," and the "false voice" are immediately recognizable. Each written assignment you tackle, whether as part of your AP class or using the practice essays in this book, is an opportunity to improve your writing. Improvement comes from revising. You must learn that the first draft is not the only draft. Question what you write and how you write it:

- Do I begin with a clear thesis statement?

- Is the body of the essay organized well and does the evidence support my thesis?

- Am I keeping to the topic or putting in irrelevant information?

- Is my conclusion clearly presented?

- Are there any examples of overwriting in the way I've phrased my answer?

- Is my style designed to inform and not impress?

- Are there any errors in grammar, punctuation, or spelling?

Revising the writing you do before the exam will prepare you for the time that your draft will be only what an AP reader scores.

Suggestions on Preparing for the Exam

You shouldn't wait until the end of the spring semester to begin preparing for the AP test. During the year, you'll read a college-level American history text and perhaps a supplemental history monograph, take multiple-choice exams, and write practice DBQs and standard essays as part of your AP class work. There are useful ways to get ready for the exam that you can do on your own or in a small group outside of class.

Test Simulations

Simulations are practice sessions in which you answer multiple-choice, DBQ, and standard essay questions as if you were taking the actual AP test. There are three complete exams in this book with annotated answers to the multiple-choice questions, which explain why the correct answer is better than the others, and sample scored essays.

The simulation *must* be done in a controlled environment. If you're working at home, turn off the TV and radio, and don't answer the phone — let someone else in your family take the call. Allot yourself the same amount of time for each section as you'll have on the exam: fifty-five minutes for the multiple-choice section, followed by the fifteen-minute mandatory reading period before you begin the free-response section. Make sure you spend only forty-five minutes on the DBQ and thirty-five minutes on each of the standard essays.

The Limited Research Paper

In addition to using simulations, you can gain writing experience by doing modest research projects. These projects should *not* be major term papers but rather should respond to questions that resemble those on the AP exam essay section. The goal is to present an informed point of view clearly and concisely and to draw on some sources of information as your evidence. Here are suggested guidelines for the limited research paper:

1. The paper should be no more than two to four typewritten pages.

2. Avoid using encyclopedias or your textbook for factual information. Use the text's list of suggested readings at the end of each chapter or the short bibliographies beginning on page 98 in this book. The internet is useful for locating sources on American history.

3. Use the public library, a nearby college or university library, or your high school library to find materials.

4. Use from four to six different sources in the paper; cite these sources using correct bibliographical form as endnotes.

5. Try to view all sides of the question, including the perspectives of different historians. A good place to find varying interpretations of the same topic is in anthologies which feature historians who disagree on the causes or consequences of a subject. Examples of anthologies are given on page 84.

6. Be specific, explain your position thoroughly, and support it from the sources you use, including the works of historians on the topic.

7. Prepare a rough draft first, and make the necessary revisions based on the points made in the discussion of writing strategies. Type the final paper.

You can use the sample essay questions in Chapter 3 for a limited research paper for each major topic in U.S. history. Here are a few possibilities to get you thinking:

- Was the American Revolution more of a political, economic, or social movement?

- "Slavery was the principal cause of the Civil War." Assess the validity of this statement.

- To what extent was the American farmer in the period 1865–1900 a victim of the economic power of business and the banks?

- Compare and contrast Theodore Roosevelt's New Nationalism with Woodrow Wilson's New Freedom.

- "The New Deal programs of Franklin Roosevelt brought the country out of the Depression." Assess the validity of this statement.

- Examining American foreign policy from 1945 to 1970, did the Containment Policy work?

Two Historical Figures

An excellent way to begin thinking interpretatively about history is to discuss the similarities and differences of two historical figures, deciding for yourself which one had the greater impact on U.S. history. The individuals may come from different eras or from the same but should offer greatly contrasting approaches to a particular problem.

In this form of essay, don't write on one individual and then the other; mesh and contrast both throughout your essay. Keep biographical information to a minimum, no more than a half page for each personality in a thousand-word essay (four pages). Your research should be based on several biographies and articles. If you quote from a source, use the appropriate footnote citation form.

Here are examples of historical figures that may be compared and contrasted:

- Ulysses S. Grant and Robert E. Lee
- Benjamin Franklin and Thomas Edison
- Jefferson Davis and Abraham Lincoln
- Elizabeth Cady Stanton and Betty Friedan
- Eugene V. Debs and John D. Rockefeller
- John Marshall and Earl Warren
- Eleanor Roosevelt and Jacqueline Kennedy
- Booker T. Washington and Martin Luther King, Jr.
- Theodore Roosevelt and Harry Truman

The list of possible comparisons is endless. Try to come up with historical pairs of your own.

Study Groups and Peer Review

The limited research paper and the historical pairs essay work well as class assignments. Both can also be used as part of a study group, which is usually made up of three or four students. The typical group reviews multiple-choice questions and holds question-response sessions, quizzing one another. Integrating peer review into the study group allows you to have your essays evaluated and critiqued outside the classroom. Everyone in the group writes on the same question, shares their essays, and discusses the strengths and weaknesses of each answer. Study groups find that they can write on the same question several times, challenging themselves to take a different interpretation. An "assess the validity" question particularly lends itself to this approach.

Your teacher may also use the peer-review method. The class is divided into two groups, each taking a different position on an essay question. It doesn't matter at this point whether you personally believe in the position you're taking. The idea is to develop the ability to take a strong stand in the essay, to acknowledge that other people may have differing views, and to convince the reader that your argument is the best one.

PART II

ANALYSIS OF EXAM AREAS

The AP U.S. History Examination gives you the opportunity to demonstrate how well you've mastered the content of a college-level course. There's no way around it — you're expected to know dates, names, and places. But the exam does go beyond memorizing historical facts. On both the multiple-choice and free-response sections, you're called on to think historically — to identify cause-and-effect relationships, understand the chronological context, determine major turning points, and evaluate documents and draw conclusions from them.

The exam is not intentionally tricky. There are, however, certain types of questions on the multiple-choice section and ways the essays are phrased in the free-response section that are important to understand. Part II first goes over the more interesting multiple-choice questions, including explanations of the correct answers and then treats the different question formats used in the free-response section. The formats are examined along with a review of documents in the DBQ and sample essays.

Multiple-Choice Question Types

Just as the exam format has undergone slight modifications, so too the types of multiple-choice questions asked may vary from year to year. In recent years, the "multiple" multiple-choice questions and questions based on a variety of graphic presentations — maps, tables, charts, graphs, political cartoons, photographs, and artwork — have not been as common as in the past. We have included them because the pendulum does swing back and forth, and, if they don't appear in the multiple-choice section, they will show up as documents in the DBQ.

"What" Questions

The multiple-choice questions are framed as a question or sentence stem where one of five possible answers correctly completes the statement. Many are straightforward and require you to remember facts about events, personalities, and significant developments in Unites States history. Students usually score quite well on this type of question.

Example 1

1. The Great Awakening was associated with

   A. Thomas Jefferson

   B. Henry David Thoreau

   C. Jonathan Edwards

   D. Lyndon Johnson

   E. William Bradford

The correct answer is **C.** This question asks you to identify an important cultural movement with its main representative. If you know that the Great Awakening was an early eighteenth-century religious revival, all the choices except Jonathan Edwards can be eliminated. None of the other individuals were known as religious thinkers and came before (William Bradford) or after (Thoreau) the eighteenth century. Lyndon Johnson is included to make sure you don't confuse the Great Society, his domestic economic program of the 1960s, with the Great Awakening. There's another way to ask the same question:

1. Jonathan Edwards was a key figure in the

    A. abolitionist movement
    B. Sons of Liberty
    C. Great Awakening
    D. Progressive party
    E. Populist party

Example 2

Factual multiple-choice questions often ask what something is about. Let's use the Great Awakening again as an example.

2. Which of the following best describes the Great Awakening?

    A. An attempt by nineteenth-century writers to create an American literature
    B. The movement among black Americans to discover their African heritage
    C. The increased emphasis on science and education after the Soviet Union launched the first satellite in 1957
    D. An eighteenth-century revival that was characterized by "fire and brimstone" sermons
    E. Lyndon Johnson's domestic program that included the "War on Poverty"

The correct answer is **D.** This question is easy if you know what the Great Awakening was. If not, you might still get the correct answer if you can place it in time — the eighteenth century.

Example 3

Here's another example of a "what" question presented as a sentence stem:

3. The Know-Nothing party

    A. wanted to limit the rights of freed slaves in the South
    B. advocated prohibiting the teaching of evolution in the public schools
    C. backed the early efforts of unskilled workers to form unions
    D. supported the claims of farmers against the railroads
    E. demanded an end to immigration into the United States

The correct answer is **E.** Established in 1854, the Know-Nothing party had strong local support in New York and New England based on an anti-immigration and anti-Catholic platform.

Example 4

"What" questions sometimes look for the definition of a term. The question may state the definition, and you select the correct term from the five choices, or it may supply the term, and you identify the appropriate definition. You're expected to know the historical context in which the term was used.

---

4. A company that buys up other businesses in the same industry is an example of

    A. horizontal integration

    B. vertical integration

    C. a corporation

    D. a joint-stock company

    E. a conglomerate

The correct answer is **A.** Examples of horizontal integration are the railroads and oil industry in the late nineteenth century. Vertical integration refers to controlling production from the raw-material stage through distribution to the consumer — for example, the steel industry under Andrew Carnegie, who owned coal mines, railroads, and steam ships as well as steel mills. Although a corporation or a conglomerate might provide valid examples, the question is asking for a more specific form of business organization.

Example 5

Here's an example where the term is given:

---

5. Which of the following most accurately describes carpetbaggers?

    A. They were former slaves who migrated to the North after the Civil War.

    B. They were black officeholders in the South during Reconstruction.

    C. They were Northerners who sought economic opportunity in the South after the Civil War.

    D. They were displaced farmers who moved to California during the Depression.

    E. They were recent immigrants who settled in the West in the late nineteenth century.

The correct answer is **C.** You should be able to associate carpetbaggers with the post-Civil War period. This eliminates answers **D** and **E.** You should also know from your reading and class lectures that carpetbaggers were Northerners.

There are literally hundreds of terms that may come up in a multiple-choice question. Your AP teacher will probably hand out a list for each unit you study, and important terms are defined beginning on page 97 of this book. As you read your text, take notes on any terms or concepts that are explained in detail. Some may be highlighted by italics or bold print.

In addition to the examples given so far, the AP exam uses multiple-choice questions that contain special markers or have a unique format. Here they are called the "reverse" multiple-choice question, the "when" question, and the "multiple" multiple-choice question.

The "Reverse" Multiple-Choice Question

The "reverse" multiple-choice question is easily identified by the words "EXCEPT" or "NOT" in all capital letters in the question or sentence stem. It basically asks you which of the five possible choices *does not belong*. Once you identify a "reverse" question, the best way to handle it is to ignore the "EXCEPT" or "NOT" marker. Then put an "X" through or cross out all of the answers that do belong. The one you're left with is correct. "Reverse" questions are very common and make up about ten percent of the multiple-choice section.

Example 1

---

1. Which of the following amendments to the Constitution was NOT part of the Bill of Rights?

    A. Freedom of speech, press, and religion

    B. Direct election of senators

    C. Protection against illegal search

    D. The right to bear arms

    E. Trial by jury

The correct answer is **B.** The direct election of senators was provided for in the Seventeenth Amendment (1913). Prior to the amendment, senators were chosen by state legislatures (indirect election). All of the other choices were among the first ten amendments to the Constitution, effective in December 1791 and commonly known as the Bill of Rights.

Example 2

> **2.** Which of the following statements about the American Federation of Labor (AFL) is NOT accurate?
>
>   **A.** The AFL was composed of skilled workers organized by craft.
>
>   **B.** The AFL used strikes to achieve its goals.
>
>   **C.** The AFL opposed restrictions on immigration into the United States.
>
>   **D.** The AFL was the largest union in the country at the end of the nineteenth century.
>
>   **E.** The AFL supported the closed shop.

The correct answer is **C.** Although Samuel Gompers, the leader of the AFL, was an immigrant himself, he and his union supported restrictions on immigration in the late nineteenth century allegedly to protect the jobs of American workers. All of the other choices accurately reflect the AFL's program. This question also requires you to know the definition of the term "closed shop" — companies could hire only workers who belonged to the union.

Example 3

> **3.** Progressives supported greater participation in the political process through all of the following EXCEPT
>
>   **A.** primary elections
>
>   **B.** recall
>
>   **C.** initiative and referendum
>
>   **D.** direct election of senators
>
>   **E.** city manager government

The correct answer is **E.** The city manager government, where a professional administrator runs local government in accordance with the policies of elected officials, reflects the Progressives' emphasis on efficiency. But since the city manager is appointed, this is not an example of greater public participation in the political process.

Example 4

> **4.** Which of the following writers is NOT considered part of the "Lost Generation"?
>
> **A.** Langston Hughes
>
> **B.** F. Scott Fitzgerald
>
> **C.** Ernest Hemingway
>
> **D.** e. e. cummings
>
> **E.** Gertrude Stein

The correct answer is **A.** This question is similar to the first example given on the Great Awakening — identify an individual with a movement or event. Four of the writers listed — Fitzgerald, Hemingway, cummings, and Stein — are associated with the "Lost Generation" of the 1920s; indeed, Gertrude Stein coined the phrase. Langston Hughes, an African-American writer, was a major figure in the Harlem Renaissance.

Example 5

> **5.** All of the following are important to understanding U.S. foreign policy from 1945 to 1970 EXCEPT
>
> **A.** brinksmanship
>
> **B.** NATO
>
> **C.** containment policy
>
> **D.** Marshall Plan
>
> **E.** McCarthyism

The correct answer is **E.** Although Senator Joseph McCarthy's campaign against alleged Communists in the government certainly reflected concerns raised by the Cold War, it had little to do with U.S. foreign policy given your other choices.

Example 6

A variant of the "reverse" multiple-choice question uses the word "LEAST," again in all capital letters. It isn't as common as the other markers. "LEAST" questions often relate to the causes/consequences of an event or the character of a period in U.S. history. Let's use U.S. post–World War II foreign policy again for an example.

6. During the period from 1945 to 1970, U.S. foreign policy planners were LEAST concerned with

   A. containing Soviet expansion

   B. trade imbalances between the United States and Japan

   C. Cuba's support for guerilla movements in Latin America

   D. wars of national liberation in Southeast Asia

   E. military conflicts in the Middle East

The correct answer is **B**. International trade didn't become an important foreign policy concern until the 1980s. All of the other choices were major foreign policy issues during the Cold War.

The "When" Question

A common type of multiple-choice question asks "when" something took place. Although history is much more than dates, students must be able to put key events in their proper chronological context. You are expected to know, for example, that the ratification of the Constitution came after the Declaration of Independence. "First," "last," "occurred," and "most recently" are obvious markers for "when" questions. These words are *not* capitalized in the question.

Example 1

1. The first permanent English colony in North America was

   A. Maryland

   B. Roanoke

   C. Jamestown

   D. Plymouth

   E. St. Augustine

The correct answer is **C**. Jamestown was founded in 1607. While Sir Walter Raleigh tried to establish a colony at Roanoke in the 1580s, the attempt failed. St. Augustine was founded by Spain (not England) in 1565. Plymouth was established in 1620 and Maryland in 1634. This question has two important clues — "permanent" and "English." If you read it too quickly and missed either clue, you probably marked the wrong answer.

Example 2

> **2.** Which of the following important events in westward expansion took place last?
>
> **A.** Annexation of Texas
>
> **B.** California gold rush
>
> **C.** Homestead Act
>
> **D.** Mexican War
>
> **E.** Oregon boundary settlement

The correct answer is **C.** The Homestead Act of 1862 offered 160 acres of public lands in the West to any citizen for a low fee. All of the other events occurred earlier: annexation of Texas (1845), Mexican War (1846), Oregon boundary settlement (1846), and California gold rush (1849). Since you can mark up the question booklet, you could put dates you know next to the event to help you eliminate the incorrect choices.

Example 3

> **3.** Which of the following occurred during the Truman administration?
>
> **A.** Yalta Conference
>
> **B.** *Brown* v. *Board of Education of Topeka*
>
> **C.** Bay of Pigs invasion
>
> **D.** Taft-Hartley Act
>
> **E.** Suez crisis

The correct answer is **D.** The Taft-Hartley Act, which significantly affected labor unions, became law in 1947 over President Truman's veto. All of the other events occurred either before (Yalta Conference) or after Truman's term as President. If you're unsure of the dates, you could arrive at the right answer by identifying the events with the correct President:

Yalta Conference — Franklin Roosevelt

Brown v. *Board of Education* — Dwight Eisenhower

Bay of Pigs invasion — John Kennedy

Taft-Hartley Act — Harry Truman

Suez crisis — Dwight Eisenhower

Example 4

A variation of the "when" question presents several lists of events, and asks which is in the correct chronological order.

---

4. Which of the following is in the correct chronological order?

   A. Japan invades Manchuria, Stimson Doctrine, NeutralityActs, Lend-Lease Act, Atlantic Charter

   B. Stimson Doctrine, Japan invades Manchuria, Lend-Lease Act, Neutrality Acts, Atlantic Charter

   C. Atlantic Charter, Stimson Doctrine, Lend-Lease Act, Neutrality Act, Japan invades Manchuria

   D. Stimson Doctrine, Atlantic Charter, Lend-Lease Act, Neutrality Acts, Japan invades Manchuria

   E. Japan invades Manchuria, Neutrality Acts, Atlantic Charter, Lend-Lease Act, Neutrality Acts.

The correct answer is **A:** Japan invades Manchuria (1931), Stimson Doctrine (1932), Neutrality Acts (1935–1939), Lend-Lease Act (1941), Atlantic Charter (1941). The Stimson Doctrine, which stated that the United States would not recognize territory acquired by force, was a direct response to Japan's invasion of Manchuria.

Example 5

"When" questions may not include one of the special markers. It's obvious from the examples presented so far that understanding when an event occurred is often an important clue to the correct answer. Dates or references to particular periods in U.S. history in the question are significant. It's a good idea to put dates that you know next to the possible answers to better define your choices.

---

5. In 1961, the most significant event affecting relations between the United States and Cuba was

   A. the discovery of Soviet missiles on the island

   B. Castro's decision to support Marxist movements in Central America

   C. the Bay of Pigs invasion

   D. the closing of the U.S. naval base at Guantánamo Bay

   E. the CIA plan to assassinate Castro

The correct answer is **C.** You might easily have answered **A** if you didn't remember that the Cuban missile crisis, which brought the United States and the Soviet Union to the brink of war, occurred in 1962.

The "Multiple" Multiple-Choice Question

In contrast to the question types reviewed so far, the "multiple" multiple-choice has not been common on recent exams. It has a format different from that of any other question. In addition to the five choices lettered **A** through **E**, there are four answers numbered I through IV; the right choice is usually a combination of those answers. There are often several correct answers presented in a "multiple" multiple-choice question. The best way to approach this type of question is to circle the correct answers and look for that combination in the lettered choices.

Example 1

1. Armed conflicts between white settlers and Native Americans were common during the seventeenth century. Which of the following involved Native Americans?

   I. Pequot War

   II. Whiskey Rebellion

   III. Bacon's Rebellion

   IV. King Philip's War

   A. I only

   B. I and IV only

   C. II and III only

   D. I, II, and III only

   E. I, III, and IV only

The correct answer is **E.** The Pequot War (1637) in Connecticut led to the tribe's virtual extermination; King Philip's War (1675–1676) involved Native American tribes in New England; Bacon's Rebellion (1675–1677) began as a conflict between settlers and Native Americans in Virginia. Even if you don't know that the Whiskey Rebellion (1794) was a farmers' revolt over taxes, you might remember that it took place after American independence and not in the seventeenth century.

Example 2

> **2.** Most immigrants arriving in the United States between 1890 and 1925 came from
>
> I.   Russia
> II. Great Britain
> III. China
> IV. Italy
>
> **A.** I only
> **B.** I and III only
> **C.** I and IV only
> **D.** II and III only
> **E.** I, II, and III only

The correct answer is **C.** This question asks about the New Immigration. From the 1890s to 1925, the overwhelming majority of immigrants came from southern and eastern Europe, for example, Russia and Italy. Chinese immigration to the United States was effectively ended by the Chinese Exclusion Act of 1882.

Example 3

> **3.** As a direct result of the Spanish-American War, the United States gained control over
>
> I.   the Philippines
> II. Cuba
> III. Puerto Rico
> IV. Hawaii
>
> **A.** I and II only
> **B.** I and III only
> **C.** I and IV only
> **D.** I, II, and III only
> **E.** I, III, and IV only

The correct answer is **B.** Cuba gained its independence as a result of the war; although Hawaii came under U.S. control in 1898, its annexation was unrelated to the war with Spain.

Example 4

4. President Hoover responded to the Depression by

   I. making loans available to financial institutions, railroads, and insurance companies

   II. supporting private relief efforts by established charities

   III. creating numerous new federal programs to provide jobs for the unemployed

   IV. taking the United States off the gold standard

   A. I and II only

   B. I and III only

   C. I and IV only

   D. II and IV only

   E. I, II, and IV only

The correct answer is **A.** Hoover's basic response to the Depression was to rely on private relief efforts. Late in his term, as the Depression continued to worsen, he did establish the Reconstruction Finance Corporation to put federal money into the economy.

Example 5

5. In the period after World War II, which of the following were intended to contain the expansion of the Soviet Union?

   I. NATO

   II. Camp David Accords

   III. United Nations

   IV. Truman Doctrine

   A. I only

   B. I and III only

   C. I and IV only

   D. III and IV only

   E. I, III, and IV only

The correct answer is **C.** NATO, the North Atlantic Treaty Organization, is the military alliance that confronted the Soviet Union and Eastern European nations of the Warsaw Pact. The Truman Doctrine committed the United States to protect Greece and Turkey and to use American military and economic resources to check the expansion of the Soviet Union. The Camp David Accords refer to the peace settlement negotiated by President Jimmy Carter between Egypt and Israel in 1979. The United Nations was not an instrument of American foreign policy.

Even with the different formats, the examples of multiple-choice questions given so far are rather straightforward. The AP exam may also use quotations, visuals (such as maps, photographs, cartoons, and artwork), and statistical data to test your ability to analyze documents, a crucial skill for the historian. Analytical questions, or "stimulus" questions as they are sometimes called, also require you to recall factual information in a different context. For example, you might be asked to locate, on a map of the thirteen colonies, where the Declaration of Independence was signed. Knowing how to handle analytical questions is important because you'll come across the same types of documents on the DBQ. If you can correctly interpret the meaning of a passage or glean information from a photograph here, you'll have little difficulty integrating documents into your essay on the DBQ.

The Quotation Question

The quotation question is based on a short passage from a written document — for example, a letter, diary, article, book, party platform, speech, or court decision.

Example 1

In many instances, the source of the quotation is not given, and you're expected to identify the author or the source from the context.

---

1. ". . . the United States is woefully unready, not only in fact but in purpose, to assert in the Caribbean and Central America a weight of influence proportional to the extent of its interest. We have not the navy, and what is worse, we are not willing to have the navy, that will weigh seriously in any disputes with those nations whose interests will conflict there with our own. We have not, and we are not anxious to provide, the defense of the seaboard which will leave the navy free for its work at sea."

   This passage was most likely written by

   A. Alfred Thayer Mahan

   B. Theodore Roosevelt

   C. Andrew Carnegie

   D. Senator Henry Cabot Lodge

   E. President William McKinley

The correct answer is **A.** The focus of the quotation is on the need for the United States to develop a strong navy. You should know from your readings that Alfred Thayer Mahan, particularly in his *The Influence of Seapower upon History,* strongly advocated this position.

Example 2

> **2.** "He has monopolized nearly all profitable employments, and from those she is permitted to follow, she receives but scanty remuneration. He closes against her all the avenues of wealth and distinction which he considers most honorable to himself. As a teacher of theology, medicine, or law she is not known. He has denied her the facilities for obtaining a thorough education, all colleges being closed to her. He allows her in Church, as well as State, but [in] a subordinate position, claiming Apostolic authority for her exclusion from the ministry, and, with some exceptions from any public participation in the affairs of the Church."
>
> This passage is most likely taken from
>
> **A.** a statement by the National Organization for Women
>
> **B.** Women's Christian Temperance Union "Declaration of Principles"
>
> **C.** Seneca Falls "Declaration of Sentiments and Resolutions"
>
> **D.** the Supreme Court decision in *Roe* v. *Wade*
>
> **E.** the "Debates of the Constitutional Convention"

The correct answer is **C.** The passage clearly deals with women's rights. Although the sentiments expressed might be echoed by the National Organization for Women, several points made in the passage don't apply to contemporary American society — women do attend college and are on the faculties of law and medical schools as well as religious seminaries. The document is from early in the women's movement, and you should know that the Seneca Falls "Declaration" (1848) was the first formal statement of women's rights.

Example 3

A quotation question might also ask you to identify the point of view of the author. Again, the source of the passage is usually not identified, and you have to use the content to determine the correct answer.

3. "Your sentiments, that our affairs are drawing rapidly to a crisis, accord with my own. What the event will be, is also beyond the reach of my foresight. We have errors to correct. We have probably had too good an opinion of human nature in forming our confederation. Experience has taught us, that men will not adopt and carry into execution measures best calculated for their own good, without the intervention of a coercive power. I do not conceive that we can exist long as a nation without having lodged some where a power, which will pervade the whole Union in as energetic a manner as the authority of the State governments extends over the several States."

Which of the following best describes the author of this passage?

    A. Federalist

    B. Jackson Democrat

    C. Abolitionist

    D. Anti-Federalist

    E. States Rightist

The correct answer is **A.** The quotation is a letter from George Washington to John Jay, dated August 1, 1786. Here Washington states his concern with the weakness of the country under the Articles of Confederation and his belief that a stronger central government was necessary. This position would soon come to be identified with the Federalists in the debate over the ratification of the Constitution.

Example 4

Quotation questions may also test your reading comprehension and ability to draw inferences from historical sources.

4. The following is from Jacob Riis's *How the Other Half Lives,* an exposé of immigrant life in New York in the 1880s:

"Six months of the year the cloakmaker is idle, or nearly so. Now is his harvest. Seventy-five cents a cloak, all complete, is the price in his shop. The cloak is of cheap plush, and might sell for eight or nine dollars over the store counter. Seven dollars is the weekly wage of this man with wife and two children, and nine dollars and a half rent to pay per month. A boarder pays about a third of it. There was a time when he made ten dollars a week and thought himself rich."

According to the passage, an immigrant family was able to make ends meet by

A. having the children go to work

B. doing piecework at home

C. taking in boarders to share the rent

D. selling cloaks directly to department stores

E. striking for higher wages

The correct answer is **C.** The approximately $3.00 a month the boarder paid in rent was the difference between the family making it or not. Boarders were often single men who were given a place to sleep and perhaps a small breakfast in return for helping with the rent and other expenses.

Tables, Charts, and Graphs

Tables, charts, and graphs are useful in determining patterns of change over time, particularly with respect to aspects of economic and social history. Your textbook almost certainly contains information on population, industrial and/or farm production, slavery, the makeup of the labor force, and immigration presented in this manner. Here are some hints on handling questions based on statistical data:

- Read the title and both the horizontal and vertical axis on a chart or graph carefully so that you understand what information is given.

- Pay particular attention to the date range. A significant event, for example, war or depression, may explain the changes shown.

- The numbers may be presented in absolute terms or in percentages. Absolute numbers are often rounded off or abbreviated. If the title of a table, for example, includes the phrase (in thousands), the number 48,000 is really 48 million.

Example 1

The simplest way to present statistical data is in a table. The most direct question requires an interpretation of the information and does not necessarily require any specific knowledge of American history.

IMMIGRATION TO THE UNITED STATES 1820–1860 BY COUNTRY OF ORIGIN					
	Great Britain	*Ireland*	*Germany*	*Italy*	*Asia*
1820	2,400	3,600	970	30	—
1830	1,150	2,720	1,900	9	—
1840	2,600	39,430	29,700	37	1
1850	51,000	164,000	72,000	431	7
1860	30,000	48,700	54,500	1,019	5,476

Source: U.S. Bureau of the Census, Historical Statistics of the United States from Colonial Times to 1970.

> 1. According to the table shown above, the greatest numerical increase in immigration was from
>
> A. Asia between 1850 and 1860
>
> B. Ireland between 1830 and 1840
>
> C. Ireland between 1840 and 1850
>
> D. Germany between 1830 and 1840
>
> E. Germany between 1840 and 1850

The correct answer is **C.** Immigration from Ireland between 1840 and 1850 increased from just over 39,000 to 164,000, a far larger increase than that of any other country listed. The same table could be used to test your factual knowledge about immigration before the Civil War. Here's an example:

> 1. The significant increase in emigration from Ireland between 1840 and 1850 was mainly due to
>
> A. opportunities for unskilled workers in U.S. factories
>
> B. the passage of the Homestead Act
>
> C. the effects of the Irish potato famine
>
> D. the British policy of settling English farmers on Irish lands
>
> E. religious oppression against the Catholic Church in Ireland

The correct answer is **C.** The failure of the Irish potato crop in 1845 led to widespread famine and emigration from the country.

Example 2

The line graph is useful to show trends over time. The horizontal axis is usually the time line, and the vertical axis is the subject of the graph. In the sample given below, the subject is energy sales expressed in millions of kilowatt-hours.

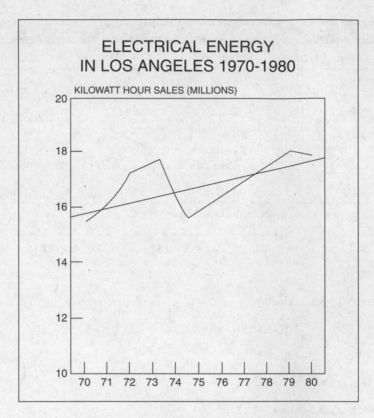

ELECTRICAL ENERGY
IN LOS ANGELES 1970-1980

KILOWATT HOUR SALES (MILLIONS)

Source: Los Angeles Department of Water and Power.

2. While the trend of increasing energy sales in Los Angeles continued during the 1970s, the accompanying graph shows a sharp decline in actual consumption during the period. The decline was most likely due to

  A. a sharp rate increase to residential customers

  B. conservation measures introduced in response to the Arab oil embargo

  C. a decline in population

  D. the effects of a serious recession

  E. the closing of plants using fuel because of air-pollution restrictions

The correct answer is **B.** This question requires that you read the graph correctly and relate the statistical information to a particular event. The sharp decline began in late 1973 and continued into 1974, a period that coincides with the Arab oil embargo. By curtailing fuel oil supplies, the embargo forced many electric utilities and local governments to institute strict energy-conservation ordinances.

Example 3

The important thing to remember about the pie chart is that the circle represents one hundred percent and the portions, or slices, of the pie represent a smaller percentage. The AP exam usually bases a question on several pie charts so that you can see changes or make comparisons. The sample given below shows the results in the presidential elections in 1904, 1908, and 1912 by the percentages each candidate received.

PRESIDENTIAL ELECTION RESULTS

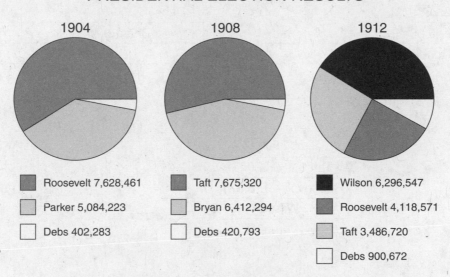

1904 1908 1912

Roosevelt 7,628,461   Taft 7,675,320   Wilson 6,296,547

Parker 5,084,223   Bryan 6,412,294   Roosevelt 4,118,571

Debs 402,283   Debs 420,793   Taft 3,486,720

Debs 900,672

Source: U.S. Bureau of the Census, *Historical Statistics of the United States from Colonial Times to 1970.*

---

3. From the election results shown above, Wilson won the presidency in 1912 mainly because

   A. voters supported his New Freedom program

   B. the Republican vote was split between Teddy Roosevelt and Taft

   C. Wilson won the southern states

   D. Eugene Debs took votes away from Taft

   E. support for the Prohibitionist candidate increased

The correct answer is **B.** Looking just at the popular vote, it seems likely that the Republicans would have won the election if the party had been unified behind a single candidate. Any votes that the Socialist Debs received wouldn't have gone to the conservative Taft, and the South had been a traditional Democratic stronghold since Reconstruction.

Statistical data can often be presented in different formats. Here's an example of a bar graph that uses the popular vote in the elections of 1904, 1908, and 1912 that could be used to ask the same question posed above. Note that while bar graphs are usually on the vertical, the data are shown in this example on the horizontal.

PRESIDENTIAL ELECTION RESULTS

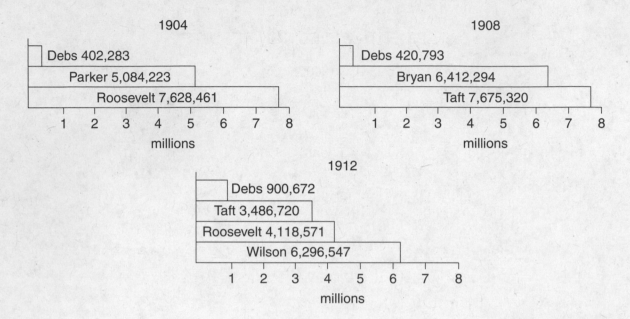

Maps

There are two types of maps used on the AP Exam: (1) maps that are historically significant themselves, for example, maps drawn by Lewis and Clark during their expedition, and (2) maps created to visually present historical information. The latter are far more common and are the type found in your textbook or a historical atlas. They are useful in describing the results of elections, the territorial growth of the United States, and military campaigns. Maps can also be used to present social and economic data — population density, agricultural and industrial development, migration patterns.

Like charts and graphs, map questions test your ability to "read" a visual document. It's important to note the title as well as the legend or key before trying to answer the question. You should be aware that this information is not provided on all maps.

Example 1

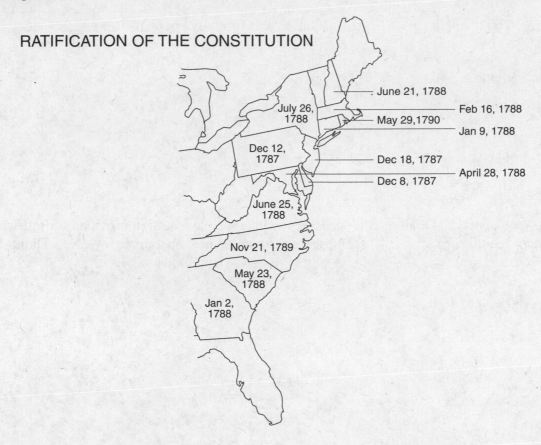

RATIFICATION OF THE CONSTITUTION

June 21, 1788

Feb 16, 1788

July 26, 1788

May 29, 1790

Jan 9, 1788

Dec 12, 1787

Dec 18, 1787

April 28, 1788

Dec 8, 1787

June 25, 1788

Nov 21, 1789

May 23, 1788

Jan 2, 1788

1. According to the map above, which was the first state to ratify the Constitution?

    A. Delaware

    B. Maryland

    C. New York

    D. Massachusetts

    E. New Jersey

The correct answer is **A.** This is an example of a straightforward map question. You can easily see which state ratified the Constitution first by the date; all you need to do is be able to name the state from the map.

Example 2

> **2.** Based on the above map, the Constitution was formally adopted after which state ratified it?
>
>   **A.** Rhode Island
>
>   **B.** Maryland
>
>   **C.** Delaware
>
>   **D.** New Hampshire
>
>   **E.** Massachusetts

The correct answer is **D.** Here you need to know that the Constitution provided for ratification by nine of the thirteen states. The ninth state to approve the Constitution was New Hampshire.

Example 3

> **3.** The shaded area on the above map refers to
>
>   **A.** states admitted to the Union after the Missouri Compromise
>
>   **B.** the area surveyed under the Land Ordinance of 1785
>
>   **C.** states where the Ku Klux Klan was strong in the 1920s
>
>   **D.** states that were formed out of the Louisiana Purchase
>
>   **E.** states that had major industrial development in the period 1800–1820

The correct answer is **B.** The shaded area is the old Northwest Territory, which was surveyed under the Land Ordinance of 1785. Illinois, Indiana, and Ohio were admitted before the Missouri Compromise, and significant industrial development was not evident in the region until after 1820.

Example 4

THE PATTERN OF SECESSION, 1860-1861

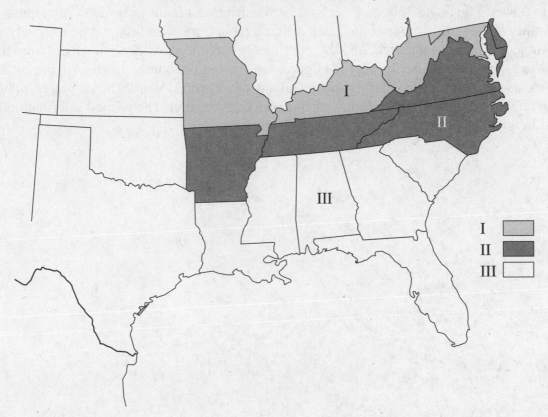

4. Which of the following statements about the states in Region II on the map is true?

   A. They were slaveholding states that remained loyal to the Union.

   B. They include Virginia, which was the first state to secede from the Union.

   C. They seceded from the Union after Fort Sumter was fired on.

   D. They seceded from the Union before Fort Sumter was fired on.

   E. They were the states with the highest number of slaves.

The correct answer is **C.** Virginia, North Carolina, Tennessee, and Arkansas seceded after the attack on Fort Sumter. South Carolina was the first state to leave the Union on December 20, 1860. Given the title of the map, it is extremely unlikely that the correct answer would deal with the slave population.

Political Cartoons, Photographs, and Artwork

The maxim that a picture is worth a thousand words is certainly true on the AP exam. Political cartoons, photographs, and artwork may be used to test your analytical skills. These types of visuals often capture the mood of a period or an event more clearly than another source if you develop the ability to "read" these documents properly.

Political cartoons have appeared in newspapers and magazines since the colonial period; they've been used to rally support for a cause and, more often than not, take a position against those in power. The artists rely on caricature or distortion and familiar symbols to emphasize their points of view. It's important to place the cartoon in time. This task can be relatively easy if the subject is clear — a caricature showing Lincoln and his generals obviously is from the Civil War — or you can use the way the figures are dressed to come up with an approximate date. It's also important to read the caption and any other printed words. In the nineteenth century, the figures in cartoons sometimes carried on a conversation. The printed information is critical in understanding the point the artist is trying to make.

Example 1

BRIBERY & CORRUPTION

NEW YORK

RIGHT UNDER HER NOSE, EVERY DAY IN THE WEEK.

Source: Library of Congress.

---

1. The political corruption attacked in the cartoon above most likely refers to

    A. the Teapot Dome scandal

    B. urban politics after the Civil War

    C. the scandals of the Grant administration

    D. the spoils system under Andrew Jackson

    E. the power of the trusts in controlling state government

---

The correct answer is **B.** A careful "reading" of the cartoon gives you the name of the artist — Thomas Nast. You should know from your reading that Nast's favorite target was William Tweed, whose Tammany Hall political machine ran New York City in the 1870s. There's nothing in the cartoon to indicate the Teapot Dome scandal or corruption in the Grant administration; you should recognize that the main figure in the cartoon is not Grant. The way the figures are dressed eliminates Andrew Jackson.

Example 2

Source: Los Angeles Department of Water and Power.

> **2.** Which of the following statements is NOT true based on the above cartoon?
>
> **A.** The term of a franchise to the gas company was set by the city charter.
>
> **B.** The cartoon opposed Charter Amendment 1-A.
>
> **C.** The gas company wants a longer franchise from the city.
>
> **D.** The gas company made excess profits under the existing franchise.
>
> **E.** The gas company will make excess profits if Charter Amendment 1-A passes.

The correct answer is **E.** This cartoon does not pertain to any well-known event in U.S. history; it's an exercise in reading a historical source. The basic information is as follows: The gas company supports an amendment to the city charter to increase the term of its franchise from twenty-one to thirty-five years. The artist opposes the amendment because twenty-one years is an "honest franchise" and because the longer franchise will result in excess profits. Note that the banner "$70,000,000 excess profits" is attached to the branch the gas company wants to "graft" onto the charter.

Example 3

Photographs are valuable tools in studying American history. They can tell us a great deal about the way people lived as well as chronicle major events, for example, Mathew Brady's Civil War photographs. Photographs are often taken for a purpose. The images of slum conditions in American cities at the turn of the century were intended in many cases to point up the need for reform. Questions often ask you to identify what is taking place in the photograph or to put the photograph in historical context.

3. Based on the photograph, which of the statements is true?

    A. The strike was over higher wages.

    B. The strike was over the refusal of the company to hire African American workers.

    C. The strike involved both labor and housing issues.

    D. The strike took place before World War I.

    E. The strike involved an 8 hour day.

The correct answer is **C.** The only clear information we have on the issues of the strike is the picket sign the woman is carrying. This clearly indicates that both low wages and high rents are the key issues. Although you may not be able to conclude with certainty that all the workers at Mid-City Realty were African Americans, the photograph does suggest this.

Example 4

4. Which of the following is the best caption for this photograph?

    A. "Life in the Coal Mines"

    B. "A Cause of Labor Unrest"

    C. "Industrialization in the Late Nineteenth Century"

    D. "The Problem of Child Labor"

    E. "Lamps and Lunch Boxes"

The correct answer is **D**. The photograph is of a group of coal miners, but the most important point is how young the miners in the photograph are. It is true that some unions did seek laws restricting the age at which children could work, but it was not a cause for strikes.

Example 5

Questions based on artwork — paintings, drawings, sculpture, architecture — are not as common as those using other types of visuals but they do come up on the exam. The types of questions are similar to those on photographs, and again it's important for you to pay attention to the details.

Source: Library of Congress.

5. The most significant impression the viewer gets from this nineteenth-century painting is that

    A. Native Americans were a serious obstacle to westward expansion

    B. wagon trains crossing the plains were small

    C. the artist had a positive image of Native Americans

    D. Native Americans provided settlers with essential supplies

    E. Native Americans were willing to trade anything for liquor

The correct answer is **E.** The key element in the painting is the empty bottles on the ground and the bottle one of the Native Americans is holding. Clearly, the artist portrays the Native Americans as a rather pathetic group, which posed no threat at all. The wagon train is shown stretching out to the distant mountains, obviously indicating that it was quite large.

Most textbooks contain large numbers of charts, tables, graphs, maps, political cartoons, photographs, artwork, and other types of sources. Since these materials are often explained or referred to in the text, studying them carefully will help you see the value of a particular document in the context of a particular era of American history. Remember that there are just so many relevant illustrations of various kinds that may turn up on the exam. Going over the ones in your textbook may give you the answer to a question on your AP exam.

Essay Question Types

You'll write three essays on the AP exam. Everyone answers the same DBQ in Section II, Part A, and you choose ONE standard essay from Part B and ONE from Part C in Section II. As in the multiple-choice section, the AP exam uses different formats in the essay section to test your knowledge of U.S. history. Here, the ways the questions can be asked are examined, and sample student essays, along with a reader's comments, are provided. The sample answers for the DBQ and standard essays are not perfect; they are typical student responses, as the possible score noted after the reader's comments indicates. Again, all the essays are scored on a 9-point scale.

Question Types for the DBQ

The DBQ is a special challenge. You are provided with evidence from a variety of sources that you must integrate into your essay along with information that doesn't come from the documents. As already pointed out, the instructions make it very clear that you **must** provide outside information. A good way for you to remember this crucial point is to answer the sample DBQ in this section and those on the practice exams in two ways: first without referring to the documents and then using the documents. The first approach is a direct test of what you know about the period or topic.

You also need to be cautious about letting the documents control you. All too often, students present the reader with a summary of what the documents say, the infamous "laundry list," and fail to analyze the sources in the context of the question. It's important to remember that historians don't give equal weight to all historical sources. They've developed techniques for evaluating the credibility of the information available to them. To give you an idea of how this process works, the value of each of the sources in the sample DBQ is reviewed. You should try to do this on your own with the DBQ documents on the practice exams.

The DBQ is much broader than the standard essay questions. No matter how well you can evaluate the documents or the depth of your knowledge of the period, the key to a high score is understanding what the question itself is asking. As with the multiple-choice questions, there are words and phrases that identify particular question types.

Assess the Validity DBQ

A challenging DBQ is one that asks you to "assess the validity" of a statement. The most direct form is a sentence taking a position on an event, personality, period, or movement in U.S. history followed by "Assess the validity of this statement." For example:

> The New Deal of Franklin Roosevelt represented a radical change in the relationship between government and society.

> Assess the validity of this statement.

The key point to remember is that there's no right or wrong answer to an "assess the validity" question. The selection of documents and your independent knowledge of the subject allow you to agree with the statement, disagree with it, or come down somewhere in between. What the reader is looking for is how well you use the sources you're given and outside information to support the position you decide to take.

In the example given above, "assess the validity" means determining whether or not the New Deal did indeed represent a "radical change." The side of the question you come down on is your thesis and should be clearly stated in the first paragraph. You also need to define here what you understand "radical change" to mean. While the documents will not necessarily lead you to a particular conclusion, it's important to recognize contrary evidence. This is the "give a little, take a lot" approach. Point out that a document or information you know about the topic may be valid, and then explain why this is not really the case.

Assess the validity questions come in different guises. Questions that ask you to examine the arguments for and against something, to measure the extent to which something is true or false, or to examine the success or failure of one person or thing against another all basically require you to take a position on a historical problem and provide the evidence to support that position.

The DBQ on the 1992 exam provides a good example of an assess the validity question phrased in a different way. It asked "to what extent" environmental factors determined the development of the West and affected the lives of the pioneers and how important other factors were. The documents, which included a physical map of the trans-Mississippi West and excerpts from the recollections of settlers, provided ample evidence of the powerful impact the environment had on the West and the people who lived there. Other documents were important clues to additional forces that were at work. President James Polk's 1845 Message to Congress on the Oregon boundary dispute obviously raises the issue of Manifest Destiny. Sections of the laws passed by the Wyoming Territorial Legislature in 1869 and 1870 giving women the right to vote and control over property was another source. The relevance of this document in the context of the question was not that Wyoming recognized women's suffrage but that the motive behind the legislation was to attract settlers.

Hints on handling additional question formats — compare and contrast and discuss/describe, for example — are covered in the discussion of the standard essays. The following sample **DBQ** gives you an analysis of the question itself and the documents as well as two student essays with a reader's comments.

Sample Document-Based Question

"The decision to intern Japanese aliens and Japanese-American citizens living on the West Coast during World War II was motivated primarily by public pressure on government officials and military leaders."

Assess the validity of this statement.

Use *both* evidence from the documents *and* your understanding of the period to compose your answer.

Document A

". . . if we go ahead and arrest the 93,000 Japanese, native-born and foreign-born, we are going to have an awful job on our hands and are very liable to alienate the loyal Japanese from disloyal. . . . I'm very doubtful that it would be common sense procedure to try and intern or to intern 117,000 Japanese in this theater. . . . I told the governors of all the states that those people could be watched better if they were watched by the police and people in the community in which they live and have been living for years. . . . and then inform the FBI or the military authorities of any suspicious action so we could take necessary steps to handle it . . . rather than try to intern all those people, men, women, and children, and hold them under military control and under guard. I don't think it's a sensible thing to do. . . . I'd rather go along the way we are now . . . rather than attempt any such wholesale internment. . . . An American citizen, after all, is an American citizen. And while they all may not be loyal, I think we can weed the disloyal out of the loyal and lock them up if necessary."

Source: Excerpt from a telephone conversation of General John L. DeWitt, head of the Western Defense Command, December 26, 1941.

Document B

A Jap is a Jap, and it makes no difference if he is an American citizen.

Source: Statement of General DeWitt before the House Naval Affairs Subcommittee on Housing, April 13, 1942.

Document C

Loyalty of alien Japanese or American-born Japanese who are Shintoists cannot be trusted it was testified yesterday by Togo Tanaka, young Japanese-American editor of the *Japanese Daily Times,* before the Tenney Committee on subversive activities at a hearing in the State Building.

Speaking, as he said, as an American citizen, he frankly admitted numerous subversive activities in which the Nisei, or second generation Japanese, had participated but explained that they themselves had felt they had been made tools of the older generation in many cases.

Testifying that he was in charge of the English language section, Tanaka admitted that some of the articles appearing during the past two years were subversive and that a Japanese yearbook and directory for 1940–1941 distributed by the paper was "nine-tenths subversive" in character.

Although he denied that the newspaper received any direct subsidy from the Japanese government, he said that he had sometimes felt that some individuals who worked on it might have been subsidized "because of some of the articles which were printed."

Source: Los Angeles Examiner, March 25, 1942.

Document D

The temporary separation of city employees of Japanese parentage from their employment should not be regarded as a serious or significant matter. Entirely too much attention has been directed to it. The employees were given an opportunity to make application for a leave of absence so that civil service status of each is fully protected and some, if not all, of the employees may be later returned to their positions with the City of Los Angeles . . . .

There will be no policy of harassment of Japanese people, whether born in Japan or in this country of Japanese parents. I feel that employment by a governmental agency is different from private employment, and hope that the action of the city will not be followed by local corporations, firms, or individual employers in dropping faithful and competent employees. . . .

The Japanese people of this community may continue to have the respect of our people and full protection so long as they properly conduct themselves. They should remember, however, that the surest safety depends upon their own acts and conduct and seeing to it that no Japanese, whether born in Japan or California, does anything detrimental to the safety, peace and dignity of the people of America.

Source: Statement of Mayor Fletcher Bowron to the Japanese people of Los Angeles, January 28, 1942.

Document E

. . . we can be assured they [the Japanese] know everything about our resources, our industrial activity, and the military objectives in the southern California area. For what have the little brown men been doing all these years but getting information and sending it through the Japanese military and naval intelligence sources?

Now that the local Japanese population has probably done its duty well and has supplied information, the Japanese are being moved out of this area and a good job the Army is doing of it, too. While, by removing the Japanese from our midsts, we are reducing the means of securing and transmitting information from the West Coast, we may at the same time, be making it more probable an air raid, because Japanese bombardiers may soon know that if they release bombs over Los Angeles they may do so with assurance that they are not killing their own countrymen. Moreover, the agitation, the public demand for the removal of Japanese from this area, where we have had the largest concentration of Japanese population in America, has stirred up ill-wind and resentment, which undoubtedly the Japanese would like to express in an effective way in the form of an air raid.

Source: Radio address of Mayor Fletcher Bowron, April 23, 1942.

Document F

As time passes, it becomes more and more plain that our wartime treatment of the Japanese and Japanese-Americans on the West Coast was a tragic and dangerous mistake. That mistake is a threat to society, and to all men. Its motivation and its impact on our system of law deny every value of democracy.

Source: Eugene V. Rostow, "Our Worst Wartime Mistake," Harper's Magazine *(September 1945).*

Document G

There is support for the view that social, economic and political conditions which have prevailed since the close of the last century, when the Japanese began to come to this country in substantial numbers, have intensified their solidarity and have in large measure prevented their assimilation as an integral part of the white population. In addition, large numbers of children of Japanese parentage are sent to Japanese language schools outside the regular hours of public schools in this locality. Some of these schools are generally believed to be sources of Japanese nationalist propaganda, culminating in allegiance to Japan. . . .

As a result of all these conditions affecting the life of the Japanese, both aliens and citizens, in the Pacific Coast area, there has been relatively little social intercourse between them and the white population. The restrictions, both practical and legal, affecting the privileges and opportunities afforded to persons of Japanese extraction residing in the United States, have been sources of irritation and may well have tended to increase their isolation, and in many instances their attachments to Japan and its institutions.

Source: U.S. Supreme Court decision, Hirabayashi v. United States (1943).

Document H

The curious thing was that there was no serious suggestion to move the Japanese off the West Coast until five or six weeks after Pearl Harbor. There were a few sporadic suggestions by Army and Navy personnel that the government should evacuate the Japanese, but not from the men who eventually persuaded Secretary of War Stimson to take the step.

Take General DeWitt, for instance, who was later to act a leading part in the evacuation. . . . He was apt to waver under popular pressure, a characteristic rising from his tendency to reflect the views of the last man to whom he talked. . . . He kept his head at first, and resisted suggestions that the Japanese be herded out of the coastal territory, which was under his jurisdiction.

. . . He [DeWitt] was a soldier, and I suppose in the face of the public clamor he decided that he could not take a chance. But I doubt whether he ever formulated precisely what that chance was. Everyone was after him on the coast to get rid of the Japs — the American Legion, the California Joint Immigration Committee, the Native Sons and Daughters of the Golden West, the Western Growers Protective Association, the California Farm Bureau, the Chamber of Commerce of Los Angeles, and the newspapers.

Source: Autobiography of Attorney General Francis Biddle, In Brief Authority *(1962).*

Document I

Instructions to all persons of Japanese ancestry living in the following area:

All of that portion of the City of Los Angeles, State of California, within that boundary beginning at the point at which North Figueroa Street meets a line following the middle of the Los Angeles River; thence southerly and following the said line to East First Street; thence westerly on East First Street to Alameda Street; thence southerly on Alameda Street to East Third Street; thence northwesterly on East Third Street to Main Street; thence northerly on Main Street to First Street; thence northwesterly on First Street to Figueroa Street; thence northeasterly on Figueroa Street to the point of beginning.

Pursuant to the provisions of Civilian Exclusion Order No. 33, this Headquarters, dated May 3, 1942, all persons of Japanese ancestry, both alien and non-alien, will be evacuated from the above area by 12 o'clock noon, P. W. T., Saturday, May 9, 1942.

No Japanese person living in the above area will be permitted to change residence after 12 o'clock noon, P. W. T., Sunday, May 3, 1942, without obtaining special permission from the representative of the Commanding General, Southern California Sector, at the Civil Control Station located at:

Japanese Union Church, 120 North San Pedro Street, Los Angeles, California.

Such permits will only be granted for the purpose of uniting members of a family, or in cases of grave emergency.

The Civil Control Station is equipped to assist the Japanese population affected by this evacuation in the following ways:

1. Give advice and instructions on the evacuation.

2. Provide services with respect to the management, leasing, sale, storage or other disposition of most kinds of property, such as real estate, business and professional equipment, household goods, boats, automobiles and livestock.

3. Provide temporary residence elsewhere for all Japanese in family groups.

4. Transport persons and a limited amount of clothing and equipment to their new residence.

The Following Instructions Must Be Observed:

1. A responsible member of each family, preferably the head of the family, or the person in whose name most of the property is held, and each individual living alone, will report to the Civil Control Station to receive further instructions. This must be done between 8:00 A.M. and 5:00 P.M. on Monday, May 4, 1942, or between 8:00 A.M. and 5:00 P.M. on Tuesday, May 5, 1942.

2. Evacuees must carry with them on departure for the Assembly Center, the following property:

   A. Bedding and linens (no mattress) for each member of the family;

   B. Toilet articles for each member of the family;

   C. Extra clothing for each member of the family;

   D. Sufficient knives, forks, spoons, plates, bowls and cups for each member of the family;

   E. Essential personal effects for each member of the family.

   All items carried will be securely packaged, tied and plainly marked with the name of the owner and numbered in accordance with instructions obtained at the Civil

Control Station. The size and number of packages is limited to that which can be carried by the individual or family group.

3. No pets of any kind will be permitted.

4. No personal items and no household goods will be shipped to the Assembly Center.

5. The United States Government through its agencies will provide for the storage, at the sole risk of the owner, of the more substantial household items, such as iceboxes, washing machines, pianos and other heavy furniture. Cooking utensils and other small items will be accepted for storage if crated, packed and plainly marked with the name and address of the owner. Only one name and address will be used by a given family.

6. Each family, and individual living alone, will be furnished transportation to the Assembly Center or will be authorized to travel by private automobile in a supervised group. All instructions pertaining to the movement will be obtained at the Civil Control Station.

Go to the Civil Control Station between the hours of 8:00 A.M. and 5:00 P.M., Monday, May 4, 1942, or between the hours of 8:00 A.M. and 5:00 P.M., Tuesday, May 5, 1942, to receive further instructions.

Source: Poster in Little Tokyo, Los Angeles, May 1942.

Analysis of the DBQ Question and Documents

Analysis of the Question

The question presents you with a rationale for the internment of the Japanese living on the West Coast during World War II. You should know that the official reason was based on the assumption of a credible threat of sabotage and espionage in a highly sensitive military area. You have to determine whether or not the position posed by the statement is valid based on the evidence. There is important outside information relevant to the question. You must include a reference to the legal instrument of internment which was Executive Order 9066, issued by President Roosevelt on February 16, 1942. Also, you might want to briefly contrast the treatment of Japanese-American citizens with that of Italian- and German-Americans, and, again briefly, comment on the treatment of Japanese in the United States prior to World War II. The fact that many Japanese-Americans were allowed to enlist in the Army and distinguished themselves in the fighting in Europe may also be relevant.

Analysis of the Documents

Document A

General DeWitt was responsible for implementing the evacuation order as head of the Western Defense Command. The excerpt from his December 1941 telephone conversation shows that he was initially opposed to internment. Because the information comes from a telephone conversation in which we assume DeWitt was freely expressing his personal views, this source is extremely credible. You will see that this is confirmed in the autobiography of Attorney General Biddle.

Document B

DeWitt has completely changed his position by April 1942, after the decision to move forward with the evacuation. We don't know if his statement reflected his personal feelings, but those feelings are really not relevant.

Document C

This testimony gives some credence to the idea that there was a credible threat from the Japanese living on the West Coast. However, the credibility of the source itself is somewhat suspect. Historians would go directly to the transcript of the testimony before the Tenney Committee rather than relying on an excerpt from a newspaper article. The attitude of the *Los Angeles Examiner* toward Japanese and Japanese-Americans is something we cannot get from the article.

Document D

Bowron's statement is significant for several reasons: the date, before Executive Order 9066 was issued, the fact that Japanese workers had been let go from city jobs in Los Angeles, and the implied threat to the Japanese community to behave itself. There is no reason to believe that the document does not reflect the position of Los Angeles civic leaders at the time.

Document E

Bowron's radio address clearly states there was a public demand for the evacuation of the Japanese.

Document F

Rostow's statement indicates that at the end of the war the legitimacy of the evacuation was questioned, at least in some quarters. It's not particularly relevant, however, to the question.

Document G

The Supreme Court decision upheld the constitutionality of the evacuation order. The Court justified the order in part because of the failure of the Japanese to assimilate, which it interpreted as evidence of the community's strong attachment to Japan. The document might also be used to see the evacuation as part of a long-standing pattern of American discrimination against Japanese.

Document H

Biddle's autobiography confirms DeWitt's early position stated in Document A. It also states that public pressure was a significant factor in the decision, pointing to specific groups that wanted the Japanese removed from the West Coast. Historians treat autobiographies with care because the motives of the author may be suspect — for example, the author may have been willing to bend the truth a bit to improve his place in history. Also autobiographies are written some time after the events they describe, and the problem of memory surfaces. Since Biddle's statement corresponds with the information we have from a highly credible source, it is assumed to be credible itself.

Document I

The poster addresses the matter of the mechanics of the evacuation process and could be included to provide the reader a sense of the scope of the order.

First Student DBQ Essay

The evacuation of all individuals of Japanese ancestry, resident aliens and Japanese-American citizens, from the West Coast in 1942 was the result of public pressure rooted in a long-standing prejudice. Military necessity and the alleged threat of sabotage rationalized the action based on a fear of the "yellow peril." This position is supported by the fact that similar action was not taken against other enemy alien groups, i.e., German or Italian-Americans, as well as the timing of the evacuation itself.

Racial prejudice against Asians was strong in the United States from the late nineteenth century. It was a key factor in ending emigration from China through the Chinese Exclusion Act of 1882. After this, Japanese in the United States felt pressure, particularly with Japan's rise to a position of world power after the turn of the century. The decision of the San Francisco school board that required Japanese (as well as Chinese and Korean) students to attend segregated schools reflects this trend. The "alienness" of the Japanese was reinforced, as the Supreme Court decision in Hirabayashi v. United States upholding the evacuation order noted, by discrimination that restricted the "privileges and opportunities" available to the Japanese. The attack on Pearl Harbor brought to the surface intense anti-Japanese feeling. A California barber offered free shaves to "Japs" with the qualification that he was not responsible for accidents. The removal of Japanese from the West Coast must be seen in this context.

The evacuation was carried out under Executive Order No. 9066 issued by President Roosevelt in February 1942. At this point, General John L. DeWitt, who was responsible for carrying out the order on the West Coast as head of the Western Defense Command, had no trouble supporting the action even if it included American citizens. He told the House Naval Affairs Subcommittee in April, "A Jap is a Jap, and it makes no difference if he is an American citizen." This is not the position he took in the weeks immediately after Pearl Harbor. At that time, he opposed interning all Japanese living under his command. The report of his telephone conversation on December 26, 1941 makes it clear that he believed that action needed to be taken only against those Japanese that were in fact disloyal. As the commander on the scene, it is significant that he saw no imminent threat of either espionage or sabotage that warranted the wholesale internment of the entire Japanese community on the West Coast.

The fact that internment was discussed by high military officials in December 1941 but not implemented for several months indicates that public pressure played a role in the decision, and that DeWitt himself succumbed to this pressure. In January, Los Angeles city employees of Japanese parentage lost their jobs; there is no indication that this applied to Italian-Americans or German-Americans, or that Mayor Fletcher Bowron's warning to the Japanese was also given to these other communities. The underlying racism behind the action comes across in the Mayor's April 1942 radio address, e.g., the reference to the Japanese as "little brown men." Bowron also states that public pressure was a factor — ". . . the agitation, the public demand for the removal of Japanese from this area . . ."

The clearest evidence on the role of public pressure is Attorney General Francis Biddle's autobiography. He points out the significant pressure DeWitt was under from a diverse collection of groups — American Legion, California Joint Immigration Committee, the Los Angeles Chamber of Commerce, and the press — to "get rid of the Japs." While we do not know Biddle's position in 1941 and the statement was written at a time when the legitimacy of the evacuation was questioned, his evaluation of DeWitt is supported by other sources, particularly the December 1941 telephone conversation.

There may have been a legitimate concern over the threat of sabotage or espionage on the West Coast. Some Japanese in the United States may have felt their first loyalty was to Japan as the Los Angeles Examiner report on the testimony of the editor of the Japanese Daily Times suggests. Neither factor seems to have been as potent a motive for the wholesale internment of over 100,000 Japanese as public pressure abetted by wartime hysteria and prejudice.

Reader's Comments on the First Student DBQ Essay

This student makes effective use of the documents and adds significant amounts of "outside" information. The first sentence clearly states the thesis, followed by setting the topic in historical context. Factual information is stated succinctly and incorporates the documentary evidence. One problem here, however, is that the student doesn't identify the documents used by their letter designation as well. Remember that the readers can devote only a limited amount of time to the essays, and the documents you cite should be clear. Always refer to the document you're using by adding the document letter at the end of the appropriate sentence — for example (Document B). The student demonstrates control over the documents by applying them to the argument, not applying the argument to the documents. Other possibilities concerning why the Japanese evacuation occurred are presented, but the essay closes with a strong restatement of the thesis.

Possible student score: 8

Second Student DBQ Essay

I agree that the decision to intern the Japanese on the West Coast was the result of public pressure on government officials and military leaders. This is clear from the documents.

Document A tells us that General DeWitt originally was opposed to the internment but soon changed his mind. He says in Document B that "A Jap is a Jap, and it makes no difference if he is an American citizen."

Even before the evacuation order was issued, Mayor Bowron of Los Angeles had fired all Japanese from their city jobs. He also warned them to behave, implying that more drastic action would be taken if they did not. This is from Document D. This is an indication of the type of pressure that General DeWitt was under. Another document that supports this is the report in the Los Angeles Examiner. Here an editor from a Japanese newspaper published in the United States admits that articles published have been subversive. This probably added to the public pressure.

Document H, which is from the autobiography of Attorney General Francis Biddle, also makes a strong case for the idea that DeWitt was under public pressure. In fact, he lists the groups and organizations that wanted the Japanese evacuated. Even the Supreme Court case in Document G shows that even the highest court in the country felt that the Japanese living on the West Coast were probably loyal to Japan because they did not assimilate, and attended Japanese schools. While some people believed that the internment of the Japanese was wrong (Document F), these sentiments were only expressed when the war was already over.

Document I tells us how the evacuation was actually carried out in Los Angeles. By May 9, 1942, all Japanese living in a specific area had to leave their homes. They were told what they could and could not bring with them. They would get transportation to an Assembly Center or could take their own cars as part of a supervised group.

Based on the documents presented, I believe that the Japanese were interned because of public pressure. There was no military or security reason to do this. It was an example of wartime hysteria.

Reader's Comments on the Second Student DBQ Essay

This student has fallen into the common trap of writing a DBQ essay as a "laundry list" of documents, stringing them together to create an essay. In this sense, the documents control the essay. The student did not evaluate the worth or relevance or even the chronology of the documents. With one exception, the documents are presented in the same order as they appear in the question. The student's thesis fails to assess the validity of the statement; instead, the essay is written as an agreement with it rather than a critical evaluation. There is no outside information.

Possible student score: 1

Question Types for the Standard Essays

In addition to the DBQ, there are two standard essays on the AP U.S. History exam. Again, these are numbered 2 through 5, and you choose one question from each part. **You can't write on both essays from either Parts B or C**. The questions in Part B cover the period through the Civil War, and those in Part C cover Reconstruction to recent American history. The suggested writing time for each question is thirty-five minutes, and both of your essays are weighted the same in the scoring. This is important. Make sure you budget your time so that you can write two coherent answers in the time allowed.

Identification/Evaluation Questions

While this type of question has come up on the AP exam before, on the 1992 exam for example, it is likely to become more common with the two-essay requirement in Section II, Parts B and C.

> Identify THREE of the following and evaluate the relative importance of each of the THREE in the decline of the Federalists and the ascent to power of the Jeffersonian Republicans.
>
> Midnight Judges
>
> The Alien and Sedition Acts
>
> The Twelfth Amendment
>
> The Virginia and Kentucky Resolutions

Your first task is to read the question carefully and *all* four factors. Then decide which *three* you'll be using in your essay. To put it another way, which one are you least comfortable with and won't use? You should indicate the three factors you've chosen and give a brief description of each in your introductory paragraph, which at least partially fulfills the question's identification requirement. You'll provide more information in the body of the essay. Your subsequent paragraphs deal with the major element of the question — evaluating the relative importance of the factors you've selected. You need to decide, and decide quickly, which one of the three you believe was the most important in contributing to the decline of the Federalists and the rise of the Jeffersonians, which was less important, and which was the least important.

This type of question can be posed in different ways. The example given above could just as easily have read

> Assess the impact of THREE of the following on the decline of the Federalists and the ascent to power of the Jeffersonian Republicans.

Here you're asked to what extent the three choices you've made are important and how they compare in importance to each other. Although you aren't specifically directed to "identify" your choices, it's obvious that you have to provide adequate facts about each to support your thesis.

There are several things to keep in mind about identification/evaluation questions:

- **There is no one correct answer.** It's entirely possible that the student next to you has chosen the same factors but assigned them the opposite order of importance or selected one that you didn't. Your score will depend on the strength of your essay and how well it persuades the AP reader that your choices, and the reasons for them, are good ones.

- **Write within the limits of the question.** You may believe that factors other than those provided, Hamilton's fiscal program for instance, were significant in the decline of the Federalists. Bringing this point in will not add to your essay and can seriously detract from it if you don't pay enough attention to the choices given.

- **Even a question that asks you to identify is not an opportunity simply to restate all the facts you know.** You are always expected to analyze or interpret the information as the question requires.

Two student answers to the same identification/evaluation question follow. You might want to try writing your own essay first and then compare yours to the sample answers and the reader's comments.

Question 1

1. Assess the impact of THREE of the following on Chinese immigration to the United States between 1850 and 1900.

    The transcontinental railroad

    The Burlingame Treaty

    Coolie labor

    The Workingmen's party of California

Note: This question could also be phrased as follows:

Identify THREE of the following and evaluate the relative importance of each of the THREE on Chinese immigration to the United States between 1850 and 1900.

First Student Essay (Question 1)

Chinese immigration effectively began with the California gold rush as Chinese prospectors joined the thousands of people coming to the California gold fields. They endured considerable discrimination because racist miners were jealous of their prospecting abilities. The state of California even passed a Foreign Miners Tax which the Chinese miners had to pay in order to work in the gold fields.

In the 1860s, the Chinese found a new opportunity for labor. The transcontinental railroad was being built. The Central Pacific Railroad needed workers to do the hard work of cutting through the Sierra Nevada range. Charles Crocker, in charge of construction, found the Chinese a reliable work force and between 1863 and 1869 employed more than 10,000 of them. Chinese railroad workers even set the record for constructing ten miles of track in one day.

As the railroad neared completion, the United States government concluded a treaty with China. This treaty, the Burlingame Treaty, marked the first agreement between China and the United States. It contained provisions for trade and for the immigration of Chinese to America. The treaty in many ways represented a high point between the two nations.

The economic depression of the 1870s produced a reaction in California against the Chinese. They were seen as economic competitors to the whites in the state. Led by Denis Kearney, California white laborers formed the Workingmen's party of California. This political party played a major role in creating the California constitution of 1879 and in agitating for Congress to pass the Chinese Exclusion Act. In 1882, Congress did pass such an act, preventing Chinese from coming to the United States for a period of ten years. The law was renewed for another ten years in 1892, and in 1902 it was renewed again, this time indefinitely. Not until World War II was this ban on Chinese immigration to the United States lifted.

Reader's Comments on the First Student Essay for Question 1

This essay has a number of problems, which are unfortunate given the student's basic understanding of the choices made. The first paragraph takes up some of the allotted time on the problems caused by the California gold rush, but the gold rush itself is not one of the factors to be discussed. As it is, the discussion of railroad construction says nothing about Chinese immigration. The assumption is that the Chinese gold miners became railroad workers when, in fact, Crocker recruited labor from China. The student has some basic facts about the Burlingame Treaty but offers little information about its effect on immigration. The information about the Workingmen's party is clearly presented and, given the time restraints, presents reasons for pushing for Chinese exclusion. Overall, the essay could have been greatly improved by eliminating extraneous details and focusing instead on why Congress decided, despite the contribution of Chinese workers and the recognition extended by the Burlingame Treaty, to end further Chinese immigration.

Possible student score: 4

Second Student Essay (Question 1)

The first transcontinental railroad, the Burlingame Treaty, and the Workingmen's party of California all had a significant impact on Chinese immigration to the United States between 1850 and 1900. Construction of the railroad created a demand for cheap labor that China could provide, while the 1868 treaty between China and the United States opened a wide door to Chinese immigration. The Workingmen's party, which campaigned on the platform "The Chinese Must Go," was a reaction to these developments. It ultimately had the greatest impact by contributing to the passage of the Chinese Exclusion Act of 1882.

One of the major problems faced by the Central Pacific Railroad, which was responsible for building the section of the transcontinental line east from Sacramento, was a shortage of labor. Company officials, Charles

Crocker and Leland Stanford, hit on the idea of importing workers directly from China. The Chinese, who worked for lower wages than whites and were rarely involved in strikes or other disruptions, were quickly recognized as an asset. By the time the transcontinental railroad was completed in 1869, some 15,000 had been hired. The prospect of jobs in America naturally encouraged other Chinese to emigrate.

The federal government encouraged the use of Chinese labor on the transcontinental railroad through the Burlingame Treaty of 1868, which guaranteed unrestricted Chinese immigration to the United States. Secretary of State Seward saw this provision as part of a larger process that would open Chinese markets to American products. Since the treaty remained in force after the railroad was completed, it continued to act as a spur to Chinese settlement in the United States. There was a significant increase in Chinese immigration between 1871 and 1880.

The growth in Chinese immigration came at a time when the economy was worsening and unemployment was high. This was particularly true in California, where it was easy to blame the Chinese for the economic problems — they were taking jobs from American workers. The Workingmen's party, which was formed in 1877, took this position and called for the exclusion of Chinese from California and the country as a whole, The California constitution, which the party played an important role in drafting, denied Chinese jobs on public works projects and stated they could not work for companies in the state. The anti-Chinese sentiment that the Workingmen's party represented influenced national policy as well.

In 1880, a new treaty with China gave the United States the right to regulate and limit Chinese immigration, and two years later, Congress passed the Chinese Exclusion Act. Although the law did not stop Chinese from entering the United States completely, it certainly brought to an end the era of open immigration that began with the construction of the transcontinental railroad and the Burlingame Treaty.

Reader's Comments on the Second Student Essay for Question 1

This student has written a strong essay. The first paragraph not only states the choices, but also presents the reader with a clear thesis statement. Logical conclusions are drawn from the information presented, and facts are used to support the thesis. Pointing out that the decision of the Central Pacific to recruit workers in China encouraged other Chinese to emigrate and connecting the growth in Chinese immigration in the 1870s to the Burlingame Treaty are examples of this. This is a well-organized essay that provides sound factual information and analysis given the time constraints of the exam.

Possible student score: 8

Other Examples of Identification/Evaluation Questions

The following are sample identification/evaluation questions for you to try. You also might try to answer the questions using factors different from those that are listed.

- Identify THREE of the following and evaluate the relative importance of each of the THREE in contributing to the economic growth of the United States in the period 1815–1860.

  - The American System

  - The transportation revolution

  - The Second Bank of the United States

  - The Tariff of 1828

- Assess the impact of THREE of the following on the status of Native Americans before the Civil War.

  - Black Hawk's War

  - The Battle of Prophetstown

  - The Trail of Tears

  - *Cherokee Nation* v. *Georgia*

- Analyze the ways in which THREE of the following indicated the tension between conservative and liberal views in American society during the 1920s.

  - The Red Scare

  - Prohibition

  - The Scopes trial

  - Flappers

- Analyze the ways in which THREE of the following supported the United States policy of containment in the post–World War II era.

  - The Truman Doctrine

  - The Marshall Plan

  - The Berlin airlift

  - The North Atlantic Treaty Organization

Discuss/Describe Questions

Essays that ask you to "discuss" or "describe" an event, period, or movement in U.S. history are deceptively straightforward. They seem to look for a recitation of factual information with little if any analysis on your part. AP essay questions are rarely so direct. It's unlikely, for example, that you'll be asked simply to discuss the causes of the entry of the United States into World War I. Although the words "discuss" and "describe" mean to tell about something, these questions aren't opportunities merely to write down everything you know on a subject. This is the same pitfall you are urged to avoid in identification/evaluation questions. Remember that Parts B and C of Section II challenge your skill in writing to the point. You won't be able to write two effective essays in the allotted time if you ramble on or bring in information that isn't pertinent to the question.

In the past, discuss/describe questions often had two parts. While this format may not be as common with the standard essays, it is still helpful to review. First, it's important, as always, to read *both* parts carefully. For example, you might be asked to discuss the political, economic, and social changes in the South from 1864 to 1877 in the first part of the question, and then to analyze the extent to which these changes survived the end of Reconstruction in the second part.

Keeping in mind that your answer shouldn't include everything you know about the South during and after the Civil War, your essay could focus on the political, economic, and social reforms, primarily instituted through Reconstruction, affecting former slaves; the second part of the question then addresses the status of African-Americans after Reconstruction.

The essay itself may be prefaced by a statement that provides framework for the answer, very similar to the assess the validity question discussed for the DBQ. Here's an example. Winston Churchill said in 1945 that the United States was at the "summit of the world." Examining the period from 1945 to 1975, what evidence is there that this was not the case?

Again, this question is not an opportunity to spit out everything you know about the United States or even American foreign policy from the end of World War II to 1975. It requires you to think about the country's position in the world in 1945 and how that changed over the next three decades. Here are some points you might make in your answer:

- Churchill's perception of the United States was correct in 1945; the United States was the strongest economic power and, with the monopoly on nuclear weapons, the strongest military power in the world.

- The position of the United States changed with the beginnings of the Cold War; the emergence of the Soviet Union as a nuclear power meant that the United States was one of two "superpowers"; containment of the Soviet Union became the goal of American foreign policy.

- Although the United States was able to contain the direct expansion of the Soviet Union, it was unable to prevent Soviet supported Communist governments from coming to power or to maintain the status quo against national liberation movements — for example, in Cuba and Vietnam.

- The United States had the resources to rebuild the economies of Western Europe (Marshall Plan) and Japan after World War II. By the 1970s, however, it was beginning to lose economic preeminence to Germany and Japan, and its economy proved vulnerable to challenges from the developing world — for example, the Arab oil embargo.

Here is an example of a discuss/describe question in the two-part format.

Question 2

2. Describe the major decisions made at the wartime conferences between the United States, Great Britain, and the Soviet Union. To what extent were these decisions responsible for the Cold War?

First Student Essay (Question 2)

The key military and political decisions that were made at the wartime conferences between the United States, Great Britain, and the Soviet Union — Teheran, Yalta, and Potsdam — were critical in shaping the post-war world. It was primarily the agreements reached on strategic planning that created the conditions for the onset of the Cold War.

Stalin's main demand from the time Germany invaded the Soviet Union in June 1941 was an allied invasion of Western Europe. The cross-Channel invasion, the "second front," was postponed several years even after the United States entered the war. The delays made Stalin suspicious of the motives of the West early in the war.

In terms of military planning, the Teheran Conference (November 1943) was crucial. Roosevelt, Churchill, and Stalin agreed that the invasion of Normandy, set for the late spring of 1944, would coincide with a Russian offensive in the east. This meant that Soviet troops would liberate Eastern Europe while the United States and Britain would liberate Western Europe. Churchill's proposal for an invasion of the "soft underbelly," i.e., Greece and the Balkans, which was intended to limit Soviet control of Central Europe, was rejected as unsound militarily by the United States.

By the time Roosevelt, Churchill, and Stalin met again at the Yalta Conference (January 1945), Russian troops were already in Eastern Europe and the Soviet Union had set up a provisional government in Poland. At Yalta, the prime concern was the planning for the peace. The allies agreed to divide a defeated Germany into four zones of occupation with the Soviet Union controlling the largest territory in the East; Berlin, which was completely within the Soviet zone, was to be administered jointly by the U.S., Britain, France, and the USSR. While the Soviet Union agreed to free elections in Poland and the establishment of democratic governments in the liberated countries, there was a basic failure to communicate on these points. Stalin's statements that the Soviet Union must have "friendly states" on its western frontier meant Communist-dominated governments. Poland was a key test. At Yalta, Britain and the U.S. agreed that the Soviet-controlled Lublin Committee would be the basis for the post-war government. The Western allies also agreed to Russian control over Outer Mongolia as well as a Russian zone of occupation in Korea as the price for a commitment from the Soviet Union that it would enter the war against Japan three months after Germany's defeat.

During the height of the Cold War, Roosevelt was accused of "selling out," giving Eastern Europe to the Soviet Union at Yalta. This is not valid. It is important to keep in mind that in January 1945 the atomic bomb had not even been tested. The planned invasion of Japan would take one million men and meant high casualties; this made the opening of a "second front" in Asia essential. The concessions made at Yalta reflected military necessity and the reality of the military situation on the ground in Eastern Europe.

The tension that was evident between the United States and the Soviet Union at Potsdam signaled the start of the Cold War. The fact was that the USSR controlled Eastern Europe. It refused to give up the territory it had acquired between 1939 and 1941; it was understood at Yalta that Poland would be compensated with German territory in the west for the Polish territory the Soviet Union took in the east. The "Iron Curtain" had indeed descended on Europe by 1945.

Reader's Comments on the First Student Essay for Question 2

Although this essay is full of factual information, it's still important to note that the student hasn't attempted to write a complete history of everything that's happened during and since World War II. The wartime conferences are discussed as well as the major policy decisions of the Allies. They lay the ground for the student's conclusion that the Cold War began as early as the Potsdam Conference.

Possible student score: 7

Here's another essay that takes a somewhat different approach to the same question.

Second Student Essay (Question 2)

Between 1943 and 1945, the leaders of the Big Three — Great Britain, the Soviet Union, and the United States — met to discuss military planning and the nature of the peace after the war was over. Although the decisions Roosevelt, Churchill, Stalin, Truman, and Clement Attlee made were crucial to maintaining the wartime alliance, the roots of the Cold War must be found in the immediate post-war years.

Roosevelt, Churchill, and Stalin met for the first time at Teheran in November 1943. Here the coordination of military operations for the invasion of Europe were set. Although some historians believe that Teheran was important to the origins of the Cold War because the strategy called for Russian troops to move into Poland, the Balkans, and attack Germany itself from the east, this is historical hindsight. The fact that Soviet troops occupied Eastern Europe did not necessarily mean they had to stay there.

At Yalta, the discussions of the Big Three focused on the post-war settlement, particularly the division of Germany into zones of occupation, the status of Poland and Eastern

Europe, and Soviet participation in the war against Japan. As in any diplomatic negotiations, there was give and take by all parties. Britain and the United States agreed that the Provisional Government created by the Soviet Union in Poland would be the basis for the post-war government. This meant a broad-based coalition that included both representatives of the Polish government-in-exile (London Poles) and Polish Communists. Stalin agreed to free elections in all of Eastern Europe. He also committed to enter the war against Japan three months after Germany was defeated in return for spheres of influence in Outer Mongolia and Korea. The agreements relating to the Far East were not made public at the time of the conference, and would cause a considerable stir in the United States some months later.

The Allies met for the last time at the Potsdam conference (July–August 1945), after Germany had been defeated. It is certainly true that the atmosphere of the conference was less accommodating than had been the case earlier, and all sides were less willing to compromise. The decisions made at Yalta with respect to the occupation of Germany were implemented; four zones of occupation were established (British, French, American, and Soviet), with Berlin (entirely within the Russian Zone), jointly administered by the four powers; the same pattern of occupation was applied to Austria. In addition, the prewar boundary of Poland was shifted to the west (Oder-Neisse line) and the Soviet Union retained its control of the territory acquired under the Nazi-Soviet Non-Aggression Pact that was in effect between 1939 and 1941.

The fact that World War II was so quickly followed by the onset of the Cold War might make it seem that the roots of the rivalry between East and West must lie during the war. While there were certainly areas of tensions between the United States and the Soviet Union, there was no decision at the wartime conferences that made the Cold War confrontation inevitable. Despite the Soviet troops in Eastern Europe, there was a window of opportunity in late 1945 and into 1946 for negotiation and even forceful diplomacy. The Soviet Union, given its tremendous losses during the war, was not a superpower in 1945 and no direct threat to the United States.

Reader's Comments on the Second Student Essay for Question 2

This essay presents a concise summary of the decisions of wartime conferences. Although it doesn't mention the planning for the United Nations, the factual presentation is otherwise strong. It is well organized and well written. The main failure is the lack of support for the thesis that the roots of the Cold War are not found at Teheran, Yalta, or Potsdam. The student may have a valid point about the "window of opportunity" immediately after the war but doesn't provide any evidence to back it up. This may be a case where the student either ran out of time or steam.

Possible student score: 5

Other Examples of Discuss/Describe Questions

Here are additional discuss/describe questions for you to try:

- The change in British imperial policy after the French and Indian War was the critical factor in bringing about the American Revolution. Discuss this change with respect to specific policies or acts of Parliament from 1763 to 1775.

- The immigrant arriving in the United States in the late nineteenth century expecting to find the "Golden Land" was often disillusioned by what he or she actually found. Describe the living and working conditions of a typical immigrant family in the 1890s that contributed to this disillusionment.

- American foreign policy is usually described as isolationist from the end of World War I to the outbreak of World War II. Discuss the evidence that supports this position.

Compare and Contrast Questions

A comparison calls for pointing out similarities; a contrast calls for noting differences. An essay might use the terms "compare," "contrast," or "compare and contrast." A question posed as "compare and contrast" obviously requires you to discuss both similarities and differences. While one side may be more significant than the other, both must be presented. Even in direct comparison questions, it's always useful to point out differences, even if just to recognize another interpretation.

The scope of your essay is sometimes limited by the question itself. An essay question that asks you to compare and contrast the economies of New England and the southern colonies shouldn't be cluttered up with information on politics, religion, or social life. The requirements to compare and contrast are often the first part of a two-part question:

> Compare and contrast the presidencies of Abraham Lincoln and Franklin Roosevelt. Which administration handled the problems it faced more effectively?

Here, the second part is really "an assess the validity" question. You have to make a judgment about the effectiveness of the two presidents and justify your position from the evidence developed in your explanation of the similarities and differences. You won't be given any extra time to answer a two-part question, and you need to condense your essay. A response to the Lincoln/Roosevelt example can be organized as follows:

- *Paragraph 1:* Make a general statement on the similarities of and differences between the two administrations, and take a position on which was more effective.

- *Paragraph 2:* Focus on similarities — for example, both Presidents came to power in times of crisis.

- *Paragraph 3:* Focus on differences — in a sense, Lincoln's election precipitated the crisis he faced, while Roosevelt's was seen as a solution.

- *Paragraph 4:* Defend your position on which handled its problems more effectively.

- *Paragraph 5:* Conclude with a statement that summarizes evidence in support of your thesis.

The best way to approach a compare and contrast question is to make a list. The similarities and differences are usually broad categories that are supported by specific evidence. After reading question 3 and the sample essay, see if you can re-create the list that the student relied on to develop the answer.

Another form of comparison is a question that asks you to examine the relative importance of two factors on an issue in U.S. history. The phrase "relative importance" should indicate to you that the question is similar to an identification/evaluation question but without its range of choices. This type of question is more limited in scope and fits nicely into the thirty-minute suggested writing time for a standard essay. For example:

> Analyze the relative importance of the Proclamation of 1763 and the passage of the Stamp Act in provoking discontent among the American colonists.

Here your first paragraph *briefly* explains what the Proclamation of 1763 and the Stamp Act were and presents a thesis statement on which had the greater effect on unrest in the colonies. The next two paragraphs go into each factor in more depth — for example, how effective was the Proclamation, what was the reaction to it, and what was the response to the Stamp Act? Your concluding paragraph again summarizes the evidence you've presented to defend the thesis.

A direct compare and contrast question and the relative importance form are used for the following student essays.

Question 3

3. Compare and contrast immigration to the United States in the period from 1800 to 1860 and from 1880 to 1924.

Student Essay (Question 3)

Immigration to the United States from 1800 to 1860 and from 1880 to 1924 were very different. First, many more people came to the United States from overseas in the later period than in the earlier period. Second, the immigrants who arrived in the late 19th and early 20th century came from other parts of Europe than the groups that came before them.

The period from 1880 to 1924 is known as the era of the New Immigration. A majority of these immigrants came from Southern and Eastern Europe — Italy, the Russian Empire, Greece, Yugoslavia, Poland, and included a large number of Eastern European Jews; the earlier immigration was made up primarily of Irish and Germans. While tens of thousands of immigrants arrived before the Civil War, the annual immigration in the later period was well over 100,000.

Because the "new" immigrants were so different from Americans in terms of religion (Judaism, Catholicism, Greek Orthodox), language (Italian, Greek, Russian, Polish), and culture, many Americans wanted an end to open immigration. Because of pressure from groups such as the Immigration Restriction League and the American Federation of Labor, which believed that immigrants were taking jobs away from

American workers, Congress finally passed the National Origins Act in 1924. This law established a quota system for the number of immigrants allowed into the country each year based on their country of origin; low quotas were given for the countries of Southern and Eastern Europe.

If we look over American history, we see that people decided to come to the United States for various reasons. The Pilgrims and the Puritans came so that they could practice their religion the way they wanted; the Irish immigrated because they faced famine in their homeland; Jews left Europe because they were persecuted and wanted a better way of life. To all these immigrants, the United States was the land of freedom and opportunity. Each immigrant group faced some type of discrimination when they settled here. The Irish were harassed because of their religion and there was anti-Semitism against the Jews.

The immigrants who came to the United States after 1880 were very different from those who came earlier in American history; they came from different countries and did not assimilate as well as the earlier immigrants.

Reader's Comments on the Student Essay for Question 3

This student really doesn't answer the question in two respects. Very little attention is paid to the similarities between the two periods of immigration, and the information that is presented seems to be tacked on in the next to the last paragraph. Almost all the attention is focused on the "new" immigration with very little of substance on the earlier immigrant experience. The student makes a good point that immigrants in both periods faced discrimination, but this needed to be developed further. Both the thesis statement and the conclusion are extremely weak and again don't address the question posed. Except for the discussion of the National Origins Act, the student doesn't present very strong evidence.

Possible student score: 3

Question 4

4. Analyze the relative importance of antitrust laws and government regulation in controlling big business during the Progressive Era.

Student Essay (Question 4)

The Progressives supported both antitrust legislation and the regulation of business as a means of limiting the power of large corporations. Presidents Roosevelt and Taft brought major prosecutions under the Sherman Anti-Trust Act, and a new law, the Clayton Anti-Trust Act, was passed under Wilson. These actions did not restore competition in any meaningful way. On the other hand, government regulation had much more success in eliminating specific abuses of big business.

Despite the Sherman Anti-Trust Act, business combination continued to grow after 1890. Indeed, court injunctions to prevent "combinations in restraint of trade" were most often used against organized labor. President Roosevelt's Square Deal did call for stricter enforcement of the antitrust laws, but he really believed that regulation was a better approach than "trust busting." He turned to the Sherman Act, in the Northern

Securities Case for example, because Congress was reluctant to pass new regulatory legislation. That victory, however, had little impact on business consolidation. The Clayton Act was enacted because the Sherman Act was not working. Perhaps its most important provision — exempting farm groups and labor unions from antitrust laws — had nothing to do with the power of big business.

The Progressive record was much stronger in the area of regulation. The Interstate Commerce Commission was made stronger through the Hepburn Act, which gave it the power to set maximum railroad rates and extended its authority to pipelines. Regulation of particular industries in the interests of consumers began with the Meat Inspection Act and the Pure Food and Drug Act. The issue of competition was also addressed outside of the antitrust laws. Wilson saw a new agency, the Federal Trade Commission, as a significant element in restoring competition in business. It defined "unfair trade practices" and could require companies to stop such practices.

The success of either antitrust legislation or regulation in controlling big business depended on the will of government. Although regulation could be meaningless if the regulations were not enforced or if representatives of the industry being regulated controlled the agency, the evidence supports the position that this was the most effective approach during the Progressive Era.

Reader's Comments on the Student Essay for Question 4

This student shows a good command of the facts even though additional information could have been brought in — Department of Commerce and Labor, Bureau of Corporations, Elkins Act. The thesis is presented clearly, and the essay keeps on track. The evidence on the antitrust legislation is somewhat weak. The fact is that major trusts were broken up at this time — for example, the Northern Securities Company and Standard Oil. The student may believe that these were simply symbolic but needs to say so if this is the case. The student makes a good point, albeit in a rather awkward sentence, that regulation is as effective as the determination of the agency.

Possible student score: 6

Other Examples of Compare and Contrast Questions

Question 3 is quite straightforward. Indeed, a comparison between the old and new immigration is covered in most textbooks. Although the AP exam doesn't shy away from direct questions, you should be ready to examine comparisons that you didn't think of before. Here are a few examples:

- African-Americans and women have both traveled a long road toward civil equality. Examine the similarities and differences in the way in which each group received the right to vote.

- In January 1917, President Wilson called for "peace without victory"; in April 1917, he stated, "The world must be made safe for democracy." Explain the differences between these two positions. Which was reflected in the Fourteen Points?

- Analyze the relative importance of the doctrine of states' rights and slavery as factors that led to the Civil War.

- Analyze the relative importance of Sinclair Lewis and F. Scott Fitzgerald in defining American culture during the 1920s.

Assess the Validity Questions

We have already discussed the "assess the validity" question form in connection with the DBQ. In the past, this type of question has also come up often as one of the standard essay choices. Because it is usually broadly framed, it may not be used as frequently in the two-essay format the AP exam now uses. In any event, you should be familiar with how an "assess the validity" question might be answered as a standard essay.

Question 5

5. To what extent was the form of government established under the Articles of Confederation successful?

Note: Questions that ask "to what extent" are usually assess the validity questions. The question could easily have been posed as follows:

The form of government established under the Articles of Confederation was successful.

Assess the validity of this statement.

Student Essay (Question 5)

The success or failure of a particular form of government is determined by how it responds to the critical problems. The Articles of Confederation simply did not give enough authority to the central government to deal with the many challenges, primarily economic, the U.S. faced after independence. While there were notable accomplishments, the fact that the Constitutional Convention decided in 1787 not simply to revise but to abandon the Articles, shows its weakness.

A case can be made that the government under the Articles was successful in important areas. The Continental Congress under the Articles did fight a war against Great Britain, and negotiate a peace settlement. The Land Ordinance of 1785 and the Northwest Ordinance of 1787 provided the basic legal framework for the territorial expansion of the country in the 19th century. Such achievements, however, did not match the weaknesses in the Articles.

The Articles gave the Congress only limited power. It was authorized to conduct foreign policy and declare war, mediate boundary disputes between the states, and deal with the Indian tribes in the territories. In all other matters, the states were in control. Congress did not have the power to tax or impose tariffs except with the unanimous agreement of the states.

At the end of the Revolution, the United States faced serious economic problems. Without the power to impose taxes, Congress had no option but to ask the states for money to pay off the national debt. Throughout the "critical period" from 1781–1787 the states either refused or were slow in making payments. Robert Morris, who was appointed Superintendent of Finance, had to use his own money to pay for the demobilization of the Continental Army. The Continental Congress also had no power to regulate foreign commerce. With each state setting its own policies, overseas trade declined and industries dependent on it, shipbuilding for example, suffered.

Even in those areas where the Confederation Congress had authority, it was not effective. British troops remained on American soil and in control of forts in the Northwest territory despite the terms of the Treaty of Paris. The government under the Articles was not able to enforce the treaties entered into with Native American tribes west of the Appalachians. Congress was also unable to resolve the dispute with Spain over the closing of New Orleans to American shipping in 1784.

Whether we examine economic or foreign policy, the government under the Articles of Confederation could not cope with many of the critical issues facing the country. This was certainly due to the weaknesses of the Articles themselves. Again, the failure of the government established is clearly demonstrated by the widespread, though certainly not unanimous, support for the major restructuring provided for in the Constitution.

Reader's Comments on the Student Essay for Question 5

This essay carefully measures the statement asking whether the Articles of Confederation acted as a basis for a successful government. The student's thesis is clearly stated in the first paragraph. The second paragraph acknowledges that some successes can be credited to the Confederation government, but it still argues that the weaknesses outweighed the strengths. The third through fifth paragraphs provide the evidence and support for the student's thesis. Finally, the student not only restates the thesis but provides a strong concluding statement. The pacing and structure of the essay are excellent; there are no digressions from the topic. The student, however, might have provided additional examples, such as Shays' Rebellion or the currency inflation caused by printing of state money.

Possible student score: 8

Other Examples of Assess the Validity Questions

Here are other examples of assess the validity questions that you should try on your own or perhaps work on in your study group:

1. "Once the United States committed itself to economic expansion, it could not avoid engaging in imperialism."

   Assess the validity of this statement.

2. Presidential elections are referendums on the political party in power and not on the programs put forward by the challenger.

   Examine this statement in light of the results of the elections in 1828, 1832, and 1840.

PART III

STUDYING UNITED STATES HISTORY

Reading United States History

Reading for factual information and interpretation is essential for success on the Advanced Placement United States History Examination. In your AP class, you'll be assigned a textbook and probably a "reader" that contains a collection of documents on U.S. history or essays by historians on particular topics. Your teacher may also require you to read a monograph, write a review of two books on the same subject, or do a short research paper that will involve additional reading.

The Textbook

Most AP teachers use a college-level textbook in their classes. There are important differences between this text and the one assigned in a regular high school course. First, the vocabulary and style of writing is more sophisticated. College texts go into much more detail and don't have "section reviews" or sample questions and essays at the end of each chapter. Review information is generally provided in separately published workbooks or study guides. At one time, the college text was distinguished from its high school counterpart by a lack of illustrative materials. This is no longer the case. The U.S. history textbooks in print today are filled with photographs, paintings, maps, charts, graphs, tables, and short excerpts from original sources. These are just the type of documents that come up on the AP exam. You should study the illustrations in the text as you read each assignment and go back over them after you finish a chapter.

A college-level textbook may challenge your vocabulary and understanding of metaphors. It's a good idea to keep a dictionary handy to look up words you don't know. The use of metaphors and idiomatic expressions make reading a textbook more interesting — as long as you understand what they mean. Take, for example, the sentence "Roosevelt's New Deal tested the waters of innovative programs during the depression." It doesn't mean that FDR developed his programs by the White House swimming pool; the author's point is that the New Deal was innovative. Don't be afraid to bring up troublesome metaphors in class or in your study group. Chances are you won't be the only one finding the reading tough going, particularly in the beginning.

Unlike other disciplines, history has no specialized vocabulary that you must master. However, there are terms and concepts that you may not be familiar with that are important to understanding a particular period in American history — headright, nullification, carpetbagger, scalawag, steerage, flapper, Hooverville, Beat Generation. Important terms and concepts are sometimes highlighted in textbooks in italics or bold print. These terms and concepts are often included in the multiple-choice section, and you'll be expected to know the definition and the chronological context.

Dozens of college history textbooks are on the market today. Visit a university bookstore, and browse through the texts different professors have ordered for their classes. You'll find one-volume hardbound, two-volume paperbacks, three-volume paperbacks suited for colleges on the quarter calendar, books that have gone through ten editions, texts with the same number of pages but a different number of chapters; one book covers the Depression and New Deal in a single chapter while another treats them separately. The experience may make you wonder just how many ways the history of the United States can be told!

While the essential facts of American history certainly don't change, textbooks do become out-dated rather quickly. Time marches on, and a book published in the 1970s can take the story only through the Ford administration. More important, the interpretation of the facts changes as new evidence is uncovered, different ways of analyzing evidence are developed — with computers, for example — or themes that were neglected by an earlier generation of historians are recognized as important. Every generation writes its own history. A textbook that came out in 1954 would prob-ably be useless in helping students today understand the country's multicultural heritage, the sta-tus of women, or environmental concerns. Such issues are not just tossed into the last chapter of the text. A fundamental rethinking may occur among historians about their impact not only on the present but also on how those issues were treated in history. Newer textbooks explore the status of minorities in the colonial period, the place of women throughout American history, and how Native Americans and pioneers interacted with the environment.

You can buy used, relatively inexpensive copies of textbooks that are just a few years old. Be aware that the previous owner probably marked up the book with marginal notes, underlining or highlighting. What one student thought was important is not necessarily what you may find important, and you don't want to be distracted by too much scribbling. Having the books avail-able gives you the chance to see how historians other than the author of the text your teacher assigned look at people and events. Comparing the way different historians approach the same topic or period is a good way to reinforce your understanding of American history and recall factual information. But don't overdo it by reading three textbooks all the way through.

United States History Survey Textbooks

Here is a list of U.S. history textbooks that have proven popular with college professors and are commonly used in AP classes. Only the name of the principal author or authors and the title of the book are given. Many texts are written by three or more historians and are revised quite of-ten. If you want to go to the expense of getting your own textbook, buy the most recent edition.

Bailey, Thomas and Kennedy, David. *The American Pageant.*

Bailyn, Bernard. *The Great Republic: A History of the American People.*

Blum, John M. *The National Experience: A History of the United States.*

Boyer, Paul S. *The Enduring Vision: A History of the American People.*

Current, Richard N. *American History: A Survey.*

Garraty, John. *The American Nation: A History of the United States.*

Kelley, Robert. *The Shaping of the American Past.*

Nash, Gary. *The American People: Creating a Nation and Society.*

Norton, Mary Beth. *A People and a Nation.*

Tindall, George B. and Shi, David E. *America: A Narrative History.*

Wilson, R. Jackson. *The Pursuit of Liberty: A History of the American People.*

How to Read a History Textbook

There's no "right" way to read a history textbook. Here are suggestions that have proved helpful to both college and AP students.

1. Instead of jumping in and tackling your initial assignment, try to get a feel for the book first. Look over the table of contents and glance through the chapters to see how the authors organize the material. You'll notice that each chapter is divided into smaller topical sections, which makes outlining easier. Some textbooks begin a chapter with a summary of what is covered, noting important events, or include a timeline. Both are useful study aids. Next, read a chapter or two from different periods. This will give you an idea of the writing style and how the information is presented.

2. Read each assignment twice. The first time through, your goal is to get an overall view of the time period covered. The second reading is for taking notes. With the section titles as a guide, write down key points and significant concepts. You want to pay close attention when the authors discuss the causes or consequences of events, summarize the character of a period, point out different interpretations, or make comparisons between one era and another. Study any maps, statistical tables, or other illustrations during the second reading.

3. The purpose of note taking is to make it easier to review what you've read and to help you retain factual information. You gain nothing if you have twenty pages of notes on a twenty-page chapter. Also, make sure your notes are well organized and clear. Notes are useless if you can't read them. It's a good idea to type up your notes on each chapter.

4. Reread the assignments before a test to reinforce your understanding of the subject matter.

5. Many college textbooks have accompanying workbooks or student manuals. These contain suggested activities for study purposes, such as true-false questions, fill-ins, identifications, chronological arrangement, and sample essays. If your teacher isn't making assignments out of a workbook, it may be helpful to use one on your own. Look in the textbook section of your local college bookstore; remember that the workbook you find may not be written for the book you're reading for your AP class.

The Reader

Readers, or anthologies, are books designed to supplement textbooks by providing students with a variety of perspectives on significant topics in American history. There are two types of readers. The first is a collection of source materials and may include official documents such as laws, treaties, and Supreme Court decisions as well as selections from diaries and journals, travel accounts, memoirs, speeches, and other contemporary records. Source readers give AP students the chance to work with documents similar to those that appear on the DBQ.

The second type of reader contains article-length essays by historians that offer either different interpretations of important issues in American history — for example, the causes of the Civil War and the decision to drop the atomic bomb on Japan — or studies on a particular subject. These interpretive readers help students understand why and how historians disagree.

Readers in United States History

The following readers are easily available at college bookstores or libraries. They are usually published in two-volume paperback editions that cover the period through Reconstruction and from Reconstruction to the present.

Source Readers

Bailey, Thomas A. and David Kennedy, eds. *The American Spirit.*

Boller, Paul F. and Ronald Story, eds. *A More Perfect Union: Documents in U.S. History.*

Commager, Henry S. and Milton Cantor, eds. *Documents of American History.*

Hofstadter, Richard, ed. *Great Issues in American History.*

Interpretative Readers

Problems in American Civilization. This series of pamphlets from D. C. Heath Company presents various interpretations of particular historical problems by prominent historians. The selections are taken from published articles and books.

American Problem Studies. Published by Holt, Rinehart and Winston, this series is very similar to the Heath pamphlets. Each has about a dozen reprinted articles presenting differing points of view. Both series approach a topic as an "either-or" question, "The Cold War: Rivalry or Morality?" for example. Topics in *American Problem Studies* include the American Revolution, ethnic/racial groups, the Civil War, and the Progressive Era.

Cords, Nicholas and Patrick Gerster, eds. *Myth and the American Experience.*

Davis, Allen F. and Harold D. Woodman, eds. *Conflict and Consensus in Modern American History.*

Fine, Sidney and Gerald S. Brown, eds. *The American Past: Conflicting Interpretations of the Great Issues.*

Frazier, Thomas R., ed. *The Underside of American History.*

Nash, Gary B. and Thomas Frazier, eds. *The Private Side of American History.*

Nash, Gary B. and Ronald Schultz, eds. *Retracing the Past: Readings in the History of the American People.*

Quint, Howard H., ed. *Main Problems in American History.*

The Monograph and Historical Series

Historians do research to contribute new information to the body of knowledge that constitutes history. This research is based on primary sources — personal papers and records of organizations, interviews with participants in events (oral history), and, increasingly, quantitative data. The materials that historians rely on may be scattered in archives and libraries across the country, ranging from the local historical society to the National Archives in Washington, D.C. Scholars working in twentieth-century American history will probably visit one of the presidential libraries, which document the administration of every president since Herbert Hoover. The product of this specialized research on a particular topic is known as a *monograph*. More often than not, these books don't wind up on the best-seller list. Historians have been accused of focusing their attention on very narrow topics, mainly of interest to other historians rather than the general public.

Monographs that are part of a historical series are written for a wider audience. While such books usually don't represent original research, they are "state-of-the-art" works that bring together the expertise of the historian and the most recent scholarship on a subject. One of the most famous efforts is Harper and Row's (now HarperCollins) New American Nation series. This is a basic history of the United States divided into several dozen monographs written by historians specializing in each topic. The "New" series succeeded the original "American Nation" series published in the early twentieth century. Some of these volumes still make worthwhile reading if only because they reflect how an earlier generation of historians viewed American history.

Other important historical series are:

> *Chicago History of American Civilization* (University of Chicago Press): Approaches American history both chronologically and topically; individual volumes deal with specific periods and cover particular topics.

> *Library of American Biography* (HarperCollins): Follows a "life and times" approach to American history from the colonial period to the present.

AP teachers often assign a history monograph or require a book review of an outside reading. A monograph not only provides you with a much more detailed picture of an aspect of American history than the textbook but also gives you an idea how historians handle evidence, organize the narrative, and present arguments. On a smaller scale, these are important elements for high scores on the DBQ and standard essays. A book review is an excellent writing assignment that helps you think critically about what you read. Look over the reviews in such journals as the *American Historical Review* or the *Journal of American History*. You'll see immediately that a review is not a summary of what the book is about; it's a concise analysis of the author's thesis and how well he or she supports it.

Reading a History Monograph

There is a select list of monographs for each time period covered in the Overview of United States History. Your textbook also has bibliographies or suggestions for further reading. Reading a monograph is different from reading a textbook; the purpose is to understand the interpretation rather than to collect factual information. Here are a few hints that should help:

1. Identify the author's thesis first. Historians usually state what they're trying to prove in the introduction or preface and restate it along with their conclusions in the last chapter.

2. Go over the table of contents and skim through the chapters to get a sense of the organization. Does the author take a chronological or topical approach to the subject? The footnotes and bibliography will tell you whether the book is a product of original research, presumably presenting new information, or a synthesis of the work of other historians.

3. Once you understand the thesis and organization, read the entire book and take notes on the main points. Does the author review what other historians have said on the topic or explain why his or her approach is different? What are the arguments the author uses to support the thesis? What subjects are covered in depth?

4. Just as with a textbook, your notes should be clear and, above all, concise.

Scholarly Journals

Historians don't just write textbooks and monographs or edit readers. Most historical writing appears as articles in scholarly journals. It's helpful to look through the journals to get an idea of what new approaches historians are taking and which topics are attracting their attention. Many articles deal with extremely narrow subjects. What a text covers in a line or two might be explored in thirty pages in a journal. Articles that assess the work done on a particular theme or period — slavery or the Progressive Era, for example, or a field of study such as diplomatic history — are often more useful to the AP student.

In addition to articles, journals contain reviews of new books published by historians, which are models of review writing. They also help students understand that just because a book appears in print, it isn't necessarily without flaws. Historian reviewers are quick to point out shortcomings in research and organization. Occasionally, an author disagrees with the reviewer to the point where a spirited exchange of letters is published. Reviews give students a quick overview of the current research in U.S. history.

You should be aware of two publications that deal exclusively with book reviews: *History: Reviews of New Books* and *Reviews in American History.* The latter has extended essays, sometimes called review articles, about several books on the same topic. Both are useful in seeing what historians have to say about the latest works in their field.

Beyond articles and reviews, the leading scholarly journals have other features worth noting. They may include bibliographies of recently published articles. It's also interesting to browse the back pages where publishers advertise their latest textbook editions and monographs. You may see your own textbook advertised here and get a sense of why it's being used in your class.

Journals are almost always published by professional organizations and usually appear quarterly. They may focus on U.S. history generally, the history of a region or state, or a particular field of study. The latter will have articles on world as well as U.S. history. The following list barely scratches the surface.

Scholarly Journals in United States History

American Historical Review. Published five times a year by the American Historical Association, its articles deal with the entire scope of history, but many are on American history. The articles are heavily footnoted and may run up to thirty pages.

Historian. A quarterly published by Phi Alpha Theta, the national history honor society, it includes articles on world and American history.

Journal of American History. Published quarterly by the Organization of American Historians, this is the leading journal for historians who do research in American history. Topics run chronologically from the colonial period to the recent past and cover cultural, diplomatic, economic, intellectual, political, and social history. Until 1964, it was called the *Mississippi Valley Historical Review.*

Journal of Southern History. Published quarterly by the Southern Historical Association, it covers the history of the South.

Pacific Historical Review. This quarterly is published by the Pacific Coast Branch of the American Historical Association and deals primarily with American history in the Pacific Coast states; it also features articles about Asia-Pacific developments.

Western Historical Quarterly. Published since 1970 by the Western History Association, it deals in broad definition with the westward movement, the frontier, and the West.

Other Regional History Journals

California History
Journal of Arizona History
New Mexico Historical Review
Pacific Northwest Historical Quarterly
Southwest Historical Quarterly

Field of Study Journals

Civil War History
Diplomatic History
Journal of American Ethnic History
Journal of Economic History
Journal of the History of Ideas (intellectual history)

Journal of Negro History

Journal of Social History

Journal of Sport History

Journal of Urban History

Journal of Women's History

Labor History

The Public Historian

Technology and Culture

AP students can find these and other journals in most college libraries. The larger the college or university, the more journals it will carry. You can see recent issues of the *American Historical Review* and the *Journal of American History* on line at http://www.historycooperative.org.

In addition to scholarly journals, there are magazines aimed at the general reading public interested in history. The most noted of the popular history journals is *American Heritage.* First published in 1954 as a bimonthly, the magazine now appears eight times a year. The articles in *American Heritage* see history as a story worth telling. They are lavishly illustrated, often in color, and cover a wide range of topics. Right behind *American Heritage* is *American History* (formerly *American History Illustrated),* published on a more modest scale but with similar attention to history as a story. Taken together, these two magazines provide interesting information in a style that puts you at ease. The main drawback is that they seldom deal with themes over which historians disagree. Instead, they take a mainstream approach, possibly noting disagreement but not addressing it as a topic for examination. Selected articles from *American Heritage* and *American History* can be reviewed on line at http://www.americanheritage.com and http://thehistorynet.com, respectively.

Audiovisual Sources

Some teachers will tell their AP students not to waste time watching film documentaries, but there are some worthwhile programs that may enhance your understanding of the past. The best of these by far is *The American Experience* series on PBS. Programs have dealt with the Fifty-Fourth Colored Infantry in the Civil War, the Johnstown flood, the Prohibition era, and World War I. *A Walk Through the Twentieth Century,* also on PBS, offers documentaries on twentieth-century American history. Individual episodes of both of these series have been marketed on videocassettes, and some may be available in your school library.

Students are advised to stay away from historical "docudramas" on commercial or cable television. In many cases these programs distort or even falsify the historical record in order to intensify their dramatic impact.

Reference Sources

Your AP teacher may require a short research assignment, or you may decide to tackle one of the limited research papers listed earlier. In any event, AP students should be familiar with the basic reference sources in American history.

The most important reference work is *America: History and Life*. Published since 1964 by the American Bibliographical Center (ABC-CLIO), this is a comprehensive bibliographic index to articles, book reviews, and dissertations in American history. It provides short abstracts (summaries) of articles in hundreds of history journals. It's well worth your time to look over *America: History and Life* and learn how to use its indexes. Reading the abstracts of the articles on a particular topic will save you considerable time The reference section of the college library is the best place to find sources of information on people, places, and events in American history. In addition to *America: History and Life,* you should be familiar with the *Harvard Guide to American History.* Originally published in 1954 and revised in 1974, the guide includes general works and specialized monographs on the major topics and periods of American history. There are also sections on historical sources, methodology, and historiography (the history of historical writing). Interpreting maps and statistical data are important skills for doing well on the AP exam. You should look over a good historical atlas such as James Truslow Adams's *Atlas of American History* to supplement your ongoing review of the maps in your text. Many of the charts, tables, and graphs in textbooks and on the exam are based on the data in *Historical Statistics of the United States: Colonial Times to 1970.* Published by the Bureau of the Census, it contains statistical tables from 1610 covering important economic and social developments. Other useful reference works include:

> *The American Heritage Encyclopedia of American History,* edited by John Mack Faragher.
>
> *Dictionary of American History,* edited by James Truslow Adams.
>
> *Encyclopaedia of American Facts and Dates.*
>
> *Encyclopedia of American History,* edited by Richard B. Morris.
>
> *Great Events from History, American Series,* edited by Frank N. Magill.
>
> *The Reader's Companion to American History,* edited by Eric Foner and John A. Garraty.

This list is far from exhaustive. Your AP teacher or the reference librarian can suggest other sources specifically on your research topic.

American History on the Internet

There are innumerable websites on the internet that can be helpful to you in preparing for the AP history exam. AP teachers and even students who have taken the exam have set up websites that may include lecture notes, important historical documents, sample DBQs and standard essays, test-taking hints, and links to relevant American history sites. These can be interesting to look at even if just to see what your peers are doing. Be aware, however, that the sites are as good as the people who put them together and may not contain the most up-to-date information about the exam.

We believe that the best use of the Internet is to locate the wide variety of primary sources in American history that an AP student should be able to handle. The National Archives and Records Administration's Digital Classroom (http://www.nara.gov/education/classrm.html) uses documents such as letters, census schedules, photographs to examine a broad range of historical questions from how barbed wire changed the West to why the United States became involved in the Korean War. The site also has worksheets that will help you learn how to analyze cartoons, maps, photographs, and text documents. The American Memory Project, the digitized historical collections from the Library of Congress (http://memory.loc.gov/ammem/amhome.html), is a tremendously rich source of information on cultural, social, economic, and political history of the United States. Finally the Yale Law School Avalon Project (http://www.yale.edu/lawweb/avalon/avalon.htm) provides access to a tremendous variety of texts from the Age of Exploration through Vietnam and the Cold War.

Here is a list of other American history sites that you might want to check out:

AMDOCS: Documents for the Study of American History
http://ukans.edu/carrie/docsamdocs-index.html

American and British History Resources on the Internet
http://www.libraries.rutgers.edu/rulib/socsci/hist/amhist.html

Archives, Documents/Databases, and Societies in American History
http://hist.unt.edu/09w-amn1.htm

History Matters
http://historymatters.gmu.edu

History On-Line
http://www.historian.org/home.htm

Hyptertext on American History
http://dour.let.rug.nl/~usa/

Making of America
http://www.umdl.umich.edu/moa

Historians and Their Work

The writing of U.S. history reflects clear-cut patterns of thought at various periods. The Puritans had their Christian interpretation of history. Early colonial leaders such as William Bradford and John Winthrop reflected this approach. In the eighteenth century, historians stressed the Enlightenment idea that reason would guide mankind along the path of progress. Historians in the next century turned to romantic beliefs in hero worship and adventure. Near the end of the nineteenth century, American historians, many of them with academic training in Germany, began to practice the teaching and writing of history as a profession. It was quite the fashion at the time to think of history writing in scientific rather than literary terms. During the Depression of the 1930s, practically every study involved an economic interpretation. As you can see, the way history is written is not static; it mirrors the ideas and characteristics of the time in which it was written.

Perhaps the most well-known school of thought is that of the Progressive historians of the late nineteenth and early twentieth century. These scholars viewed American history in terms of conflict — rich vs. poor, farmer vs. merchant, debtor vs. creditor, democracy vs. aristocracy. They believed that progress was inevitable, that the United States was moving toward a more ideal order. To the Progressive historian, all periods in American history could be divided into two clear and distinct phases: periods of active reform and periods of conservative consolidation.

Many Progressive historians were themselves committed to reform movements in the early 1900s and tended to view their own era in terms of a struggle by the people to free themselves from the large corporate monopolies. They read back into history the same conflict between the masses and the upper classes that seemed to be taking place before their own eyes. An excellent analysis of this group is Richard Hofstadter's *The Progressive Historians,* which focuses on Frederick Jackson Turner, Charles Beard, and Vernon L. Parrington.

After World War II, historical writing in the United States became more conservative. Historians such as Daniel Boorstin and Richard Hoftstadter viewed American history in terms of consensus rather than conflict. They deemphasized class and sectional divisions, arguing instead that there was never any class struggle in the United States as there had been in Europe. They were cynical about the optimistic view of the Progressive historians. The war, nuclear weapons, and the apathy of the masses during the 1950s made them see their predecessors' views as too simple. The Conservative historians claimed that Americans have fought only over the means of reaching their basic objectives but that the goals have always been the same. Their writing shows a need to prove national unity among the American people.

The Revisionists are in sharp contrast to the Conservative historians of the 1940s and 1950s. Revisionism occurs when a historian challenges the accepted understanding of an event or issue. Revisionist historians such as Howard Zinn, William Appelman Williams, and Eugene Genovese offer new versions that on occasion overwhelm conventional understanding and become the new standard interpretation. A subject that revisionists have written extensively on is the involvement of the United States in World War II. The United States entered the war after the Japanese attack on Pearl Harbor on December 7, 1941. The conventional interpretation is that Japan began the war with an unfair "sneak attack" that was part of a policy of aggression in the Pacific. The Revisionists maintain that President Franklin Roosevelt, through inept and racist foreign policies, placed Japan in a no-win position where the only alternative was to attack. Some historians also maintain that the United States knew about Japan's plans to attack Pearl Harbor but did nothing so as to provide a reason for getting involved in the war in Europe.

Students interested in the current work of American historians should examine *The New American History (1997),* which was edited for the American Historical Association by Eric Foner. It contains essays reviewing the latest scholarship both by time period and subject, e.g., women's history, labor history, diplomatic history. Each essay includes an extensive bibliography of books and articles.

The Varieties of History

History texts and many monographs and articles deal with a few areas of historical study: political, economic, social, and intellectual history. Today, many new fields have become objects of study by historians. These include ethnic history, women's history, environmental history, and psychohistory (which seeks to explain the past by examining the motives of individuals).

The use of oral history has also become significant, both as an aid to traditional research and a field of study in its own right. The recollections of people who were involved in significant events adds greatly to the historical record. Moreover, oral history gives a voice to people who didn't appear in history because they didn't leave written records.

Quantitative historians practice what they call "cliometrics," using such records as election returns, ship passenger lists, and a wide variety of other statistical sources to make conclusions about historical patterns in immigration, population movements, demography (where people live), persistence patterns (how long people live in one place), and economic status. Their work is characterized by numerous tables, charts, and graphs, which narrative historians sometimes claim makes their work unreadable. The quantitative historians reply that narrative is often inexact and imprecise when it come to the analysis of data.

History as an academic discipline in the United States is just over a century old. While most historians teach, others make their livelihood outside of the college or university community. The books of Barbara Tuchman and David McCullough have become national bestsellers. Public, or applied, history is a comparatively new field. Public historians are not based in a university but work for government agencies, private corporations, historical societies and museums, and as independent consultants. They may develop corporate archives, write a company or agency history, provide expert testimony in a lawsuit, or tackle numerous other assignments that involve the application of the historian's research and analytical skills to real-world issues.

You should be aware that there are people who use history for their own purposes. They knowingly twist facts, make up their own, and consciously misinterpret data to convince people that history happened in a certain way. The fake historians usually take an extreme view on topics that at first glance would seem unquestionable. The most notorious example of this type of writing is the effort to "prove" that the Holocaust, the extermination of six million Jews during World War II, never happened.

Some Prominent American Historians

There is no way to create a definitive list of historians without leaving out significant scholars or areas of research. But even a partial list of original and influential historians would include the following:

- **Charles A. Beard**

  Beard achieved lasting and controversial fame when he published *An Economic Interpretation of the Constitution of the United States* in 1913. Instead of dealing with the Constitution as a political document, he studied it in economic terms and concluded that the framers were motivated by economic self-interest. Even today, any discussion of the Constitution remains incomplete without acknowledgment of Beard's work.

- **Bruce Catton**

  While not a particularly original researcher, Catton wrote numerous studies on the Civil War distinguished by a very high level of quality writing. His works, including the three-volume *Centennial History of the Civil War,* are of continuing interest.

- **Henry Steele Commager**

  A specialist in American intellectual history, Commager is perhaps best known for his classic textbook and his *Documents in American History,* which has gone through numerous editions and remains an excellent collection of primary sources.

- **John Hope Franklin**

  For many years, Franklin was the leading African-American historian in the United States, and his works, particularly *From Slavery to Freedom* (1947), are basic to understanding African-American historiography.

- **Richard Hofstadter**

  Hofstadter had the rare talent of writing on a number of subjects, primarily in intellectual history, and having each of his books influence the work of his colleagues. Among his many books are *The American Political Tradition, The Age of Reform,* and *Anti-Intellectualism in American Life.*

- **William Leuchtenburg**

  A specialist in recent American history, Leuchtenburg is best known for his informative and readable *Perils of Prosperity, 1914–1932* (1958) and his contribution to the New American Nation series, *Franklin D. Roosevelt and the New Deal, 1932–1940* (1963).

- **Patricia Nelson Limerick**

  Limerick gained attention in the early 1980s with her major revisions of Frederick Jackson Turner's view of western history. Her *Legacy of Conquest: The Unbroken Past of the American West* is considered a major contribution to western historiography.

- **Arthur S. Link**

  Link is the major interpreter of the life of Woodrow Wilson. He is writing a multi-volume biography of Wilson, and his significant monographs includes *Woodrow Wilson and the Progressive Era.* Link is the chief editor of the Wilson papers. Any study of Wilson must begin with Link's work.

- **Vernon Parrington**

  The leader of the Progressive historians, Parrington's major work is *Main Currents in American Thought* (1927–1930). His negative interpretation of the Puritans influenced the views of a generation of other scholars.

- **Arthur Schlesinger, Jr.**

  The son of a noted historian, Schlesinger gained early attention with his *Age of Jackson.* His *Age of Roosevelt,* a three-volume study of Franklin Roosevelt and the New Deal, is an outstanding example of history writing that has captured a popular audience. An advisor to President Kennedy, he has also written *A Thousand Days: John F. Kennedy in the White House.*

- **Frederick Jackson Turner**

  In 1893, Turner delivered a path-breaking address to the American Historical Association entitled "The Significance of the Frontier in American History." For many years afterward, his ideas of the frontier as the determining factor in shaping the American character were discussed and debated among historians. Never a prolific writer, Turner's essays have been collected in several books, the most important of which is *The Frontier in American History.*

Although it might appear from the list that American historical writing is dominated by men, women historians have certainly made and continue to make important contributions to the field. Women's history encompasses both general surveys of women in American life and monographs on such topics as women in the workplace. Leading American women historians include Susan Hartmann, Alice Kessler-Harris, and Susan Ware.

An Overview of United States History

The following overview of U.S. history concentrates on political and economic developments. Each of the twelve sections contains a brief outline of things to know about the period, a list of important individuals, events, and concepts, key definitions, and a short bibliography of helpful monographs for further reading. Tables present information about the Age of Exploration, the founding of the British colonies, the background to the American Revolution, the Supreme Court decisions of Chief Justice Marshall, events leading up to the Civil War, and the programs of the New Deal. If you want a more detailed summary of American history, we suggest you use *Cliffs Quick Review U.S. History I and II (1998, 1999)* by the authors.

The overview is best used as a study guide for tests in your AP class and for the AP exam itself. As you read your text, identify the items listed under Key Terms and Concepts in a sentence or two. Since it's impossible to include all the people, places, and things or define all the terms that you or your teacher find important, add to those provided here. You may want to use three-by-five index cards to better organize this part of your notes. Also, try your hand at making up additional tables — Supreme Court decisions dealing with civil rights or major American writers, for example. Tables are a good way of summarizing information on a theme or broad subject in U.S. history, particularly one that covers a long period of time.

Exploration and Colonization, 1492–1763

Things to Know

1. *Factors in the European Age of Exploration (fifteenth–sixteenth centuries):* importance of trade with Asia; need for new routes; improvements in maritime technology; rise of nation-states.

2. *Major voyages of exploration and conquest:* explorers, dates of voyages, countries they represented, results; consequences of first contact — Great Biological Exchange.

THE AGE OF EXPLORATION			
Date	**Explorer**	**Country**	**Results**
1487	Diaz	Portugal	rounds southern tip of Africa
1492	Columbus	Spain	first to explore Western Hemisphere
1497	da Gama	Portugal	sea route to India by sailing around Africa
	Cabot	England	explores Newfoundland and Nova Scotia
1499	Vespucci	Spain	explores coast of South America
1500	Cabral	Portugal	Portugal's claim on Brazil
1519	Cortes	Spain	conquest of Aztecs
	Magellan	Spain	circumnavigates world
1531	Pizarro	Spain	conquest of Peru (Incas)
1535	Cartier	France	explores St. Lawrence River
1539	de Soto	Spain	explores lower Mississippi River
1540	Coronado	Spain	explores the Southwest

3. *Establishment of English colonies of North America:* motives in founding colonies (economic and religious); when and how the colonies were established.

ENGLISH COLONIES IN NORTH AMERICA		
Colony	**Founded By**	**Significance**
Jamestown (1607)	Virginia Company	first permanent English colony
Plymouth (1620)	Pilgrims	Mayflower Compact
Massachusetts Bay (1630)	Massachusetts Bay Company	Puritans
Maryland (1634)	Lord Baltimore	first proprietary colony; Catholics
Rhode Island (1636)	Roger Williams	religious toleration
Connecticut (1636)	Thomas Hooker	Fundamental Orders of Connecticut
Delaware (1638)	Swedes	under English rule from 1664
Carolinas (1663)	proprietary	North and South given separate charters in the eighteenth century
New York (1664)	Duke of York	under Dutch control as New Amsterdam from 1621 to 1664
New Hampshire (1664)	John Mason	royal charter in 1679
New Jersey (1664)	Berkeley and Carteret	overshadowed by New York
Pennsylvania (1681)	William Penn	Quakers
Georgia (1732)	James Oglethorpe	buffer against Spanish Florida

4. *Economic basis of colonies:* differences between New England, middle colonies, and southern colonies; role of agriculture, industry, and trade.

5. *Colonial society:* labor force — indentured servants and slaves; ethnic diversity — Germans, Scotch-Irish, Jews; status of women; relations between colonists and Native Americans; religious dimension — religious conformity vs. religious dissent; Puritanism, Great Awakening.

6. *Relations with Great Britain:* mercantilism and its early impact on colonies; impact of events in England — Restoration (1660) and Glorious Revolution (1688); colonial political institutions — assemblies and governors; Anglo-French rivalry in North America — French and Indian War.

Key Terms and Concepts

Mesoamerica

Great Biological Exchange

Line of Demarcation

Treaty of Tordesillas

lost colony of Roanoke

Virginia Company

Virginia House of Burgesses

William Bradford

Mayflower Compact

John Winthrop

"City on a Hill"

Salem witch trials

Roger Williams

Thomas Hooker

Pequot War

King Philip's War

Bacon's Rebellion

New Amsterdam

"Peaceable Kingdom"

Society of Friends

Maryland Toleration Act (1649)

Fundamental Orders of Connecticut (1639)

Restoration colonies

Dominion of New England

John Peter Zenger

Jonathan Edwards

George Whitefield

Leisler's Rebellion

Albany Plan of Union

Benjamin Franklin

Treaty of Paris (1763)

Important Definitions

Antinomianism: An interpretation of Puritan beliefs that stressed God's gift of salvation and minimized what an individual could do to gain salvation; identified with Anne Hutchinson.

enumerated articles: Under the English Navigation Acts, those commodities that could be shipped only to England or other English colonies; originally included sugar, tobacco, cotton, and indigo.

Great Awakening: Religious revival movement during the 1730s and 1740s; its leaders were George Whitefield and Jonathan Edwards; religious pluralism was promoted by the idea that all Protestant denominations were legitimate.

Great Migration: Settlement of over twenty thousand Puritans in Massachusetts Bay and other parts of New England between 1630 and 1642.

Half-Way Covenant: In 1662, Puritans permitted the baptized children of church members into a "half-way" membership in the congregation and allowed them to baptize their children; they still could not vote or take communion.

headright system: Method of attracting settlers to Virginia; after 1618, it gave fifty acres of land to anyone who paid for their own passage or for that of any other settlers who might be sent or brought to the colony.

indentured servants: Individuals who sold their labor for a fixed number of years in return for passage to the colonies; indentured servants were usually young, unemployed men and could be sold.

joint-stock company: The company sold shares of stock to finance the outfitting of overseas expeditions; colonies founded by joint-stock companies included Jamestown (Virginia Company) and New Amsterdam (Dutch West India Company).

mercantilism: Economic policy that held that the strength of a nation is based on the amount of gold and silver it has; also, that the country needs a favorable balance of trade and that colonies exist for the good of the mother country as a source of raw materials and a market for manufactured goods.

Middle Passage: The sea route followed by slave traders from the west coast of Africa to the Western Hemisphere.

proprietary colony: A colony founded as a grant of land by the king to an individual or group of individuals; Maryland (1634) and Carolina (1663) were proprietary colonies.

Separatists: Those who wanted to break all connections with the Church of England as opposed to most Puritans who believed it was possible to reform the church; the Pilgrims were Separatists.

triangular trade: Trade pattern that developed in the colonies; New England shipped rum to the west coast of Africa in exchange for slaves that were sent to the West Indies for molasses that was sold in New England.

Readings on Exploration and Colonization

Bailyn, Bernard. *The Peopling of British North America: An Introduction* (1986).

Boorstin, Daniel J. *The Americans: The Colonial Experience* (1958).

Greene, Jack P. and J. R. Pole, eds. *Colonial British America* (1984).

Hofstadter, Richard F. *America at 1750: A Social Portrait* (1971).

Nash, Gary B. *Red, White, and Black: The Peoples of Early America* (1982).

The American Revolution, 1763–1787

Things to Know

1. *British Empire in North America in 1763:* debts resulting from wars with France and increased cost of administering the colonies; western land issues — Pontiac's Rebellion and Proclamation Line of 1763.

2. *Britain's attempt to exercise greater control over the colonies and increase revenues:* policies of Grenville and Townshend; reaction of the colonies, particularly evidence of greater unity; debate on relations between Britain and colonies — rights of Englishmen vs. virtual representation and Declaratory Act.

BRITISH IMPERIAL POLICY, 1764–1774	
Parliamentary Act	*Colonial Reaction*
Sugar Act (1764): expanded the list of enumerated articles; stricter enforcement of trade regulations	
Currency Act (1764): colonies prohibited from issuing paper money	
Stamp Act (1765): tax on printed materials and legal documents	Virginia Resolves; Stamp Act Congress; Sons of Liberty
Quartering Act (1765): colonies to provide British troops with housing and provisions	
Townshend Acts (1767): external taxes on colonial imports	non-importation agreements; *Letters of a Farmer in Pennsylvania*
Tea Act (1773): monopoly to East India Company for tea sold in colonies	Boston Tea Party
Coercive Acts (1774): British response to Boston Tea Party, intended to punish Boston	First Continental Congress

3. *The American Revolution:* Key political and military events of the American Revolution, 1775–1783; change in attitude on independence; social consequences of Revolution — slavery, status of women; growth of religious toleration.

4. *United States under the Articles of Confederation:* accomplishments under the Articles — land policy and foreign relations; weaknesses of the Confederation; immediate background to the Constitutional Convention.

Key Terms and Concepts

Pontiac's Rebellion

Proclamation Line of 1763

Paxton Boys

North and South Carolina Regulators

Letters of a Farmer in Pennsylvania

Samuel Adams

Sons of Liberty

Gaspee incident

Boston Massacre

circular letter

Committees of Correspondence

Thomas Jefferson

Patrick Henry

Continental Association

Lexington and Concord

Ticonderoga

Olive Branch Petition

Bunker Hill

Trenton and Princeton

Oriskany

Benedict Arnold

Saratoga

Treaty of Alliance (1778)

Savannah

Yorktown

General Cornwallis

Treaty of Paris (1783)

western land claims

Land Ordinance of 1785

Northwest Ordinance

Shays' Rebellion

Important Definitions

Committees of Correspondence: First established in Boston in 1772, the committees became a way for the colonies to state and communicate their grievances against Great Britain.

Critical Period: Term used by historians to describe the United States under the Articles of Confederation.

direct tax: British-imposed tax directly on the colonies that was intended to raise revenue; the Stamp Act was the first attempt by Parliament to impose a direct tax on the colonies.

indirect tax: A measure that raised revenue through the regulation of trade — the Sugar Act, for example.

Loyalists: Also known as Tories, the term refers to those Americans who remained loyal to Great Britain during the Revolution.

non-importation agreements: A form of protest against British policies; colonial merchants refused to import British goods.

"No taxation without representation": The assertion that Great Britain had no right to tax the American colonies as long as they did not have their own representatives in Parliament.

virtual representation: The British argument that the American colonies were represented in Parliament, since the members of Parliament represented all Englishmen in the empire.

Whig ideology: Idea that concentrated power leads to corruption and tyranny; emphasis on balanced government where legislatures check the power of the executive.

Writs of Assistance: Search warrants that allowed British soldiers to search the houses or businesses of colonists.

Readings on the American Revolution

Alden, John. *The American Revolution* (1969).

Bailyn, Bernard. *The Ideological Origins of the American Revolution* (1967).

Fiske, John M. *The Critical Period of American History, 1783–1789* (1883).

Higginbotham, Don. *The War of American Independence* (1971).

Jameson, John Franklin. *The American Revolution Considered as a Social Movement* (1926).

MacLeod, Duncan J. *Slavery, Race and the American Revolution* (1974).

Middlekauff, Robert. *The Glorious Cause: The American Revolution, 1763–1789* (1982).

Quarles, Benjamin. *The Negro in the American Revolution* (1961).

The Constitution and the Federalists, 1787–1800

Things to Know

1. *The Constitution:* major compromises of the Constitutional Convention — representation, slavery, election of the President; principles embodied in the Constitution — separation of power and checks and balances; ratification –– Federalists vs. Antifederalists; amendments to the Constitution.

2. *Washington as President:* development of the Cabinet; economic problems facing the early Republic and Hamilton's response; relations with Great Britain and France.

3. *Rise of political parties:* election of John Adams; issues that led to Republican opposition; relations with France and the Alien and Sedition Acts and Republican response; Jefferson and the "Revolution of 1800."

The Structure of Government under the Constitution

Article I: Legislative Branch (Congress)

House of Representatives: Members elected for two-year terms; number of representatives for each state based on population; all revenue bills originate in the House.

Senate: Two senators from each state, chosen by state legislatures; serve six-year term; Vice President is President of the Senate and votes only in the event of tie; tries all impeachment cases; ratifies treaties and confirms appointments.

The President's veto of a law passed by Congress can be overridden by a two-thirds vote of both houses.

Principal powers of Congress (enumerated powers): Collect taxes; regulate foreign and inter-state commerce; coin money; establish post offices and post roads; declare war; raise and support army and navy; make all laws necessary to carry out above ("necessary and proper" clause).

Limitations on Congress: Cannot prohibit importation of slaves prior to 1808; cannot suspend the writ of habeas corpus; cannot enact bill of attainder or ex post facto law.

Article II: Executive Branch (President and Vice President)

President: Elected for four-year term; elected by electors from each state; the candidate who receives second highest total votes becomes Vice President.

Powers of the President: Commander-in-chief of army, navy, and state militia; make treaties and appointments of ambassadors, executive departments, and Supreme Court with "advice and consent of the Senate."

Article III: Judicial Branch (Supreme Court)

Supreme Court established; Congress given authority to create inferior courts; Supreme Court has original jurisdiction in cases involving ambassadors and the states; in all other cases, the Supreme Court has appellate jurisdiction; trial by jury is provided for, and treason is defined.

Article IV: Relations with States

Position of states and territories; each state will give "full faith and credit" to acts and court actions of the states; privileges and immunities of citizens in the states; fugitive slave provision; Congress shall control territories and admit new states; government to protect states from foreign invasion or domestic violence.

Article V: Amendment Process

Amendments proposed by two-thirds vote of Congress or application by two-thirds of state legislatures; amendments ratified by three-fourths of state legislatures.

Article VI: Supremacy Clause

The Constitution, laws passed by Congress, and treaties entered into by the United States supreme law of land; no religious test for holding office.

Article VII: Ratification of Constitution

Ratification of Constitution requires nine of the thirteen states.

Amendments to the Constitution

Amendment I (1791): Freedom of religion, speech, press, and assembly; right of petition.

Amendment II (1791): Right to bear arms (militia).

Amendment III (1791): Limit on quartering of troops.

Amendment IV (1791): Protection against unreasonable search and seizure.

Amendment V (1791): Due process; double jeopardy; self-incrimination.

Amendment VI (1791): Right to speedy trial.

Amendment VII (1791): Trial by jury in civil cases.

Amendment VIII (1791): No excessive bail or fine; no cruel or unusual punishment.

Amendment IX (1791): People retain rights.

Amendment X (1791): Powers not delegated to United States to states or people.

Amendment XI (1798): States cannot be sued by individuals.

Amendment XII (1804): Electoral College.

Amendment XIII (1865): Abolition of slavery.

Amendment XIV (1868): Equal protection under the law.

Amendment XV (1870): Right to vote guaranteed irrespective of race, color, or former condition of slavery.

Amendment XVI (1913): Income tax.

Amendment XVII (1913): Direct election of senators.

Amendment XVIII (1919): Prohibition.

Amendment XIX (1920): Women gain right to vote.

Amendment XX (1933): End to lame-duck session of Congress; change in when President and Congress take office.

Amendment XXI (1933): Repeal of prohibition.

Amendment XXII (1951): Two-term limit for President.

Amendment XXIII (1961): Voting for President in District of Columbia.

Amendment XXIV (1964): Abolition of poll tax in national elections.

Amendment XXV (1967): Presidential succession.

Amendment XXVI (1971): Lower voting age to eighteen.

Amendment XXVII (1992): Congressional salaries.

Key Terms and Concepts

Virginia Plan

New Jersey Plan

Connecticut Compromise

3/5 Compromise

census

Federalists

Antifederalists

Federalist Papers

Alexander Hamilton

John Jay

James Madison

Bill of Rights

Judiciary Act of 1789

Executive departments — State, Treasury, War, Attorney General

Bank of the United States

strict/loose construction

protective tariff

Whiskey Rebellion

impressment

Citizen Genêt

Jay's Treaty

Pinckney's Treaty

XYZ Affair

John Adams

Democratic-Republicans

Alien and Sedition Acts

Kentucky and Virginia Resolutions

Aaron Burr

election of 1800

Important Definitions

Antifederalists: Opposed to a strong central government; saw undemocratic tendencies in the Constitution and insisted on the inclusion of the Bill of Rights. Included Thomas Jefferson, James Monroe, and Patrick Henry.

checks and balances: System embodied in the Constitution through which the power of each branch of government is limited by the other; the President's authority to veto legislation and Congress's power to override that veto are examples.

Compact theory of government: The idea that the Constitution was a compact of sovereign states, and when the government exceeded its limited powers, the states had the right to take action. This idea is reflected in the Virginia and Kentucky Resolutions.

enumerated powers: Powers specifically given to Congress in the Constitution; including the power to collect taxes, coin money, regulate foreign and interstate commerce, and declare war.

Federalists: Supporters of a strong central government; stressed the importance of maintaining the social order and the rights of property. Included George Washington, Alexander Hamilton, and James Madison.

loose construction: Constitution is broadly interpreted, recognizing that it could not possibly anticipate all future developments; relies on idea of implied powers and the "necessary and proper" clause. Both views on how to interpret the Constitution came up during the debate on chartering the Bank of the United States.

protective tariff: A tax on goods imported into the country that is intended to protect manufacturing and industry from foreign competition.

separation of powers: The structure of the government provided for in the Constitution where authority is divided between the executive, legislative, and judicial branches; idea comes from Montesquieu's Spirit of the Laws.

strict construction: Constitution is narrowly interpreted to give the federal government only those powers specifically delegated to it.

supremacy clause: The Constitution, treaties entered into by the United States, and laws passed by Congress are superior to state laws.

Readings on the Constitution and the Federalists

Appleby, Joyce. *Capitalism and a New Social Order: The Republican Vision of the 1790s* (1984).

Beard, Charles A. *An Economic Interpretation of the Constitution of the United States* (1913).

Collier, Christopher and James Collier. *Decision in Philadelphia* (1986).

Cunliffe, Marcus. *The Nation Takes Shape, 1789–1837* (1959).

Main, Jackson T. *The Anti-Federalists* (1961).

Miller, John C. *The Federalist Era, 1789–1800* (1960).

Morris, Richard. *Witnesses at the Creation: Hamilton, Madison, Jay and the Constitution* (1985).

Jeffersonian and Jacksonian Democracy, 1800–1840

Things to Know

1. *Jefferson as President:* attitude toward Federalist programs; Louisiana Purchase and reaction to it; foreign policy and neutral rights.

2. *The Supreme Court under John Marshall:* major cases and significance of decisions.

KEY DECISIONS OF THE SUPREME COURT UNDER JOHN MARSHALL	
Case	*Significance*
Marbury v. Madison (1803)	first time an act of Congress declared unconstitutional; establishes principle of judicial review
Fletcher v. Peck (1810)	first time a state law declared unconstitutional; contract clause of the Constitution overrode state law
Dartmouth College v. Woodward (1819)	the charter of a private corporation is protected under the Constitution
McCulloch v. Maryland (1819)	upheld constitutionality of Bank of the United States; example of loose construction of the Constitution
Gibbons v. Ogden (1824)	affirmed federal control of interstate commerce under commerce clause of the Constitution

3. *Presidencies of James Madison and James Monroe:* foreign-policy background and results of War of 1812 and Monroe Doctrine; economic nationalism — development of national transportation system and tariff policy; shift from cottage industry to factory system.

4. *The Age of Jackson:* election of 1824 — "corrupt bargain"; political views of Democrats; strong executive — veto as instrument of political power; Second Bank of the United States; nullification crisis; Indian policy; Whig party.

Key Terms and Concepts

Judiciary Act of 1801

midnight judges

judicial review

Lewis and Clark Expedition

Embargo Act of 1807

Non-Intercourse Act

Henry Clay

John C. Calhoun

Daniel Webster

Francis Scott Key

Battle of New Orleans

Treaty of Ghent

Hartford Convention

Rush-Bagot Agreement

factory system
National Road
Erie Canal
Adams-Onís Treaty
Monroe Doctrine
Noah Webster
Washington Irving
James Fenimore Cooper

Democrat-Republicans
National-Republicans
Trail of Tears
spoils system
Maysville Road veto
Tariff of Abominations
Webster-Hayne debate
Independent Treasury Act

Important Definitions

American System: Economic program advanced by Henry Clay that included support for a national bank, high tariffs, and internal improvements; emphasized strong role for federal government in the economy.

corrupt bargain: Refers to the claim from the supporters of Andrew Jackson that John Quincy Adams and Henry Clay had worked out a deal to ensure that Adams was elected President by the House of Representatives in 1824.

Era of Good Feelings: Refers to the period after the War of 1812, during the presidency of James Monroe, when competition among political parties was at a low ebb.

impressment: British practice of taking American sailors from American ships and forcing them into the British navy; a factor in the War of 1812.

internal improvements: Included roads, canals, railroads; essentially, an internal transportation network that would bind the country together.

judicial review: The right of the Supreme Court to declare a law passed by Congress unconstitutional; the principle was established in *Marbury v. Madison*.

Kitchen Cabinet: Informal group of friends who advised Jackson during his administration. Jackson believed that the "official" Cabinet's main function was to carry out his orders.

nullification: The theory advanced by John Calhoun in response to the Tariff of 1828; states, acting through a popular convention, could declare a law passed by Congress "null and void"; the roots of the idea go back to Jefferson's compact theory of government.

pet banks: A term used by Jackson's opponents to describe the state banks that the federal government used for new revenue deposits in an attempt to destroy the Second Bank of the United States; the practice continued after the charter for the Second Bank expired in 1836.

spoils system: Essentially, political patronage; public offices went to political supporters during Jackson's presidency.

War Hawks: Those nationalist members of Congress who strongly supported war with Great Britain on the eve of the War of 1812; included Henry Clay and John C. Calhoun.

Readings on Jeffersonian and Jacksonian Democracy

Brodie, Fawn. *Thomas Jefferson: An Intimate History* (1974).

Dangerfield, George. *The Era of Good Feelings* (1952).

Ellis, Richard. *The Jeffersonian Crisis: Courts and Politics in the Young Republic* (1971).

Horsman, Reginald. *The Causes of the War of 1812* (1962).

May, Ernest R. *The Making of the Monroe Doctrine* (1975).

Remini, James C. *Andrew Jackson and the Course of American Democracy, 1833–1845* (1984).

Schlesinger, Arthur M., Jr. *The Age of Jackson* (1945).

Taylor, George Rogers. *The Transportation Revolution* (1955).

Ward, John William. *Andrew Jackson: Symbol for an Age* (1955).

Sectionalism and Expansion, 1840–1860

Things to Know

1. *Rise of sectionalism:* economic issue — industrial North vs. agricultural South; immigration and nativism; slavery and sectionalism — Missouri Compromise; slavery in the territories after the Mexican War — Compromise of 1850.

2. *Manifest Destiny:* Texas independence and the issue of annexation; election of James Polk — Texas and Oregon as issues; acquisition of Oregon; war with Mexico — Treaty of Guadalupe Hidalgo.

3. *Intellectual and cultural trends:* rise of an American literature — major writers; major reform movements — abolitionists; temperance; women's rights; utopian communities; rise of public education.

4. *The coming of the Civil War:* key events after 1850: *Uncle Tom's Cabin;* Kansas-Nebraska Act; Dred Scott decision; Lincoln-Douglas debates; John Brown's raid; election of Lincoln.

Key Terms and Concepts

cotton gin

Nat Turner's rebellion

American Colonization Society

Elias Howe

Irish potato famine

Know-Nothing party

Wilmot Proviso

popular sovereignty

Free Soil party

Stephen Douglas

Compromise of 1850

Fugitive Slave Law

Webster-Ashburton Treaty

Mormons

Joseph Smith

Brigham Young

Treaty of 1846

Texas independence

Mexican cession

Gadsden Purchase

Edgar Allan Poe

Nathaniel Hawthorne

Herman Melville

Henry David Thoreau

Ralph Waldo Emerson

Walt Whitman

Dorothea Dix

William Lloyd Garrison

Frederick Douglass

Sarah Grimké

Elizabeth Cady Stanton

Lucretia Mott

Seneca Falls Declaration of Sentiments

Horace Mann

Harriet Beecher Stowe

Dred Scott decision

Important Definitions

"Bleeding Kansas": The virtual civil war that erupted in Kansas in 1856 between proslavery and free soilers as a consequence of the Kansas-Nebraska Act.

"Fifty-four forty or fight": Political slogan of the Democrats in the election of 1844, which claimed fifty-four degrees, forty minutes as the boundary of the Oregon territory claimed by the United States. The Treaty of 1846 with Great Britain set the boundary at the forty-ninth parallel.

Freeport Doctrine: The position on slavery taken by Stephen Douglas during the debates with Lincoln in 1858. Slavery could not exist if local legislation did not accept it. Douglas refused to say whether he believed slavery was right or wrong.

"free soil": The idea surfaced after the Mexican War that Congress had the authority to ban slavery in the newly acquired territories. It was embodied in the Wilmot Proviso. The advocates of "free soil" formed their own political party in 1848, and Martin Van Buren was their candidate for President.

Kansas-Nebraska Act (1854): Created two new territories with slavery decided by popular sovereignty; it effectively repealed the Missouri Compromise as it applied to slavery north of the Compromise line.

Manifest Destiny: Americans had the God-given right to spread their institutions and culture across the continent; it was the ideological justification for territorial expansion in the 1840s.

nativism: Response to the increased immigration in the 1840s, it reflected a fear that the United States was being taken over by foreigners. Nativism found a political expression in the American party, also known as the Know-Nothing party, which was founded in 1854 on a program of controlling immigration and requiring a longer naturalization period; the party was strongly anti-Catholic.

popular sovereignty: Proposed by Senator Lewis Cass, it meant that the decision to permit slavery in a territory was up to the territorial legislature; it was incorporated into the Compromise of 1850 for New Mexico and Utah territories.

transcendentalism: American expression of the Romantic movement that emphasized the limits of reason, individual freedom, and nature; best represented by Ralph Waldo Emerson and Henry David Thoreau, the author of *Walden* and *Civil Disobedience*.

Readings on Sectionalism and Expansion

Blassingame, John. *The Slave Community: Plantation Life in the Ante-Bellum South* (1972).

Elkins, Stanley. *Slavery: A Problem in American Institutional and Intellectual Life* (1959).

Melder, K. E. *The Beginnings of Sisterhood* (1977).

Merk, Frederick. *Manifest Destiny and Mission in American History* (1963).

North, Douglass C. *The Economic Growth of the United States* (1961).

Potter, David. *The Impending Crisis, 1848–1861* (1976).

Civil War and Reconstruction, 1860–1877

Things to Know

1. *Outbreak of the Civil War:* pattern of secession after Lincoln's election; relative strengths and weaknesses of the North and South at the outbreak of the war.

2. *The Civil War, 1861–1865:* military strategy and major battles; economic impact of the war on the North and South; response to war in Europe; Emancipation Proclamation — position of African-Americans during the war.

3. *Reconstruction:* Lincoln's views on treatment of the South; difference between Congressional and Presidential Reconstruction; implementation of Reconstruction; status of former slaves; national politics and the end of Reconstruction.

Key Terms and Concepts

Fort Sumter

Jefferson Davis

Anaconda Plan

First Battle of Bull Run

Antietam

U. S. Grant

Robert E. Lee

George McClellan

Thomas J. "Stonewall" Jackson

Shiloh

Vicksburg

Monitor

Merrimac

Sherman's March to the Sea

Gettysburg

Chancellorsville

Appomattox

Mathew Brady

Morrill Land Grant Act

Pacific Railroad Act

National Bank Act

Wade-Davis Bill

John Wilkes Booth

Thirteenth-Fifteenth Amendments

Civil Rights Act of 1866

Andrew Johnson

Radical Republicans
Freedmen's Bureau
Reconstruction Acts (1867)
tenant farms

contract labor system
Ku Klux Klan
Force Acts
election of 1876

Important Definitions

Black Codes: Passed by state legislatures in 1865–1866; granted former slaves right to marry, sue, testify in court, and hold property but with significant qualifications.

Border States: Slave states — Delaware, Maryland, Kentucky, Missouri — that remained loyal to the Union; the secession of these states would have considerably strengthened the South.

Carpetbaggers: Derogatory term for Northern Republicans who were involved in Southern politics during Radical Reconstruction.

Compromise of 1877: Rutherford B. Hayes and other Republicans agreed that U.S. troops would be withdrawn from the South, agreed to appoint a Southerner to the Cabinet, and pledged federal projects to the South in return for an end to Democratic opposition to official counting of the electoral votes for the disputed election of 1876.

Copperheads: Northern Democrats, also known as Peace Democrats, who opposed Lincoln's war policies and were concerned with the growth of presidential power. In the election of 1864, General George McClellan was nominated by the Democrats with their support.

Ex Parte Milligan (1866): Supreme Court decision involving presidential war powers; civilians could not be tried in military courts in wartime when the federal courts were functioning.

Presidential Reconstruction: Put forward by Andrew Johnson, it included repeal of ordinances of secession, repudiation of Confederate debts, and ratification of the Thirteenth Amendment. By the end of 1865, only Texas had failed to meet these terms.

Radical Reconstruction: Provided for dividing states into military districts with military commanders to oversee voter registration that included adult African-American males for state conventions; state conventions to draft constitutions that provided for suffrage for black men; state legislatures to ratify the Fourteenth Amendment.

Scalawags: Term used to describe Southern white Republicans who had opposed secession.

sharecropping: Common form of farming for freed slaves in the South; received a small plot of land, seed, fertilizer, tools from the landlord who decided what and how much should be planted; landlord usually took half of the harvest.

"Ten-Percent Plan": Lincoln's Proclamation of Amnesty and Reconstruction (December 1863) provided that new state governments could be established in the South when ten percent of the qualified voters in 1860 took an oath of loyalty.

Readings on the Civil War and Reconstruction

Commager, Henry S., ed. *The Blue and the Gray: The Story of the Civil War as Told by Participants* (1950).

Cox, Lawanda. *Lincoln and Black Freedom* (1981).

Franklin, John Hope. *Reconstruction After the Civil War* (1961).

Litwack, Leon. *Been in the Storm So Long: The Aftermath of Slavery* (1980).

McKitrick, Eric L. *Andrew Johnson and Reconstruction* (1963).

McPherson, James M. *Battle Cry of Freedom: The Civil War Era* (1988).

Randall, James G. and David Donald. *The Civil War and Reconstruction* (1969).

Stampp, Kenneth. *The Era of Reconstruction, 1865–1877* (1965).

The Gilded Age, 1877–1900

Things to Know

1. *Developments in the West and South:* successive frontiers — mining frontier and cattle kingdom; relations with Native Americans and development of federal policy; status of African-American — rise of segregation and African-American response — for example, W. E. B. Du Bois vs. Booker T. Washington.

2. *United States as industrial power:* advances in technology and rise of new industries — oil and steel; development of new forms of business organization; regulation of business; industrialization and labor — rise of early labor unions; labor disputes of the period — railroad strikes, Haymarket Square riot, Homestead steel strike, Pullman strike.

3. *Farmers revolt:* farmer organizations — Grange, farmer alliances; position on inflation — Greenbacks and silver; Populist party.

4. *Politics in the Gilded Age:* party positions and issues in presidential elections, 1876–1896; urbanization and urban politics — boss system; reform movements of the late nineteenth century.

Key Terms and Concepts

Comstock Lode	Sand Creek massacre
Central Pacific Railroad	Battle of the Little Bighorn
Union Pacific Railroad	Nez Percé
Promontory Point	Chief Joseph
long drive	Helen Hunt Jackson
Joseph Glidden	Wounded Knee
Great American Desert	Jim Crow laws

1883 *Civil Rights Cases*

Plessy v. Ferguson (1896)

Thomas Edison

John D. Rockefeller

Standard Oil

Andrew Carnegie

J. Pierpont Morgan

Horatio Alger

horizontal/vertical combinations

Social Darwinism

Sherman Anti-Trust Act

National Labor Union

Knights of Labor

Terence Powderly

American Federation of Labor

Samuel Gompers

company town

closed shop

The Grange

long vs. short haul

Munn v. Illinois

Interstate Commerce Commission

subtreasury plan

William Jennings Bryan

spoils system/merit system

Greenback party

Pendleton Civil Service Act

Grand Army of the Republic

Sherman Silver Purchase Act

McKinley Tariff

William Marcy Tweed

Social Gospel

Salvation Army

YMCA

New Immigration

Chinese Exclusion Act

Important Definitions

Atlanta Compromise: Argument put forward by Booker T. Washington that African-Americans should not focus on civil rights or social equality but concentrate on economic self-improvement.

craft unions: Labor organizations whose members were skilled workers in a particular craft — for example, carpenters, masons, or cigar makers. The American Federation of Labor was composed of individual craft unions.

"Crime of '73": Through the Coinage Act of 1873, the United States ended the minting of silver dollars and placed the country on the gold standard. This was attacked by those who supported an inflationary monetary policy, particularly farmers, and believed in the unlimited coinage of silver.

Dawes Act (1887): Changed the reservation system by granting 160 acres and U.S. citizenship to Native American heads of families who agreed to give up their tribal allegiance.

Gilded Age: The name applied to the 1870s and 1880s during which national politics was characterized by party rivalries, the spoils system, and unregulated business competition. The term comes from the title of a novel written by Mark Twain and Charles Dudley Warner.

long vs. short haul: The railroad practice to charge higher rates on lines where there was no competition than on routes where several lines were operating. This often meant that the cost of shipping goods a short distance was greater than over a long distance.

Mugwumps: Reform Republicans who refused to support James Blaine, the party's candidate in the election of 1884.

"Rum, Romanism, and Rebellion": An insult made against New York Irish-Americans by a Republican clergyman in the 1884 election; Republican candidate James Blaine's failure to repudiate this statement lost him New York and contributed to his defeat by Grover Cleveland.

Social Gospel: Religious response to the problems created by industrialization and urbanization in the late nineteenth century; supporters of the Social Gospel supported child labor laws, civil service reform, and control of the trusts.

Stalwarts and Half-Breeds: Factions in the Republican party that emerged by 1880; the Stalwarts, led by Senator Roscoe Conkling, supported the spoils system, while the Half-Breeds claimed to represent the idea of civil service reform.

trust: A form of business organization in which a group of corporations in the same industry gave their stock in the individual companies to a board of trustees in return for stock certificates that earned dividends. The trust effectively eliminated competition by giving control to the board. The earliest example is the Standard Oil Trust that controlled ninety percent of the oil refineries and pipelines.

Turner Thesis: The historian Frederick Jackson Turner argued that the frontier was the key factor in the development of American democracy and institutions; he maintained that the frontier served as a "safety valve" during periods of economic crisis.

Readings on the Gilded Age, 1877–1900

Billington, Ray Allen. *Westward Expansion* (1967).

Foner, Philip. *Women and the American Labor Movement* (1979).

Hays, Samuel P. *The Response to Industrialism, 1884–1914* (1957).

Hicks, John D. *The Populist Revolt* (1931).

Hofstadter, Richard. *Social Darwinism in American Thought* (1955).

Kaufman, S. B. *Samuel Gompers and the Origins of the American Federation of Labor* (1973).

Morgan, H. Wayne. *From Hayes to McKinley: National Party Politics, 1877–1896* (1969).

The United States at Home and Abroad, 1896–1920

Things to Know

1. *Overview of the Progressive movement:* political, economic, and social programs — direct democracy and government efficiency, regulation of big business, social justice (women's rights, child labor, temperance).

2. *Roosevelt, Taft, Wilson as Progressives:* Roosevelt's Square Deal — "trust-buster," conservation, consumer protection; Taft — tariff policy, business regulation, income tax; election of 1912 — New Nationalism vs. New Freedom.

3. *United States becomes a world power:* foreign policy before Spanish-American War (1898) — relations with Great Britain, Latin America, and Pacific; causes and consequences of Spanish-American War — extent of American empire, Caribbean policy, Panama Canal, Philippine insurrection, relations with China and Japan, Mexico.

4. *United States in World War I:* background to the war in Europe; American neutrality and immediate causes of U.S. entry in the war; war and the home front — mobilizing economy and public opinion; Wilson and the peace — Paris Peace Conference, Fourteen Points, battle over ratification.

Key Terms and Concepts

Robert M. La Follette

Ida Tarbell

Lincoln Steffens

Upton Sinclair

Frank Norris

progressive constitutional amendments:
Sixteenth–Nineteenth Amendments

Gifford Pinchot

Northern Securities case

Hepburn Act

Meat Inspection Act

Pure Food and Drug Act

Payne-Aldrich Tariff

Eugene Debs

Bull Moose party

Underwood Tariff

Clayton Anti-Trust Act

Federal Reserve Act

Federal Trade Commission

Josiah Strong

Alfred Thayer Mahan

De Lôme Letter

Teller Resolution

Emilio Aguinaldo

Open Door Policy

Boxer Rebellion

Treaty of Portsmouth

Gentlemen's Agreement

Platt Amendment

Roosevelt Corollary

Pancho Villa

General John J. Pershing

Lusitania

Sussex pledge

Zimmermann telegram

unrestricted submarine warfare

Treaty of Brest-Litovsk

Selective Service Act

War Industries Board

Creel Committee

Fourteen Points

Paris Peace Conference

Treaty of Versailles

Henry Cabot Lodge

Important Definitions

The Big Four: Refers to the allied leaders at the Paris Peace Conference: Wilson (United States), Georges Clemenceau (France), David Lloyd George (Great Britain), Vittorio Orlando (Italy).

Dollar Diplomacy: President Taft's policy of promoting U.S. interests overseas by encouraging American business to invest in foreign countries, particularly in the Caribbean and Central America.

Insular Cases: The Supreme Court cases (1901–1903) that dealt with the constitutional rights in the newly acquired overseas territories. The Court ruled that the Constitution did not necessarily follow the flag, and therefore Congress was to determine how to administer the territories.

Irreconcilables: Senators opposed to ratification of the Treaty of Versailles on any grounds; lead by isolationists William Borah, Hiram Johnson, and Robert La Follette.

Muckrakers: A group of investigative reporters who pointed out the abuses of big business and the corruption of urban politics; included Frank Norris (*The Octopus*), Ida Tarbell (*A History of the Standard Oil Company*), Lincoln Steffens (*The Shame of the Cities*), and Upton Sinclair (*The Jungle*).

New Freedom: Woodrow Wilson's program put forward during the election of 1912; business competition could be restored by breaking up the trusts, but Wilson did not

believe in having the federal government control the economy.

New Nationalism: Program that Theodore Roosevelt ran on in the election of 1912; large corporations had to be controlled and regulated by a strong President and the federal government that would protect the rights of women, labor, and children.

referendum, recall, direct primary: Ways in which the Progressives hoped to bring about direct democracy; *referendum* gives the voters the right to accept or reject a piece of legislation; *recall* is a mechanism for removing an officeholder before the end of his or her term; *direct primary* allows the voters rather than the political bosses to nominate a party's candidate for office.

Reservationists: Members of the Senate who were ready to ratify the Treaty of Versailles with modifications; the group is often divided into the "mild" Reservationists, who wanted only minor changes, and the "strong" Reservationists, who favored the significant changes advocated by Henry Cabot Lodge.

yellow journalism: Refers to the treatment of the Cuban Revolution that exaggerated the Spanish atrocities; the sensational stories in William Randolph Hearst's *New York Journal* and Joseph Pulitzer's *New York World* were a factor in the U.S. declaration of war against Spain in 1898.

Readings on the United States at Home and Abroad, 1896–1920

Bailey, Thomas A. *Woodrow Wilson and the Great Betrayal* (1972).

Beale, Howard K. *Theodore Roosevelt and the Rise of America to World Power* (1956).

Freidel, Frank. *The Splendid Little War* (1958).

Link, Arthur S. *Woodrow Wilson and the Progressive Era, 1900–1917* (1954).

Mowry, George. *The Era of Theodore Roosevelt, 1900–1912* (1958).

Murphy, Paul L. *World War I and the Origin of Civil Liberties* (1979).

Prosperity and Depression, 1920–1940

Things to Know

1. *Politics of prosperity:* period of Republican ascendancy — Harding, Coolidge, Hoover; political scandals, economic policy ("business of America is business"), election of 1928 and Al Smith.

2. *Social and cultural aspects of prosperity:* "Roaring Twenties" vs. conservativism — background of Red Scare, immigration policy, KKK, Scopes trial, religious fundamentalism; writers of the "Lost Generation"; consumer culture.

3. *The coming of the Depression:* problems in agriculture and other indicators of economic weakness — stock speculation and stock market crash; Hoover's response to the onset of the Depression.

4. *Roosevelt and the New Deal:* New Deal — conservative or revolutionary; major New Deal legislation and agencies; New Deal and the Supreme Court; did the New Deal end the Depression?

ALPHABET SOUP: NEW DEAL AGENCIES, 1933–1938	
Acronym	*Agency*
AAA	Agricultural Adjustment Administration (1933)
CAA	Civil Aeronautics Authority (1938)
CCC	Civilian Conservation Corps (1933)
CWA	Civil Works Administration (1933)
FCC	Federal Communications Commission (1934)
FDIC	Federal Deposit Insurance Corporation (1933)
FERA	Federal Emergency Relief Administration (1933)
FHA	Federal Housing Administration (1934)
FSA	Farm Security Administration (1937)
NLRB	National Labor Relations Board (1934–1935)
NRA	National Recovery Administration (1934)
NYA	National Youth Administration (1935)
PWA	Public Works Administration (1935)
REA	Rural Electrification Administration (1935)
SEC	Securities and Exchange Commission (1934)
TVA	Tennessee Valley Authority (1933)
WPA	Works Progress Administration (1935)

Key Terms and Concepts

Ohio Gang

Teapot Dome scandal

Secretary of the Treasury Andrew Mellon

Budget and Accounting Act

Bureau of the Budget

Dawes Plan

Veterans Bureau

Bonus bill

Hawley-Smoot Tariff

A. Mitchell Palmer

National Origins Act of 1924

Sacco and Vanzetti

Charles Lindbergh

T. S. Eliot

F. Scott Fitzgerald

Theodore Dreiser

Sinclair Lewis

Ernest Hemingway

Gertrude Stein

Harlem Renaissance — Langston Hughes

Marcus Garvey

McNary-Haugen Bill

Reconstruction Finance Corporation

bank holidays

Harry Hopkins

Huey Long

Father Coughlin

Francis Townsend

John Steinbeck

Indian Reorganization Act

Social Security Act

Secretary of Labor Frances Perkins

Congress of Industrial Organizations (CIO)

Alf Landon

Important Definitions

Bonus Army: Unemployed World War I veterans who came to Washington in the spring of 1932 to demand the immediate payment of the bonus Congress had voted them in 1922. The veterans were forcibly removed from Anacostia Flats by federal troops.

court packing proposal: In the wake of Supreme Court decisions that declared key piece of New Deal legislation unconstitutional, Roosevelt proposed increasing the number of justices. If a justice did not retire at age seventy, the President could appoint an additional justice up to a maximum of six.

deficit spending: The English economist John Maynard Keynes proposed that governments cut taxes and increase spending in order to stimulate investment and consumption. The effect was to increase the deficit because more money was spent than was taken in.

Hoovervilles: Shantytowns that the unemployed built in the cities during the early years of the Depression; the name given to them shows that the people blamed Hoover directly for the Depression.

Lost Generation: Term coined by Gertrude Stein to describe American expatriate writers of the 1920s; include T. S. Eliot, F. Scott Fitzgerald, Ernest Hemingway, and Stein herself.

100 Days: Period from March to June 1933 when Congress passed major legislation submitted by Roosevelt to deal with the Depression.

Return to Normalcy: Campaign theme of Warren Harding during the election of 1920; it reflected the conservative mood of the country after the constant appeals to idealism that characterized both the Progressive Era and Wilson's fight over the League of Nations.

Roaring Twenties: Popular image of the decade as a period of prosperity, optimism, and changing morals; symbolized best by the "flapper."

Share the Wealth: Program of Huey Long that proposed the redistribution of income of the rich to give every American a guaranteed annual income of $2,000 to $3,000, old-age pensions, money for a college education, and veterans benefits.

Sick Chicken Case: In *Schechter Poultry v. U.S.,* the Supreme Court struck down the National Industrial Recovery Act as unconstitutional. The decision encouraged Roosevelt to consider ways to change the makeup of the Court.

Readings on Prosperity and Depression, 1920–1940

Allen, Frederick Lewis. *Only Yesterday* (1931).

Graham, Otis L., Jr. *An Encore for Reform: The Old Progressives and the New Deal* (1967).

Leuchtenburg, William. *The Perils of Prosperity, 1914–1932* (1958).

____. *Franklin D. Roosevelt and the New Deal, 1932–1940* (1963).

Schlesinger, Arthur M., Jr. *The Age of Roosevelt* (3 vols., 1958–1960).

Ware, Susan. *Holding Their Own: American Women in the 1930s* (1982).

America at War, 1941–1945

Things to Know

1. *Background to war:* American foreign policy in the 1920s — isolationist or not; disarmament, war debts and reparations, policy toward Latin America; response to aggression — nonintervention and neutrality legislation; change in policy after September 1939.

2. *United States at war:* major military campaigns in Pacific and European theaters and military leaders; wartime diplomacy — conferences between the "Big Three," problems that arose, plans for the United Nations.

3. *The home front:* mobilization for war — industrial conversion, wage and price controls, key wartime agencies; social effects of the war — status of women, African-Americans, internment of Japanese-Americans; elections of 1940 and 1944.

Key Terms and Concepts

Washington Disarmament Conference	Lend-Lease Act
London Naval Conference	Atlantic Charter
Kellogg-Briand Pact	America First Committee
Dawes and Young Plans	Casablanca Conference
Clark Memorandum	Operation Overlord
Stimson Doctrine	Teheran Conference
Good Neighbor Policy	Yalta Conference
Nye Committee	Potsdam Conference
Neutrality Acts, 1935–1937	Manhattan Project
Panay incident	J. Robert Oppenheimer
"Quarantine the Aggressor"	Hiroshima and Nagasaki
Neutrality Act of 1939	Executive Order 9066

Manzanar
A. Philip Randolph
War Production Board
Office of Price Administration

Office of War Information
War Labor Board
Wendell Willkie
Thomas Dewey

Important Definitions

blitzkrieg: German term meaning "lightning war"; term applied to the rapid German military advance into Poland, Denmark, Norway, Belgium, Netherlands, and France in 1939 and 1940.

Bracero Program: Wartime agreement between the United States and Mexico to import farm workers to meet a perceived manpower shortage; the agreement was in effect from 1941 to 1947.

cash and carry: Key provisions of the Neutrality Act of 1939 that allowed the United States to sell arms and other contraband as long as nations paid cash and shipped the goods on their own vessels.

Europe First: Military strategy adopted by the United States that required concentrating on the defeat of Germany while maintaining a holding action against Japan in the Pacific.

Final Solution: Plan for the extermination of the Jewish population in Nazi-occupied Europe; a total of six million Jews were killed in death camps such as those established at Auschwitz, Belzec, Majdanek, Sobibor, and Treblinka.

internment: Detaining enemy aliens during wartime; term specifically applied to Japanese aliens and Japanese-Americans living on the West Coast who were sent to relocation centers (Manzanar) in 1942 allegedly because of possible disloyalty.

kamikaze: Literally "divine wind," Japanese term for fighter pilots who crashed their planes into American warships during the latter stages of World War II.

merchants of death: Term used by Senator Gerald P. Nye to describe the munitions-makers whom he blamed for forcing the United States into World War I. Nye headed a committee that investigated the industry from 1934 to 1936.

Rosie the Riveter: Term that came to symbolize all women who worked in defense plants and other industries during World War II.

second front: British and American invasion of France to relieve pressure on the Soviet Union in the east; Stalin had insisted on opening the second front from June 1941, but the invasion of Normandy (Operation Overlord) did not take place until June 1944.

Readings on America at War, 1941–1945

Alperovitz, Gar. *Atomic Diplomacy* (1965).

Blum, John Morton. *V Was for Victory: Politics and American Culture During World War II* (1976).

Dalfiume, Richard M. *Desegregation of the U.S. Armed Forces* (1975).

Dallek, Robert. *Franklin D. Roosevelt and American Foreign Policy, 1932–1945* (1979).

Daniels, Roger. *Concentration Camp U.S.A.* (1971).

Dower, John W. *War Without Mercy: Race and Power in the Pacific War* (1986).

Hartmann, Susan M. *The Home Front and Beyond* (1982).

Prange, Gordon. *At Dawn We Slept: The Untold Story of Pearl Harbor* (1981).

Smith, Gaddis. *American Diplomacy During the Second World War* (1965).

The United States As a Superpower, 1945–Present

Things to Know

1. *Cold War policy:* relations with the USSR — containment, brinksmanship, collective security (United Nations and NATO), summit conferences, detente; arms race and arms limitations.

2. *Cold War events:* Europe — NATO vs. Warsaw Pact, status of Berlin, Hungarian uprising, Prague Spring, "fall of communism"; Asia — "loss of China," Korean War, Nixon and China, U.S.-Japan trade issues; Middle East — Suez crisis, relations with Israel, oil and Islamic fundamentalism; Western Hemisphere — Alliance for Progress, Organization of American States, Cuba and Central America, Panama Canal.

3. *Vietnam:* U.S. involvement, 1954–1975 — policies of Kennedy, Johnson, Nixon, Ford; significant military events — Tet offensive, bombing of North Vietnam, Cambodia; negotiating peace settlement.

Key Terms and Concepts

San Francisco Conference	Secretary of State John Foster Dulles
Central Intelligence Agency	SEATO
Marshall Plan	CENTO
Berlin airlift	ANZUS
Warsaw Pact	Suez crisis
Korean War	U-2 incident

Bay of Pigs invasion

Cuban missile crisis

Limited Nuclear Test Ban Treaty

Berlin Wall

Peace Corps

Six-Day War

Yom Kippur War

Dien Bien Phu

Vietminh

Vietcong

Gulf of Tonkin Resolution

Ho Chi Minh Trail

Tet offensive

My Lai massacre

Khmer Rouge

Paris Peace Accords

Henry Kissinger

Salvador Allende

SALT

ABM Treaty

OPEC

Arab oil embargo

Solidarity

Camp David Accords

Iranian hostage crisis

Panama Canal Treaty

Grenada invasion

Sandinistas/Contras

Iran/Contra

glasnost

perestroika

Important Definitions

brinksmanship: The policy associated with Secretary of State John Foster Dulles that stressed that Soviet aggression would be met by massive nuclear retaliation; Dulles was opposed to simply "containing" the USSR and wanted to liberate the countries under Soviet control.

containment: American foreign policy adopted after World War II to restrain the expansion of the Soviet Union. It was based on the belief that the USSR does not take risks and would back down if faced with determined opposition. The policy was developed by Foreign Service officer George Kennan in 1947.

detente: Policy toward the USSR developed by President Nixon and Henry Kissinger focused on easing tensions through negotiations, particularly on arms reductions — for example, the first **SALT** treaty (1972).

Eisenhower Doctrine: The United States was prepared to use force in the Middle East against aggression from any country controlled by the Soviet Union (1957).

military-industrial complex: In his farewell address in 1961, Eisenhower warned of the danger posed by a strong defense industry and the armed forces; despite his own background, Eisenhower wanted to control military spending.

shuttle diplomacy: Henry Kissinger's diplomatic efforts in the Middle East in early 1974 led to the withdrawal of Israeli troops from the west bank of the Suez Canal and disengagement between Israel and Syria on the Golan Heights.

summit diplomacy: Meetings between world leaders, usually the United States and the Soviet Union, to discuss bilateral issues and matters of mutual concern — for example, nuclear disarmament; the first summit conference took place in 1955 in Geneva.

Truman Doctrine: In response to the Greek Civil War in 1947, the United States provided economic and military aid to both Greece and Turkey. The United States would support "free peoples" against armed minorities or outside pressure.

Vietnamization: President Nixon's policy of withdrawing troops from Vietnam and turning the fighting over to the South Vietnamese with massive amounts of American supplies.

Readings on the United States as a Superpower, 1945–Present

Gaddis, John Lewis. *Strategies of Containment: A Critical Appraisal of Postwar American National Security Policy* (1982).

Halberstam, David. *The Best and the Brightest* (1972).

Herring, George C. *America's Longest War: The United States and Vietnam, 1950–1975* (1979).

Hoopes, Townsend. *The Devil and John Foster Dulles* (1973).

Kennedy, Robert. *Thirteen Days* (1969).

LaFeber, Walter. *America, Russia, and the Cold War, 1945–1980* (1987).

Szulc, Tad. *The Illusion of Power: Foreign Policy in the Nixon Years* (1978).

Contemporary America, 1945–Present

Things to Know

1. *Domestic politics*, 1945–1968: programs and legislation associated with the Fair Deal, Modern Republicanism, New Frontier, Great Society, New Federalism; Cold War at home — House Un-American Activities Committee and McCarthyism; counterculture of the 1950s and 1960s — Beat Generation and New Left.

2. *Domestic politics*, 1968–present: new national issues — environment, energy policy, abortion, AIDS; domestic response to war in Vietnam; Watergate; economic policy — recession, inflation, supply-side economics, deficit, international trade.

3. *Civil rights movement*: African-Americans — legislation, Supreme Court decisions, leaders and tactics; affirmative action vs. reverse discrimination; issues of gender and race — feminism, Hispanics (immigration policy), Native Americans.

Key Terms and Concepts

GI Bill of Rights

Taft-Hartley Act

McCarran Act

HUAC

Alger Hiss case

Rosenbergs

Youngstown Sheet and Tube v. Sawyer

Adlai Stevenson

Senator Joseph McCarthy

Brown v. Board of Education

AFL-CIO

Gideon v. Wainwright

Office of Economic Opportunity

War on Poverty

Medicare

Immigration Act of 1965

Jack Kerouac

Students for a Democratic Society (SDS)

Woodstock

Environmental Protection Agency

revenue sharing

energy crisis

WIN

Kent State

hippies

Chicago Democratic Convention

CREEP

Reaganomics

Rosa Parks

Martin Luther King, Jr.

Civil Rights Act of 1964

Voting Rights Act of 1965

black power

Black Muslims — Malcolm X

Board of Regents v. Bakke

National Organization for Women

Betty Friedan

ERA

Roe v. Wade

Cesar Chavez — UFW

American Indian movement

Important Definitions

baby boom: The significant increase in the birth rate from 1946 through 1957; the rise in population contributed to the growth of the suburbs, consumer culture, and the sharp increase in college enrollments in the 1960s.

Dixiecrats: Southern Democrats who bolted the party following the adoption of a civil rights plank at the 1948 convention; ran Strom Thurmond as their candidate in 1948 as the States' Rights party.

Fair Deal: President Truman's domestic policy (1948) that included civil rights and an extension and enlargement of the New Deal — health insurance, federal aid to education, public housing, and repeal of the Taft-Hartley Act.

Great Society: President Johnson's domestic program that included Medicare, civil rights legislation, the War on Poverty; funding for the programs suffered because of the costs of the Vietnam War.

Modern Republicanism: Represented by President Eisenhower, it combined acceptance of the basic features of the New Deal with a conservative economic policy, particularly controlling government spending.

125

New Federalism: President Nixon's program to return power and tax dollars to the states and cities; the key aspect was revenue sharing, which distributed $30 billion in revenues to the states.

stagflation: High inflation combined with high unemployment and a declining gross national product; used to describe economic condition of the country in the mid-1970s.

supply-side economics: President Reagan's economic policy; reduction in taxes would give people more spendable income and in turn lead to business expansion and more jobs. The policy did increase the federal deficit.

Warren Court: Under Chief Justice Earl Warren (1953–1969), an activist Supreme Court became an important instrument of social and political change, particularly in the areas of civil rights and civil liberties.

Readings on Contemporary America, 1945–Present

Acuntildea, Rodolfo. *Occupied America: A History of the Chicanos* (1988).

Berry, Mary Frances. *Why ERA Failed: Politics, Women's Rights, and the Amending Process of the Constitution* (1986).

Branch, Taylor. *Parting the Waters: America in the King Years, 1954–1968* (1988).

Dallek, Robert. *Ronald Reagan* (1984).

Goldman, Eric. *The Crucial Decade and After: America, 1945–1960* (1961).

O'Neill, William L. *Coming Apart: An Informal History of America in the 1960s* (1971).

Schlesinger, Arthur M. *The Imperial Presidency* (1973).

White, Theodore. *The Making of the President, 1960* (also see volumes for 1964, 1968, and 1972).

FOUR FULL-LENGTH PRACTICE TESTS

Following are four complete practice AP U.S. History exams. The best way to use the practice exams is to take them as simulations. This means having the right tools — two number 2 pencils and two good quality, medium-point pens. Time yourself with an alarm clock. Follow the hints for answering questions — that is, avoid wild guessing, mark questions you do skip so that you can go back to them, and mark up the questions to eliminate wrong answers. After you finish the multiple-choice section, take the required fifteen minutes to read over the DBQ and the standard essay questions if possible. Use the suggested writing times in Section II as a guide.

When you complete the entire exam, check your multiple-choice answers using the answer key and go over the explanations of all the answers, paying special attention to those you got wrong. This will help you determine if you have a weakness in a particular area of U.S. history or have trouble with a certain type of question. Compare your essays to the student DBQ and standard essays and go over the reader's comments. Again, look for weaknesses. Are your essays organized as well as they could be? Did you provide enough factual information to support your thesis? If you have a study group, it will be particularly helpful for each member to take a simulation on the same day and then exchange essays for review and comment. Once you understand what your strengths and weaknesses are, you should try to answer the essays again using your textbook or other materials for support. Do the same with the essays in Parts B and C that you didn't answer. Remember that the more experience you have in writing essays and revising what you write, the higher you'll score on the exam itself.

Practice Test 1

Section I: Multiple-Choice Questions

Time: 55 Minutes

80 Questions

Directions: Select the best answer for the following questions or incomplete statements from the five choices provided. Indicate your answer by darkening the appropriate space on the answer sheet.

1. Which of the following was the most broadly based labor organization in the late nineteenth century?

   A. American Federation of Labor

   B. Knights of Labor

   C. The Grange

   D. Congress of Industrial Organizations

   E. Industrial Workers of the World

2. The Seneca Falls "Declaration of Sentiments and Resolutions" dealt with

   A. the abolition of slavery

   B. colonial opposition to British taxes

   C. working conditions of children in factories

   D. the concern of farmers over railroad rates

   E. women's rights

3. The principle of separate but equal facilities for blacks and whites was set down in

   A. the Dred Scott decision

   B. *Bakke v. Board of Regents*

   C. *Brown v. Board of Education*

   D. *Plessy v. Ferguson*

   E. *Roe v. Wade*

4. All of the following statements about indentured servitude in colonial America are true EXCEPT:

   A. Indentured servants were primarily young men.

   B. Indentured servants provided most of the labor in tobacco cultivation in the seventeenth century.

   C. Indentured servants could not be sold as property.

   D. Indentured servants came primarily from the unemployed and lower classes.

   E. Indentured servants were replaced by black slaves in the southern colonies by the early eighteenth century.

GO ON TO THE NEXT PAGE

5. Woodrow Wilson won the presidency in 1912 largely because

   A. there was broad support for his New Freedom program

   B. he promised to keep the United States out of a European war

   C. he received the endorsement of the Socialist party

   D. the Republican vote was split between William H. Taft and Theodore Roosevelt

   E. the political bosses in the cities paid recent immigrants to vote twice

6. The mood of the "Beat Generation" is best reflected in which of the following?

   A. Jack Kerouac's *On the Road*

   B. J. D. Salinger's *Catcher in the Rye*

   C. F. Scott Fitzgerald's *This Side of Paradise*

   D. James Joyce's *Ulysses*

   E. Arthur Miller's *Death of a Salesman*

7. The Virginia Resolves

   A. declared Virginia's secession from the Union

   B. created the House of Burgesses

   C. protested against the Stamp Act of 1765

   D. put forward Virginia's claim to western lands

   E. stated the Loyalist position during the American Revolution

8. The fear of left-wing subversion during the 1920s was reflected in the

   A. America First Committee

   B. trial of Sacco and Vanzetti

   C. Scopes trial

   D. Palmer raids

   E. Army-McCarthy hearings

9. The "Trail of Tears" refers to

   A. the removal of the Cherokees and other Native American tribes to Oklahoma

   B. the difficulties new immigrants faced in getting to the United States

   C. the migration of freed slaves to the North after the Civil War

   D. child labor in nineteenth-century factories

   E. conditions on slave ships coming to the colonies in the seventeenth century

10. Middle-class concern for the conditions of the working class in a period of rapid industrialization and urbanization was shown in all of the following EXCEPT

   A. Social Gospel

   B. Salvation Army

   C. settlement house movement

   D. Social Darwinism

   E. Young Men's Christian Association

Questions 11–12 refer to the following table.

Unemployment in the United States, 1929–1941		
	Number Unemployed (in thousands)	*Percentage of Labor Force Unemployed*
1929	1,550	3.2
1930	4,340	8.7
1931	8,020	15.9
1932	12,060	23.6
1933	12,830	24.9
1934	11,340	21.7
1935	10,610	20.1
1936	9,030	16.9
1937	7,700	14.3
1938	10,390	19.0
1939	9,480	17.2
1940	8,120	14.6
1941	5,560	9.9

Source: U.S. Bureau of the Census. Historical Statistics of the United States from Colonial Times to 1970.

11. According to the information in the above table, the worst year of the Depression was

A. 1931

B. 1932

C. 1933

D. 1938

E. 1940

12. The most likely explanation for the decline in unemployment between 1940 and 1941 is

A. the New Deal public works projects

B. that fewer people were looking for jobs

C. mobilization of industry for World War II

D. that more women were going into the labor market

E. the 1940 presidential election

GO ON TO THE NEXT PAGE

13. Which of the following historians is most closely associated with the idea that economic factors have shaped American history?

    A. Frederick Jackson Turner

    B. William Bradford

    C. Charles Beard

    D. Arthur Schlesinger, Jr.

    E. Alfred Thayer Mahan

14. The first proprietary colony was

    A. Jamestown

    B. Carolina

    C. Maryland

    D. Massachusetts Bay

    E. New Amsterdam

15. Which of the following was the LEAST significant factor in the demand for restrictions on immigration from 1880 to 1924?

    A. Immigrants were a threat to jobs of American workers.

    B. Immigrants could not assimilate into American society.

    C. Immigrants were radicals and a threat to the government.

    D. Immigrants were racially inferior to Anglo-Saxons.

    E. Immigrants owed loyalty to the Pope.

16. Gerald Ford's main liability in the 1976 presidential election was

    A. his inexperience in foreign policy

    B. the Republican party's position on civil rights

    C. the war in Vietnam

    D. the Watergate scandal

    E. his support for a national health-insurance plan

17. Which of the following was NOT a reason given by President Franklin Roosevelt in his attempt to "pack" the Supreme Court?

    A. He believed he had a mandate after the 1936 election.

    B. Most Supreme Court justices were interpreting the Constitution too broadly.

    C. He wanted to ease the work load of the Court's older members.

    D. Most of the Supreme Court justices were conservative.

    E. The Court was declaring too many New Deal programs unconstitutional.

18. The Compromise of 1850 provided a concession to the South by

    A. allowing slavery in New Mexico and Utah

    B. permitting the slave trade to continue in the District of Columbia

    C. having slavery in Nebraska and Kansas determined by popular sovereignty

    D. creating a new Fugitive Slave Law

    E. determining how new states would be admitted to the Union

19. Dorothea Dix is most closely associated with which area of social reform in the first half of the nineteenth century?

    A. Temperance movement

    B. Women's rights

    C. Settlement house movement

    D. Abolitionist cause

    E. Prisons and asylums

20. The income tax amendment to the Constitution adopted in 1913

    A. applied the same tax rate to all incomes

    B. redistributed wealth from the rich to the poor

    C. recovered revenue lost by reducing the tariff

    D. paid for the social-welfare programs of the Wilson administration

    E. was repealed at the beginning of the Depression

21. The United Nations was able to provide military assistance to South Korea in 1950 because

    A. the USSR opposed the North Korean invasion of the south

    B. the USSR boycotted the session of the Security Council at which the decision was made

    C. the United States outvoted the Soviet Union

    D. the General Assembly approved the decision

    E. other nations in Southeast Asia pledged their support

22. Which of the following statements about the Emancipation Proclamation is NOT accurate?

    A. It immediately freed all slaves living in the United States.

    B. It freed slaves only in the Confederacy or in areas of active rebellion.

    C. It led to the creation of all-black units in the Union Army.

    D. It was issued in part because slave labor was helping the Confederate cause.

    E. It gave the North a high moral reason for continuing the war.

23. The Pendleton Act was enacted in response to

    A. efforts to raise tariffs on imported cloth

    B. the assassination of President James Garfield

    C. protests against civil service examinations

    D. complaints about currency deflation

    E. the loss of public support for both political parties

GO ON TO THE NEXT PAGE

24. According to the Proclamation of 1763,

    A. colonial militiamen were required to put down Pontiac's Rebellion

    B. colonial paper money could not be printed

    C. contact between colonials and Indians was strictly forbidden

    D. settlers were prohibited from crossing the Appalachians

    E. speculators were allowed to purchase certain lands from trans-Appalachian tribes

25. The Indian Reorganization Act of 1934 represented a significant change in policy because it

    A. ended the government's allotment policy

    B. divided Indian lands into individual plots

    C. weakened the legal basis for tribal sovereignty

    D. undercut existing barriers to the exploitation of Native Americans

    E. expanded the role of the Bureau of Indian Affairs

26. The term "scalawag" was used to describe

    A. homeless unemployed freedmen in the South

    B. former plantation owners who had lost their lands

    C. native white Southerners who cooperated with the Republicans

    D. Union soldiers who occupied the South during Reconstruction

    E. Northerners who came to the postwar South to take lucrative federal appointments

27. Which of the following is a direct social change brought about by the American Revolution?

    A. The emancipation of slaves who fought against the British

    B. The elimination of property qualifications for voting

    C. An end to religious requirements for holding political office

    D. Recognition of the right of women to inherit property

    E. Complete separation of church and state

28. Which of the planks from the 1892 Populist party platform showed a concern with issues raised by organized labor?

    A. Graduated income tax

    B. Restrictions on immigration

    C. Government ownership of the railroads

    D. Unlimited coinage of silver

    E. Direct election of senators

29. The Monroe Doctrine stated all of the following policies EXCEPT:

    A. North and South America were no longer open to European colonization.

    B. Existing colonies would not be bothered by the United States.

    C. The United States would intervene in the problems South American countries had with other nations.

    D. The colonies Europeans had had in the Western Hemisphere were forever lost.

    E. The United States would not involve itself in the affairs of European nations.

30. The most significant increase in immigration in recent years has come from

    A. Latin America and Southeast Asia

    B. Eastern Europe

    C. the Middle East

    D. newly independent states of Africa

    E. northern Europe

31. The Pilgrims were also known as Separatists because they

    A. wanted to separate Plymouth from the Massachusetts Bay Colony

    B. believed in the complete separation of church and state

    C. broke all ties with the Church of England

    D. were the first to declare independence from Great Britain

    E. tried to isolate the Native Americans from white settlers

32. In *Marbury v. Madison,* Chief Justice John Marshall argued successfully that the Supreme Court could

    A. declare federal laws unconstitutional

    B. remove federal officials who would not or could not perform their duties

    C. determine cases involving interstate commerce

    D. decide whether debts should be considered in contracts

    E. uphold the authority of the federal government over the states

33. Which of the following best illustrates government support for the construction of the first transcontinental railroad?

    A. Open immigration from China

    B. The exchange of Union Pacific stock for federal bonds

    C. Creation of the Crédit Mobilier construction company

    D. The grant of thousands of acres of public lands to the railroads

    E. Preference in hiring to Union Army veterans

34. The most important consequence of the Boston Tea Party was the

    A. repeal of the tax on tea

    B. failure of other colonies to support Boston's action

    C. opening of negotiations between Britain and Massachusetts

    D. enactment by Parliament of the Coercive Acts

    E. reopening of the Port of Boston to foreign trade

35. The outcome of the disputed election of 1876 was significant because it

    A. was the last victory for the Radical Republicans

    B. meant the end of Reconstruction

    C. marked the beginning of a long line of Democratic Presidents

    D. demonstrated that black voters held the balance of power in Southern politics

    E. showed that the North and South were able to reconcile

GO ON TO THE NEXT PAGE

36. All of the following were New Deal agencies EXCEPT

   A. CCC
   B. RFC
   C. WPA
   D. NRA
   E. TVA

37. "If I'd only bought a hundred instead of fifty shares, I'd be up two hundred dollars. I'll buy fifty more now. Doubles or quits. If I lose what I'm ahead now, I'll quit. 44, 43½, 43. Now I'm behind a little. . . . Why am I so greedy? No one ever got poor taking a profit. 43½, 44, 44½, 44¾. Come on, boy, right through the roof."

   The above quotation was most likely written in

   A. 1837
   B. 1920
   C. 1928
   D. 1931
   E. 1985

38. The outcome of the election of 1824 between John Quincy Adams and Andrew Jackson was decided by

   A. the Electoral College
   B. a plurality of the popular vote
   C. the Senate
   D. the House of Representatives
   E. the "corrupt bargain"

39. In addition to the Embargo Act of 1807, a significant factor in the development of American industry in the period 1800–1820 was

   A. the invention of the cotton gin
   B. the development of railroads
   C. the availability of cheap immigrant labor
   D. protective tariffs
   E. the Louisiana Purchase

40. The South hoped to gain diplomatic recognition and active support from Great Britain because

   A. slavery was still legal in the British Empire
   B. British public opinion generally supported the South
   C. British factories needed Southern cotton
   D. Britain wanted the help of the South to regain the Oregon Territory
   E. the North had placed high tariffs on British goods

41. The theory of nullification, according to which a state can reject a federal law, is associated with

   A. John C. Calhoun
   B. Daniel Webster
   C. Andrew Jackson
   D. James Madison
   E. John Marshall

42. Which of the following was the principal target of Thomas Nast's political cartoons?

   A. Slavery

   B. President Andrew Johnson

   C. New immigrants

   D. Boss Tweed

   E. The trusts

43. Chautauqua movement was

   A. an early form of adult education

   B. an effort to prevent the teaching of evolution

   C. a late nineteenth-century religious revival

   D. a literary movement of expatriate American authors

   E. a school of fiction based in the Midwest

44. Which of the following statements about colonial politics in the eighteenth century is true?

   A. The right to vote for representatives to the colonial assemblies was severely restricted by high property qualifications.

   B. The colonial assemblies controlled taxes and expenditures.

   C. The colonial assemblies had the right to elect the governors.

   D. The governors had unlimited authority as agents of the king.

   E. The requirements for office holding were the same as those for voting.

45. The Battle of Saratoga resulted in

   A. an embarrassing defeat for the Continental Army

   B. an unsuccessful peace overture from Lord North

   C. France entering the war on the side of the colonies

   D. renewed efforts of the Loyalists to enlist colonial support

   E. the treason of Benedict Arnold

46. The decline in agricultural prices after World War I was due primarily to

   A. overproduction

   B. lack of overseas markets

   C. decline in small farms

   D. crop failures in the Midwest

   E. high transportation costs

47. Which statement best summarizes the Open Door Policy?

   A. The United States should have its own sphere of influence in China.

   B. Japan should be excluded from trading with China.

   C. All nations should be granted equal trading rights in China.

   D. China should be punished for its support of the Boxer Rebellion.

   E. The United States should control international trade in the Pacific.

GO ON TO THE NEXT PAGE

48. The Neutrality Act of 1939

    A. maintained the ban against trade with countries at war

    B. was passed by Congress in response to the outbreak of war in Europe

    C. provided for the exchange of naval bases for destroyers between the United States and Great Britain

    D. was enacted over President Roosevelt's veto

    E. provided for the cancellation of war debts

49. Ratification of the Constitution

    A. required unanimous approval of the states

    B. was put to a nationwide referendum

    C. was agreed to by the delegates to the Constitutional Convention

    D. was determined by electors from each state

    E. needed the approval of nine states

50. Which of the following civil liberties protected by the Bill of Rights was in the Constitution as originally ratified?

    A. Freedom of the press

    B. The right to bear arms

    C. Freedom of religion

    D. Protection against self-incrimination

    E. Trial by jury

51. Which of the following states seceded from the Union first?

    A. South Carolina

    B. North Carolina

    C. Kentucky

    D. Georgia

    E. Virginia

52. When President Taft called for dollar diplomacy, he advocated

    A. that American businessmen should invest in underdeveloped countries rather than lend those countries U.S. dollars

    B. that American government money be loaned to underdeveloped countries

    C. purchasing foreign-owned territories

    D. the rejection of the Open Door Policy

    E. encouraging foreign exports by reducing tariffs

53. In responding to the Depression, President Hoover placed primary emphasis on

    A. reducing the tariff

    B. cutting federal taxes

    C. regulating the sale of stocks

    D. increasing federal income tax rates

    E. encouraging private volunteer efforts

54. Thomas Paine's *Common Sense*

    A. was a call for the abolition of slavery

    B. insisted that the British allow the colonies to elect their own representatives to Parliament

    C. criticized the weaknesses of the Articles of Confederation

    D. blamed George III for the colonies' problems and urged Americans to declare their independence

    E. demanded that a strong executive be included in the Constitution

55. After 1815, such factors as time, cost, and distance in moving people and goods

    A. were increased because of the lack of internal improvement

    B. resulted in excessive land speculation

    C. were significantly reduced by the transporation revolution

    D. mattered less as new market centers were developed

    E. caused a downturn in the growth of eastern cities

56. Hinton R. Helper's book *The Impending Crisis of the South* was intended as

    A. a refutation of Harriet Beecher Stowe's *Uncle Tom's Cabin*

    B. an argument against slavery as an economic institution

    C. a rallying cry against abolitionism

    D. a condemnation of the violent acts of Preston Brooks

    E. a rational defense of the practice of slavery

57. Which of the following was the main issue in *Munn v. Illinois?*

    A. Suppression of a major strike by the federal government

    B. Monopolistic practices of the Standard Oil Company

    C. State regulation of labor unions

    D. State regulation of grain elevator operators and railroad rates

    E. State prosecution of a federal official

58. The participation of the United States in World War I was ended

    A. through a separate treaty with Germany alone

    B. by a treaty with all of the Central Powers

    C. when the Senate ratified the Treaty of Versailles

    D. through a joint resolution of Congress

    E. by a treaty with the other members of the Big Four

GO ON TO THE NEXT PAGE

59. The Opposition tells us that we ought not to govern a people without their consent. I answer, The rule of liberty that all just government derives its authority from the consent of the governed, applies only to those who are capable of self-government. . . . And, regardless of this formula of words made only for enlightened, self-governing people, do we owe no duty to the world? Shall we turn these peoples back to the reeking hands from which we have taken them? Shall we abandon them, with Germany, England, Japan, hungering for them?

This speech is referring to

A. territory acquired from Mexico as the result of the Mexican War

B. land included in the Louisiana Purchase

C. the purchase of Alaska by Secretary of State Seward

D. colonies acquired after the Spanish-American War

E. American intervention in the Caribbean and Central America

60. Which of the following best describes the position of William Lloyd Garrison?

A. Immediate abolition of slavery with compensation to slave owners

B. Immediate abolition of slavery without compensation to slave owners

C. Compensated liberation of slaves over a period of time

D. Prohibition of slavery in newly acquired territories

E. Freedom for all slaves in the states that had seceded from the Union

61. The decisive factor in bringing about the resolution of the dispute with Great Britain over the Oregon Territory in 1846 was

A. the Lewis and Clark Expedition forty years earlier

B. the major influence exercised by the Hudson's Bay company

C. the American claim of prior discovery

D. the heavy influx of American settlers after 1818

E. British reluctance to go to war against the United States

62. Andrew Jackson's view of the presidency emphasized

A. strong Cabinet leadership

B. strengthening the power of the states

C. support for the nullification doctrine

D. congressional partisan leadership

E. leadership by the executive branch in the interests of the people

63. After the Civil War, the practice of sharecropping

A. turned African-Americans into a labor force with housing and supplies provided by white planters

B. taught African-Americans and whites to work together as farmers

C. made it possible for African-Americans to save enough money to buy their own farms

D. required African-Americans to form groups to work as gang labor

E. forced African-Americans to migrate to the North

64. President Lyndon Johnson received authorization for the use of force in Vietnam through

   A. the Southeast Asia Treaty Organization

   B. the Truman Doctrine

   C. the Gulf of Tonkin Resolution

   D. a declaration of war by Congress

   E. the United Nations Security Council

65. The first federal agency established to regulate business was the

   A. Pure Food and Drug Administration

   B. Federal Power Commission

   C. Federal Reserve System

   D. Interstate Commerce Commission

   E. Securities and Exchange Commission

Source: Library of Congress

66. According to this cartoon, the trusts

   A. were good for the economic growth of the United States

   B. were too powerful and contributed to the impoverishment of the country

   C. were in control of the food industry

   D. opposed restrictions on child labor

   E. were positive examples of Social Darwinism at work

67. The novels of William Faulkner are set in

   A. Paris during the 1920s

   B. the South

   C. the frontier after the Civil War

   D. New England

   E. small towns in the Midwest

GO ON TO THE NEXT PAGE

68. Which of the following made the Soviet Union suspicious of the motives of the United States and Great Britain during World War II?

    A. The delay in opening the second front in Europe

    B. The refusal to grant the Soviet Union lend-lease aid

    C. The American monopoly on atomic bomb technology

    D. The adoption of the Europe-first strategy

    E. The failure of the West to accept changes in the borders of Poland

69. In the post-Civil War period, the idea that African-Americans should concentrate on economic betterment rather than political or social equality was advanced by

    A. W. E. B. Du Bois

    B. Frederick Douglass

    C. Booker T. Washington

    D. Marcus Garvey

    E. William Lloyd Garrison

70. Which of the following best represents the Realist school of American literature?

    A. *The Red Badge of Courage*

    B. *The Gross Clinic*

    C. *Looking Backward*

    D. *The Grapes of Wrath*

    E. *Moby Dick*

71. Which of the following colonies was founded as a haven for Catholics?

    A. Plymouth

    B. New Amsterdam

    C. Pennyslvania

    D. Rhode Island

    E. Maryland

72. Which of the following is in the correct chronological order?

    A. Bay of Pigs invasion; Gulf of Tonkin Resolution; U.S. intervention in Dominican Republic; limited nuclear test ban treaty

    B. Gulf of Tonkin Resolution; Bay of Pigs invasion; limited nuclear test ban treaty; U.S. intervention in Dominican Republic

    C. Bay of Pigs invasion; limited nuclear test ban treaty; Gulf of Tonkin Resolution; U.S. intervention in Dominican Republic

    D. Bay of Pigs invasion; U.S. intervention in Dominican Republic; Gulf of Tonkin Resolution; limited nuclear test ban treaty

    E. U.S. intervention in Dominican Republic; Gulf of Tonkin Resolution; Bay of Pigs invasion; limited nuclear test ban treaty

73. The Sherman Anti-Trust Act of 1890 was

    A. effective in restoring competition

    B. declared unconstitutional by the Supreme Court

    C. supported by John D. Rockefeller

    D. not immediately successful in limiting business concentration

    E. passed by Congress over the veto of President Benjamin Harrison

74. The key issue in Youngstown Sheet and *Tube v. Sawyer* was the

    A. constitutionality of the Taft-Hartley Act

    B. right of the President to seize private property

    C. power of the states to limit the number of hours worked by children

    D. authority of Congress to impose quotas for hiring based on race

    E. validity of state right-to-work laws

75. Which of the following was the most significant foreign-policy accomplishment of President Jimmy Carter?

    A. Paris Peace Accords

    B. Panama Canal Treaties

    C. SALT I Treaty

    D. Camp David Accords

    E. *Mayaguez* incident

76. The countries shaded on the map were

    A. acquired by the United States as a result of the Spanish-American War

    B. U.S. protectorates at various times between 1898 and 1933

    C. places where the United States intervened to prevent a Communist takeover

    D. the only countries in the Caribbean to join the Alliance for Progress

    E. locations of important American military bases in the 1960s

GO ON TO THE NEXT PAGE

77. Which of the following is properly considered the main purpose of the Navigation Acts?

   A. The promotion of trade among the colonies

   B. The protection of American manufacturing from foreign competition

   C. To guarantee that England alone would profit from trade with the colonies

   D. To raise revenue for maintaining the British Empire

   E. The regulation of the slave trade in the colonies

78. The principle of freedom of the press in colonial America was established by the

   A. Articles of Confederation

   B. Bill of Rights

   C. Virginia House of Burgesses

   D. trial of Peter Zenger

   E. Mayflower Compact

79. Michael Harrington's *The Other America* (1962) had a significant impact on public policy because it

   A. vividly described the plight of Native Americans on the reservations

   B. addressed the problems of environmental pollution

   C. drew attention to the persistence of poverty in the United States

   D. dealt with the effectiveness of the Jim Crow laws in the South that denied African-Americans voting rights

   E. highlighted the difficulties faced by migrant workers

80. The economic program that emphasizes increasing government expenditures to spur growth and employment is known as

   A. supply-side economics

   B. deficit spending

   C. protectionism

   D. voodoo economics

   E. stagflation

IF YOU FINISH BEFORE TIME IS CALLED, CHECK YOUR WORK ON THIS SECTION ONLY. DO NOT WORK ON ANY OTHER SECTION IN THE TEST.

Section II: Essay Questions

Part A

(Suggested writing time — 45 minutes)

Directions: Write an essay based on your analysis of Documents A–J as well as your knowledge of the period covered by the question. It is important for you to include information on the topic not provided by the documents.

1. In *Letters from an American Farmer,* St. John de Crèvecoeur wrote:

    He is an American, who, leaving behind him all his ancient prejudices and manners, receives new ones from the new mode of life he has embraced, the new government he obeys, and the new rank he holds . . . . Here individuals of all nations are melted into a new race of men, whose labors and posterity will one day cause great changes in the world.

    Assess the validity of this early statement of the melting-pot theory of acculturation using *both* the documents *and* your knowledge of immigration during late nineteenth- and twentieth-century U.S. history.

Document A

The rapidity with which the democratic ideas are taken on by immigrants under the influence of our institutions is remarkable. These races have certainly taken advantage of their opportunities among us in a fashion to promise well for their final effect upon this country. The French-Canadian has become a sufficiently good American to have given up his earlier programs of turning New England into a new France — that is, into a Catholic province or of returning to the province of Quebec. He is seeing something better than a racial or religious ideal in the freedom of American citizenship; and on one or two occasions, when he had political power in two municipalities, he refrained from exercising it to the detriment of the public-school system.

Source: Percy Stickney Grant, "American Ideas and Race Mixture," North American Review (1912).

Document B

The district can yet be called a "Little Italy." Social life centers around the Catholic Church of Our Lady Help of Christians, on 10th and Wash. streets, the main business places being on 7th Street, between Franklin and Carr. It is there that one finds the Rome Drug store, the Viviano Macaroni establishment, the Selvaggi and Coppolino steamship agencies, the wholesale house of Costa and Siales, Dr. Cataldi's office, the "pasticceria" and several groceries and butcher shops. One of the main events of the colony is the

GO ON TO THE NEXT PAGE

145

celebration of the Congregation of Santa Fara, the patroness of the town of Cinisi. . . . For the occasion solemn vespers are sung, a colorful parade takes place and fireworks galore remind the immigrant of his days in the "old country." But Santa Fara is not the only Saint that is venerated. Almost every one of the groups from the towns mentioned above has its "patron" or "patroness" saint in whose honor large amounts of money are lavished each year.

Source: Giovanni Schiavo, The Italians in Missouri *(1929).*

Document C

There were approximately 33,000,000 people in the country in 1910 who were either born abroad or under foreign home conditions and neighborhood environment. In all there are 38 different language groups in the United States, supporting publications which have a total circulation approximated at 10,982,000.

Source: New York Times, *February 2, 1919.*

Document D

The societies which are organized and maintained by the members of different nationalities, and which flourish in some form in every community where there are large groups of immigrants, are a factor in helping the immigrant through the trials of immigration and the difficulties of adjustment to new conditions. The chief reason among all nationalities for the formation of these societies is insurance against sickness and death, but most of them combine with this some other objects. Nearly all of them outline an educational and civic program. They may lack the means to carry this out, yet the statement of these purposes has an influence upon the members. Cooperation with these organizations on the part of American agencies would help the immigrant in solving his own problems, and might mean carrying out these larger ideals.

Source: Report of the Commission on Immigration on the Problem of Immigration in Massachusetts (1914).

Document E

The present immigrant organizations represent a separateness of the immigrant groups from America, but these organizations exist precisely because they enable the immigrants to overcome this separateness. They are signs, not of the perpetuation of immigrant groups here, but of their assimilation. We know of no type of immigrant organization which is able to live without some feature related to the needs of the immigrant in America. If we give the immigrants a favorable milieu, if we tolerate their strangeness during their period of adjustment, if we give them freedom to make their own connections between the old and new experiences, if we help them to find points of contact, then we hasten their assimilation. This is a process of growth as against the "ordering and forbidding" policy and the demand that the assimilation of the immigrant shall be "sudden, complete, and bitter."

Source: Herbert A. Miller and Robert E. Park, Old World Traits Transplanted *(1921).*

Document F

When our immigrant's son looks back at his early life to consider his environment, his recollections in most cases are not very encouraging. The best he can think of is the sight of the East Side of New York or of any other Eastern city where immigrants are massed together. The rich surroundings of traditions characteristic of his race do not exist for him; he experiences a sort of spiritual starvation from which he tries to escape.

Often he cannot understand his own parents; thought and manners and this situation at times becomes really tragic. He is no longer at home in his own family. That peaceful united homelife which we still believe is the real foundation of happiness and society is never experienced by many of these young people.

Source: Mario Petruzzelli, Atlantica *(May 1937).*

Document G

Source: Library of Congress

VEGETABLE STAND IN THE MULBERRY STREET BEND, NEW YORK, 1890.

GO ON TO THE NEXT PAGE

Document H

In any summary of the work of the Polish schools it is evident that the knowledge of the Polish language among the American-born youth has created a better contact with their parents who immigrated from oppressed Poland and settled here permanently, building churches, schools, newspapers, and community centers, but who never ceased to long for their newly freed homeland, the Republic of Poland. Knowing that they will not return to their native land, what is more natural than their desire to pass on to their children this proud and splendid heritage of culture and to make them realize that in making a part of American culture they are adding to the latter rather than subtracting from its prominence? The immigrant generation is happy to see their youth absorb Polish along with American culture and take pride in the homeland of their forefathers, thus assured of their becoming better and more contented citizens of America.

Source: A.M. Skibinska, "Polish Language Supplementary Schools" in Poles of Chicago *(1937).*

Document I

The growing sense of superiority on the part of the boy to the Hebraic part of his environment extends itself soon to the home. He learns to feel that his parents, too, are "greenhorns." In the struggle between the two sets of influences that of the home becomes less and less effective. He runs away from the supper table to join his gang on the Bowery, where he is quick to pick up the very latest slang; where his talent for caricature is developed often at the expense of his parents, his race, and all "foreigners," and like his glorious countrymen in general, he is quick to ridicule the stranger. He laughs at the foreign Jew with as much heartiness as at the Italian; for he feels that he himself is almost as remote from the one as from the other.

The boys not only talk together of picnics, of the crimes of which they read in the English newspapers, of prizefights, of budding business propositions, but avoid the Yiddish theater, seek the uptown places of amusement, dress in the latest American fashion, and have a keen eye for the right thing in neckties.

Source: Hutchins Hapgood, The Spirit of the Ghetto: Studies in the Jewish Quarter of New York *(1902).*

Document J

By the first decade of the twentieth century, the Lower East Side had become an immigrant Jewish cosmopolis. Clustered in their separate Jewries, they were set side by side in a pattern suggesting the cultural, if not the physical, geography of the Old World. Hungarians were settled in the northernmost portion above Houston Street, along the numbered street between Avenue B and the East River, once indisputably [Little Germany]. Galicians lived to the south, between Houston and Broom, east of Clinton, on Attorney, Ridge, Pitt, Willet and the cross streets. To the west lay the most congested Rumanian quarter . . . on Chrystie, Forsyth, Eldrige, and all streets, flanked by Houston Street to the north and Grand Street to the south, with the Bowery gridironed by the overhead elevated to the west. The remainder of the great Jewish quarter, from Grand Street reaching south to Monroe, was the preserve of the Russians — those from Russia, Poland, Lithuania, Byelorussia, and the Ukraine — the most numerous and heterogeneous of the Jewries of Eastern Europe.

Source: Moses Rischin, The Promised City: New York's Jews 1870–1914 *(1962).*

Part B

(Suggested writing time — 35 minutes, including a 5-minute planning period)

Directions: Choose ONE question from this part. Cite relevant historical evidence in support of your generalizations and present your arguments clearly and logically.

2. The election of Thomas Jefferson is sometimes called he "Revolution of 1800." To what extent is this description accurate?

3. Assess the impact of THREE of the following on the decision of the United States to go to war with Mexico.

   Manifest Destiny

   The Rio Grande boundary dispute

   The annexation of Texas

   Slidell's mission

Part C

(Suggested writing time — 35 minutes, including a 5-minute planning period)

Directions: Choose ONE question from this part. Cite relevant historical evidence in support of your generalizations and present your arguments clearly and logically.

4. The Populist party platform in 1892 stated, "The interests of rural and civic [urban] labor are the same; their enemies are identical." Given the political and economic conditions of the 1890s, to what extent was this true?

5. Analyze the relative importance of Supreme Court decisions and congressional action during the 1950s and 1960s in bringing about significant change in the civil rights of African-Americans.

IF YOU FINISH BEFORE TIME IS CALLED, CHECK YOUR WORK ON THIS SECTION ONLY. DO NOT WORK ON ANY OTHER SECTION IN THE TEST.

Answer Key For Practice Test 1

Section I: Multiple-Choice Questions

1.	B	30.	A
2.	E	31.	C
3.	D	32.	A
4.	C	33.	D
5.	D	34.	D
6.	A	35.	B
7.	C	36.	B
8.	B	37.	C
9.	A	38.	D
10.	D	39.	D
11.	C	41.	A
12.	C	42.	D
13.	C	43.	A
14.	C	44.	B
15.	E	45.	C
16.	D	46.	A
17.	B	47.	C
18.	D	48.	B
19.	E	49.	E
21.	B	50.	E
22.	A	51.	A
23.	B	52.	A
24.	D	53.	E
25.	A	54.	D
26.	C	55.	C
27.	A	56.	B
28.	B	57.	D
29.	C	58.	D

59. D	**71.** E
61. D	**72.** C
62. E	**73.** D
63. A	**74.** B
64. C	**75.** D
65. D	**76.** B
66. B	**77.** C
67. B	**78.** D
68. A	**79.** C
69. C	**80.** B
70. A	

Section II: Essay Questions

Student essays and analysis appear beginning on page 31.

Answers and Explanations for Practice Test 1

Section I: Multiple-Choice Questions

1. B. The Knights of Labor (1869) was open to "all producers," including skilled and unskilled workers, African-Americans, and women. The American Federation of Labor (1886) organized skilled workers by craft. The Congress of Industrial Organizations, which was founded in the 1930s, is outside the time frame of the question.

2. E. You should be familiar with the Seneca Falls Declaration from your reading. Modeled after the Declaration of Independence, it was a strong call for equality between men and women and went beyond the issue of the right to vote. It was written by Elizabeth Cady Stanton and Lucretia Mott and adopted by the Seneca Falls Convention in 1848.

3. D. All the cases listed deal with civil rights issues, and three pertain to the rights of African-Americans. The Dred Scott decision was a key event leading to the Civil War but does not relate to the question. In *Plessy v. Ferguson* (1896), the Court ruled that "separate but equal" facilities did not violate the Fourteenth Amendment. The decision was overturned in *Brown v. Board of Education,* which in 1954 required the desegregation of public schools "with all deliberate speed."

4. C. Indentured servants were an important part of the labor force in the southern colonies in the seventeenth century; there is ample evidence in the historical records that indentured servants were in fact sold from one planter to another despite the terms of their labor contracts.

5. D. Wilson received less than fifty percent of the vote in the election against President William Howard Taft and Theodore Roosevelt. Roosevelt's decision to run as a Progressive after failing to get the Republican nomination gave the Democrats the election.

6. A. Kerouac is the father of the "Beat Generation." Fitzgerald and Joyce reflect the literature of the 1920s. J. D. Salinger's *Catcher in the Rye* is an important 1950s novel about conformity, but he is not identified with the "Beat Generation."

7. C. The Virginia Resolves were protests against the Stamp Act adopted by the House of Burgesses; the main point was that Virginians were Englishmen and could be taxed only by their own representatives.

8. B. You should be able to eliminate several of the answers based on chronology. The America First Committee was an isolationist group formed on the eve of Word War II, and the Army-McCarthy hearings are associated with the "Second Red Scare" of the early 1950s. The Palmer raids took place in 1919, under Woodrow Wilson's Attorney General. The Scopes trial concerned the teaching of evolution, and while it reflected the conservative tide of the 1920s, it did not revolve around a fear of left-wing subversion. By this process of elimination, the trial of Sacco and Vanzetti is the correct answer.

9. A. The "Trail of Tears" refers to the removal of Native Americans primarily from the southeast to lands west of the Mississippi between 1830 and 1838 under the provisions of the Indian Removal Act and related treaties.

10. D. Unlike the other movements or organizations listed, the Social Darwinists would not show particular compassion for the problems of the working class. They would argue that workers were in the position they were because of natural selection and their inability to compete.

11. C. This question requires you only to read the table. 1933 was the year with the highest unemployment.

12. C. Here, you have to come up with an interpretation of the data based on your knowledge of the period. The downward trend in the unemployment numbers was primarily due to increased spending on defense-related industry with the outbreak of the war in Europe. The jump in unemployment in 1938 can be seen as evidence that the New Deal programs were not effective in dealing with the country's basic economic problems.

13. C. All the answers are historians whose works you should know. Beard's views are set down in his classic *An Economic Interpretation of the Constitution* (1913); Turner is associated with the "Frontier Thesis" of American history.

14. C. A proprietary colony was one founded by an individual or group of individuals by a grant from the king. Maryland was established by George Calvert (Lord Baltimore) in 1634. Carolina was also a proprietary colony (1663); Jamestown, Massachusetts Bay, and New Amsterdam were all established by joint-stock companies.

15. E. Anti-Catholic sentiment was important in the calls for immigration restriction in the 1840s and 1850s, particularly in the program of the Know-Nothing party; while anti-Catholicism was probably a factor in the later period as well, it was not as significant as the other choices.

16. D. 1976 was the first presidential election after the Watergate scandal; Ford assumed the presidency on the resignation of Richard Nixon. Jimmy Carter campaigned on the pledge that he would never lie to the American people, an obvious reference to Watergate.

17. B. Roosevelt would probably not have tried to "pack" the Supreme Court if the justices were following a loose construction of the Constitution; the problem was that they were interpreting the Constitution too narrowly, as far as Roosevelt was concerned, and invalidating many of the New Deal programs — for example, the Agricultural Adjustment Act and the National Industrial Recovery Act.

18. D. The federal Fugitive Slave Act made it a federal crime to assist runaway slaves. The Northern states greatly reduced its effectiveness, however, by refusing to support or enforce it. Although slavery was allowed to continue in the District of Columbia, the slave trade was banned there under the Compromise of 1850.

19. E. Dix began an investigation of prisons and asylums in Massachusetts in the 1840s. Her report to the state legislature in 1843 led to improvements in the conditions in these institutions.

20. C. With the reduction of tariff rates, the federal government paid its expenses with revenue generated from the new personal income tax. The income tax was a "progressive" tax in the sense that the tax rate was higher for higher-income individuals.

21. B. The decision of the United Nations to send troops to South Korea required approval of the Security Council. Each of the five permanent members of the Security Council — the United States, France, Great Britain, the USSR, and China (Taiwan at that time) — had the power to veto this action. The Soviet Union would have exercised its veto but was boycotting the sessions because of the failure of the United Nations to recognize the People's Republic of China (Communist China).

22. A. The Emancipation Proclamation applied only to the Confederate states. Slavery remained legal in such states as Kentucky and Delaware until the ratification of the Thirteenth Amendment in 1865. All of the other choices are accurate statements about the Proclamation.

23. B. Garfield's assassination (July 1881) by a deranged and disappointed office seeker led to the passage of the Pendleton Act (1883), the first significant federal civil service reform law. Garfield's nomination by the Republicans in 1880 touched off a major debate in the party over the spoils system between the Stalwarts and Half-Breeds.

24. D. The Proclamation of 1763 attempted to create a boundary between the colonies and the Native American tribes in the trans-Appalachian region newly acquired from France after the French and Indian War. Choice **C**, taken literally, is incorrect, since white/ Native American contact east of the Appalachians already existed.

25. A. The legislation brought major reforms to the government's policy toward Native Americans, rejuvenated the tribal structure, and ended the disastrous policy of allotting acreage to individual Native Americans that had been the keystone of the Dawes Severalty Act of 1887.

26. C. This is a question where you have to define the term. All of the choices pertain to the post-Civil War period, but you should know that "scalawag" was a derogatory term used against whites in the South who cooperated with Reconstruction policies.

27. A. The idea of equality championed by the American Revolution did improve the status of women without granting them any additional rights. While separation of church and state was strengthened, several states continued to support established churches, and non-Christians could not hold office in some states as well. The only direct social change was the granting of freedom to slaves who fought with the Continental Army.

28. B. The Populist party tried to include the concerns of urban workers in its 1892 platform. With the exception of the direct election of senators and restrictions on immigration, the other choices were primarily of interest to farmers, the Populists' main constituency. Organized labor, particularly the American Federation of Labor, was most concerned with legislation that would restrict immigration because it was felt that immigrants were taking jobs from American workers.

29. C. The policy of intervention in Latin-American affairs occurred when Theodore Roosevelt became President in 1901 and was given its justification in Roosevelt's Corollary to the Monroe Doctrine (December 1904), not in the original provision of the Monroe Doctrine.

30. A. The Immigration Act of 1965 abolished the national origins quota system in place since 1924. It eliminated the racial provisions that had restricted immigration from Asia in the past. Although the law put limits on immigration from the Western Hemisphere for the first time, immigration, both legal and illegal, from Mexico and Central America rose sharply after 1965 because of political upheavals and economic problems.

31. C. While the Puritans were determined to rid the Church of England of all Catholic influences, to purify it, the Pilgrims did not believe the Church could be reformed and therefore separated themselves from it. The Pilgrims, in contrast to the Puritans, were a fringe group.

32. A. Major Supreme Court cases almost always come up on the AP exam, and you're expected to know the main points of the decisions. *Marbury* v. *Madison* states the principle of judicial review — that is, the Supreme Court has the authority to determine the constitutionality of laws passed by Congress.

33. D. The Pacific Railroad Act of 1862 provided the Union Pacific and Central Pacific railroads with land grants that could be sold to prospective settlers. Justification for this decision was based on the fact that the railroads would run through unoccupied territory that would be economically worthless unless the railroads could offer them for sale.

34. D. Following the Boston Tea Party, Parliament passed a series of laws specifically to punish Massachusetts. These were known as the Coercive Acts in Great Britain but as the Intolerable Acts in the colonies and included closing the port of Boston until the destroyed tea was paid for.

35. B. A political bargain was struck that resulted in the Republicans putting Rutherford B. Hayes in the presidency and freeing the South from military rule, a bargain known as the Compromise of 1877.

36. B. You need to know the "Alphabet Soup" of the New Deal programs: CCC = Civilian Conservation Corps, WPA = Works Progress Administration, NRA = National Recovery Administration, TVA = Tennessee Valley Authority. The RFC is the Reconstruction Finance Corporation, which was established under Herbert Hoover in 1932. It was authorized to lend money to banks, railroads, and insurance companies.

37. C. The quotation clearly captures the stock speculation mania of the late 1920s that contributed to the stock market crash of 1929.

38. D. Because no candidate won a majority in the Electoral College, the election was decided by the House of Representatives as provided for in the Constitution. This question requires you to know not only the facts about the election of 1824, but the provisions of the Constitution as well. The "corrupt bargain" was a charge that Jackson's supporters made after the House vote and not the way in which the election was decided.

39. D. This question tests your sense of chronology as well as your knowledge of American economic history. The development of railroads and cheap immigrant labor were not factors in American industrialization until after 1820; the cotton gin and the Louisiana Purchase were more relevant to the growth of American agriculture than that of industry. The protective tariffs imposed after the War of 1812, on the other hand, were particularly significant to the protection of infant American manufacturing from British competition.

40. C. Although the South hoped that Britain's need for cotton would encourage the British government to provide recognition and aid, British factory owners had stockpiled cotton in anticipation of the war. The South's hope for British aid failed.

41. A. Calhoun outlined the theory of nullification in his "South Carolina Exposition and Protest" (1828), which was a response to the so-called Tariff of Abominations.

42. D. William Marcy Tweed, "Boss Tweed," was the political boss of New York City for a brief period in the late 1860s and early 1870s and became the symbol of the corruption in urban politics at the time. There are probably cartoons on Tweed by Nast in your textbook.

43. A. This question addresses an aspect of late nineteenth-century social/cultural history. The Chautauqua movement began in 1874 and over the years featured touring lecturers who spoke on literature, science, economics, and government. It also offered correspondence courses for adults.

44. B. Colonial assemblies had the power to tax and approve expenditures. This power gave them some control over the governors, who were appointed by the crown. Although there were property qualifications for voting, these did not significantly limit the right of free white males to vote. Qualifications for office holding were somewhat higher than those for voting.

45. C. The Battle of Saratoga (1777) was a major American victory and is considered a turning point in the Revolution because it led to a formal alliance with France (1778).

46. A. The war-produced demand for agricultural products combined with improvements in farm technology — increased mechanization and use of chemical fertilizers — led to serious overproduction during the 1920s. With production up and demand down, prices for farm products fell sharply.

47. **C.** The policy tried to persuade, without much effect, the nations that already had their own spheres of influence in China to agree to respect the trading rights of all countries, including the United States. The Open Door Policy was outlined by Secretary of State John Hay in 1899. Following the Boxer Rebellion (1900), Hay announced in another series of Open Door notes that the United States supported the preservation of the territorial integrity of China.

48. **B.** The Neutrality Act of 1939 reflected a shift in U.S. policy brought about by the outbreak of World War II in Europe in September 1939. It provided that the United States could trade with belligerents as long as those countries paid cash for the goods and carried them on their own ships.

49. **E.** The Constitution itself provided for the ratification process, which required the approval of nine of the thirteen states. New Hampshire was the ninth state to approve the Constitution in June 1788. Remember that the Articles of Confederation required unanimous approval before they were adopted.

50. **E.** Article III, Section 2, of the Constitution states that "trial of all crimes, except impeachment, shall be by jury." The Bill of Rights in Amendment VI expands on what trial by jury means — speedy and public — and specifies the rights of the accused.

51. **A.** South Carolina seceded on December 20, 1860; Kentucky, although a slave state, remained in the Union; North Carolina and Virginia seceded after the surrender of Fort Sumter (April 14, 1861), while Georgia left the Union before Fort Sumter (January 19, 1861). It's not important to know the specific dates of secession but rather the pattern of secession.

52. **A.** Taft believed that foreign markets could provide an outlet for American business to profitably penetrate other countries without the expense of maintaining colonies.

53. **E.** Hoover believed strongly in self-help and community efforts and opposed direct federal relief efforts as demoralizing to the individual. Here you have two directly opposite choices.

54. **D.** Prior to the publication of Paine's *Common Sense* (January 1776), most Americans believed that Parliament was the colonies' main enemy. The pamphlet attacked royal authority for the first time and contributed significantly to the move for independence.

55. **C.** The transportation revolution — canals, steamboats, improved roads, railroads — dramatically lowered costs and made trade between distant parts of the country economically feasible.

56. **B.** Helper argued that slavery was an outmoded practice the South could not sustain in the coming industrial age. He believed that slavery led nonslaveholding white Southerners into poverty.

57. **D.** In this landmark 1877 decision, the Supreme Court found that state laws regulating businesses that operated in the public interest were constitutional.

58. **D.** The key fact relevant to this question is that the United States did not ratify the Treaty of Versailles. The only possible answer is a joint resolution of Congress.

59. **D.** This quotation is from the debates on American imperialism following the Spanish-American War. The key clue is the last sentence; the reference to Germany, England, and Japan eliminate all of the choices except **D.**

60. **B.** Garrison took an uncompromising position for the immediate freedom for slaves without paying the owners the so-called market prices for slaves.

61. **D.** Between 1818 and 1846, thousands of people had taken the Oregon Trail to new homes in the Pacific Northwest. Beaver trapping declined in the region during that time as well, making it feasible for Great Britain to agree to a westward boundary extension of the forty-ninth parallel.

62. **E.** Jackson argued that while political factions could divide Congress on issues, the President represented all of the people. His use of the veto underscored his belief in a strong executive branch.

63. **A.** Sharecropping and tenant farming became the principal forms of African-American agriculture in the South after the Civil War. This question asks for a definition of sharecropping. You should know that the significant migration of African-Americans from the rural South to northern cities did not take place until World War I and that independent black-owned farms were almost unknown in the post-Civil War South.

64. **C.** The official authorization for the buildup of U.S. forces in Vietnam was the Gulf of Tonkin Resolution (August 1964). It gave the United States the right to repel an armed attack against its forces and to prevent further aggression. Congress never declared war against North Vietnam, and the United States never sought the backing of international organizations. The Truman Doctrine (1947) applied to Greece and Turkey, although the theory behind it — U.S. support for free peoples resisting armed minorities — was applicable to Vietnam.

65. **D.** This is a "when" question. The Interstate Commerce Commission was established in 1887 to regulate the railroads. It was the result of the Supreme Court decision in *Wabash v. Illinois,* which held that states could not regulate the rates of railroads engaged in interstate commerce, since control of such commerce was reserved for the federal government under the Constitution.

66. **B.** This cartoon draws a sharp contrast between the "two ends of the national table": the powerful trusts, depicted by a large, muscular figure, and the frail figure, probably representing the rest of the country. The artist uses the tattered and worn tablecloth at one end to illustrate poverty.

67. **B.** Faulkner, along with Thomas Wolfe, made the South the focus of his writing. Faulkner lived most of his life in Oxford, Mississippi.

68. **A.** The Soviet Union had wanted the allies to open a "second front" in Europe almost as soon as Germany invaded in June 1941. Although this was not possible until the United States entered the war after Pearl Harbor, it did not take place until June 1944. The "second front" refers to the invasion of German-occupied France.

69. **C.** This position, which is sometimes called "accommodation," was formally put forward by Booker T. Washington in 1895. The exactly opposite view was taken by W. E. B. Du Bois. You should know that both Garrison and Douglass are associated with the pre-Civil War abolitionist movement, while Garvey was involved with the "Back to Africa" movement that found support after World War I.

70. A. Melville's *Moby Dick* is representative of the American Renaissance in literature in the mid-nineteenth century, while John Steinbeck's *The Grapes of Wrath* captures the mood of the Depression of the 1930s. Although Bellamy's *Looking Backward* (1888) is in the right period, the utopian novel hardly represents the Realist school. *The Gross Clinic* by Thomas Eakins is an example of the Realist school in art.

71. E. Maryland, established as a proprietary colony by the Calvert family, was specifically founded for English Catholics who faced discrimination. The only other possible choice is Rhode Island, which was founded by Roger Williams for religious dissenters from Massachusetts and respected religious tolerance.

72. C. Bay of Pigs invasion (1961), limited nuclear test ban treaty (1963), Gulf of Tonkin Resolution (1964), U.S. intervention in Dominican Republic (1965).

73. D. The legislation had little immediate success. There was a new surge of business mergers and combination after the law was passed, including the U.S. Steel Corporation and the so-called "Money Trust" under J. P. Morgan.

74. B. In the face of a strike by steel workers during the Korean War, President Truman ordered the seizure of the mills by the federal government. The Court ruled that there was no authority for the President to take such action even in his role as commander-in-chief.

75. D. The choices include two significant foreign-policy actions of the Carter administration. The Camp David Accords, which brought an end to the state of war between Israel and Egypt (March 1979) was a more important accomplishment than the Panama Canal Treaty by which the United States agreed to turn over the canal to Panama.

76. B. The United States established protectorates in Cuba, Haiti, the Dominican Republic, Panama, and Nicaragua for varying periods of time from the Spanish-American War to the establishment of the Good Neighbor Policy in 1933. Only Puerto Rico (not shaded) became an American possession, and U.S. military bases have been only in Panama and Guantánamo Bay, Cuba.

77. C. The Navigation Acts, first enacted in 1651, gave England and English merchants a monopoly on trade with the colonies. Certain products, such as sugar, tobacco, cotton, and indigo, could be shipped only to England or to other British ports.

78. D. The acquittal of Peter Zenger on the charge of seditious libel in 1735 established the principle of freedom of the press. The time frame of the question, the colonial period, eliminates the Bill of Rights as a plausible answer.

79. C. *The Other America* described mass poverty that existed in our "affluent society." The book played a role in stimulating the antipoverty programs of the Kennedy-Johnson administrations, including food stamps.

80. B. Deficit spending assumes that increased federal expenditures — on public works programs, for example — will stimulate the economy by providing jobs; the employed will spend their money, leading business to increase production and hire more workers.

Section II: Essay Questions

Part A

Student DBQ Essay

The melting pot as stated by de Crèvecoeur assumes that immigrants who settle in the United States lose their national identity, and are transformed into something completely different by the experience of living here — Americans. Whether or not the melting pot idea is a valid theory of acculturation depends on the perspective of time. While the attachment to the old world culture was strong among the immigration generation, it lost its hold on their children rather quickly.

In his classic study on immigration, Oscar Handlin described the newcomer to America as "uprooted"; an individual taken from known surroundings and transplanted in an alien environment. Under these circumstances, it was natural for the immigrant to cling to what was familiar. Aside from the obvious economic reasons, this was the key factor in the emergence of distinct immigrant neighborhoods. Every large city, particularly in the Northeast and Midwest had its "Little Italy," Jewish quarter, section where Greeks lived. It was not just that Italians lived with Italians but people from the same region or even town congregated together. This is clearly described in Moses Rischin's description of the living patterns of East European Jews on New York's Lower East Side (Document J). Similarly, in an Italian neighborhood in Missouri, the Festival of Santa Fara, the patron saint of Cinisi, was a reminder of the "old country" for immigrants from that town. (Document B)

To the outsider, there was little evidence that the melting pot was working in these immigrant neighborhoods. The fact that the immigrants continued to speak their native languages and read foreign-language newspapers, that the signs on the storefronts were in Italian, Greek, Russian, or Yiddish, and that each immigrant group formed their own network of self-help organizations could easily have been seen as proof that the new immigrants were unassimilable. But the "education and civic" programs mentioned in the Report of the Massachusetts Commission on Immigration (Document D) were often classes in English and citizenship. While both the number and readership of foreign-language newspapers grew during the new immigration, the New York Times report (Document C) does not go into their content. The Jewish Daily Forward, for example, had a regular column on English and carried articles about baseball and how the Constitution worked.

Both the Massachusetts Report and Miller and Park in Old World Traits Transplanted (Document E) argue that the institutions the immigrants created were essential to their adjustment to America. Miller and Park also point out that assimilation did not take place overnight and that the immigrant institutions, while they might appear to encourage separatism, were in fact bringing about the integration of the immigrant into American society. Patience was not necessary for the children of immigrants. Both Mario Petruzzelli and Hutchins Hapgood note that a gulf developed between the immigrant and the second generation, which reflected how quickly each became Americanized. Knowledge of the language was not necessarily passed down (Document F) and the sons and daughters considered themselves

Americans while the parents remained "greenhorns." (Document I)

America as a melting pot is a valid theory of acculturation but not in the way de Crèveceour stated. Clearly, the new immigrants did not leave behind "their ancient prejudices and manners." They brought them with them and they became important elements in adjusting to America. For the children of the immigrants, however, the fact of living in the United States was a powerful force toward acculturation. This is obvious from the sources.

Reader's Comments

In qualifying Crèvecoeur's statement, the student has written a strong essay demonstrating that immigration was an experience in which acculturation, if not assimilation, was a process validated by the second generation. The essay is well organized and is a useful model on how to structure an answer:

> Paragraph 1: Introduction that clearly states the thesis.
>
> Paragraphs 2–4: Evidence to support the thesis.
>
> Paragraph 5: Conclusion that restates the thesis.

The student makes effective use of Oscar Handlin's *The Uprooted* and analyzes the documents rather than simply restates what they say. Describing the documents while providing their letter designation is a good technique that can help students avoid the "laundry list" approach to the DBQ.

The one weak spot in the essay is the focus on European immigration. Although the documents themselves focus on the classic period of the New Immigration (1880–1924), the question itself is not so limited. Late nineteenth- and twentieth-century immigration does include immigrants from Latin America and Asia. Bringing these groups into the essay would have earned high marks for outside information, which is somewhat limited in the essay as written. The end result is a good essay that falls just a bit short of a top score.

Possible student score: 8

Part B

Question 2 Student Essay

The idea that the election of Thomas Jefferson in 1800 represented a "revolution," which means radical and rapid change, is difficult to support. Although portrayed as a dangerous radical during the campaign, there is little evidence that he was able to completely abandon the programs the Federalists had put in place. The smooth transition from Federalist to Republican control of the government may have been "revolutionary" in the context of the times, but Jefferson's own actions were not.

There were basic differences between the Federalists and Republicans over economic policy. Jefferson had opposed Hamilton on excise taxes on whiskey to produce revenues and the national bank, which he challenged on constitutional grounds as giving too much power to the Federal government. Further, Hamilton's vision of an America in which manufacturing, supported by protective tariffs, would play a key role contrasted with Jefferson's emphasis on the agrarian ideal — U.S. as a nation of yeoman farmers. Despite these sharp differences, the only part of Hamilton's program that Jefferson ended was the whiskey tax and other excises. Jefferson accepted the bank as a necessary convenience and continued to rely on tariffs. The Embargo of 1807, which was not very successful in ending trade with Europe or keeping the United States out of the European war, was a factor in the long term in encouraging American industrialization. Clearly, in terms of the economic policies he followed, Jefferson did not bring about radical change.

In another area, Jefferson showed that he was more a practical politician than a revolutionary. The most important accomplishment of his administration was the Louisiana Purchase (1803), which doubled the size of the country. The acquisition of the territory did present him with a problem. Republican concerns over a strong central government made them take a strict view of the Constitution; the authority of the Federal government was limited to the powers specifically mentioned in the Constitution. The Constitution made no provision for the purchase of the new territory. Jefferson used a loose construction argument — the power of the president to make treaties — to justify the purchase. His willingness to compromise did not go over well with his own party. After the victory in 1804, some Republicans believed that the national government was continuing to grow at the expense of the states and individual liberty. This indicates that even among his supporters, there was a feeling that Jefferson was not going far enough to put Republican principles into practice.

Reader's Comments

This essay has several problems. The student doesn't point out that the concept of the "Revolution of 1800" was Jefferson's own. With this information, the answer might have been better framed as a contrast between what Jefferson hoped to accomplish and what he was able to do. The evidence presented to support the thesis is limited; the student doesn't mention Jefferson's actions with respect to the Alien and Sedition Acts, for example, nor does he/she note the fact that the Louisiana Purchase, by opening more land to farming, was an attempt to support Jefferson's agrarian vision of the United States.

It's always helpful in this type of essay to recognize the other point of view. The "Revolution of 1800" concept has validity if examined on ideological grounds — the importance of individual liberty and democracy and the idea of a unified government with the demise of the Federalists after 1804.

The most glaring shortcoming of the essay is the lack of a concluding paragraph. The essay just ends without any recap. This is so obvious that points would certainly be taken off in the scoring. You might want to try to write a conclusion for this essay as it is presented. Also, rewrite the essay as an exercise, using these comments and information from your textbook and lecture notes as a guide.

Possible student score: 4

Part B

Question 3 Student Essay

The American people were not wholly united on the issue of war with Mexico, but events in the mid-1840s resulted in support of the government's decision to go to war. These events included the annexation of Texas and the dispute over the exact boundary of the Rio Grande. Although not an "event" in the literal sense of the word, the view of Manifest Destiny also caught the imagination of many people at this time. This was the idea that the North American continent would some day be under the U.S. flag and that the United States would extend from the Pacific to the Atlantic coast.

The United States recognized the independence of Texas as soon as the Lone Star Republic successfully established itself following the Battle of San Jacinto. Although Mexico refused to admit the reality of an independent Texas, this was not in itself a cause for war with the United States. Texas functioned as an independent nation for nine years. Early in 1845, President Tyler proposed the annexation of Texas, a move that met with favor in Texas but which was opposed by many people in the United States, especially the Whig party. This was because the admission of Texas was seen as adding another slave state to the union. After Polk became President, however, the Democrats put through the annexation. Mexico could do nothing about this because its government was experiencing another in a series of political upheavals. Therefore, although the annexation provoked Mexico, it was not an immediate cause of war.

The Rio Grande boundary dispute was related to the annexation of Texas, but in an odd way. Without conceding the loss of Texas, Mexico maintained that the true southern boundary of Texas was not the Rio Grande, but instead was the Nueces River, some three hundred miles to the north. In between was disputed territory. Did this area belong to Texas — and after annexation, the United States? Or did it belong to Mexico because the Texans were claiming an improper boundary? This dispute did not immediately escalate into war. Soldiers from both the United States and Mexico patrolled the disputed region. In April 1846, however, Mexican soldiers fired upon Americans in the area, providing the "spark" that started the war. Abraham Lincoln, serving his only term in the House of Representatives as a member of the minority Whig party, sponsored the "Spot Resolution" — a resolution calling for a monument on the "spot" of American soil where blood was shed starting the war. This was the Whig way of scolding the Democrats for upholding the claim of the Rio Grande boundary.

Perhaps the most significant cause of the war was the general (but not unanimous) feeling of Manifest Destiny, a term that first became popular in the early 1840s. Americans had migrated to Texas and become the majority population there; the British were caving in on the Oregon question, even with Polk compromising on the 54° 40' issue; reports were being published by explorers and frontiersmen describing the unknown western half of the continent. Mexico claimed much of the southwest but, except for a few isolated communities, had done little to colonize it. The land was ripe for the taking, and the Polk administration wanted it. The annexation of Texas contributed to the tension between the two countries, and the Rio Grande boundary dispute provided a spark for war. But the belief in Manifest Destiny provided a justification, however wrong in hindsight it may have been, for the war to take place.

Reader's Comments

This is a well-written essay that could have been better had the student chosen to organize the ranking of the factors more clearly. As it is, the essay begins with the weakest of the impact factors and places the major argument at the end. This was apparently done because the student placed the factors in a chronological framework, which wasn't necessary, given that the question asks the writer to "assess the impact." On that basis, the student essay would have been more assertive had it begun with the strongest argument first and placed the other factors as subordinate reasons. The conclusion, however, does wrap up the argument neatly and makes its point.

Possible student score: 7

Part C

Question 4 Student Essay

In order to broaden its base of support, the Populist Party included the demands of organized labor into its 1892 platform — the 8-hour day, restrictions on immigration, and an end to the use of Pinkerton detectives to break up strikes. The platform went further than this, and stated that workers and farmers had the same concerns and enemies. The fact that the Populists did not get a significant percentage of the vote of urban workers in 1892 indicates the weakness of this position.

The Populists' appeal to workers was more than just a tactical move in an election campaign; they sincerely believed that farmers and labor as producers had a common cause against their exploiters — banks, big business, corrupt politicians. The Populists did not fully understand, however, that workers were also consumers. There were parts of the platform that were directly contrary to the interests of workers as consumers.

Farmers had long supported inflation. Increasing the amount of paper money in circulation and the unlimited coinage of silver meant higher prices, making it easier for them to pay off their debt. Hourly workers are the ones hardest hit by inflation. Unskilled workers in particular, frequently unemployed or able to find only seasonal jobs, barely earned enough in the late 19th century to meet basic expenses such as food, rent, clothing, and medicine. It is doubtful their real wages would have increased to meet the additional costs caused by high inflation.

The Populists also supported the subtreasury plan, which was actually a federal subsidy for agriculture. Since overproduction was the key cause of declining farm prices, they wanted the government to establish warehouses where commodities could be stored until market prices rose. While higher prices for bread and other foodstuffs would have helped the farmer, it would only have added to the financial problems of urban workers.

The Depression of 1893 seemed to put farmers and workers in the same boat. Falling prices meant that it cost farmers more to plant crops and grow livestock than they could sell them for; wages fell faster than the cost of food. Buying power began to disappear, and with that came either wage cuts or unemployment as factories closed. The response of the Populists to these conditions during the election of 1896, however, supports the idea that there was a clash of interests between the two groups.

William Jennings Bryan ran on both the Democratic and Populist Party tickets in 1896. The cornerstone of his campaign was the free and unlimited coinage of silver, captured in his famous "Cross of Gold" speech at the Democratic convention. Although he used the Populist idea of "producers," he believed that the future of the country lay in the farmers rather than the cities. The Republican McKinley, on the other hand, stressed that free silver meant higher prices and directly appealed to the workers with the slogan "a full dinner pail." Rather than showing the shared concerns of workers and farmers, the election of 1896 almost pitted the two groups against each other.

Despite the Populists' conviction that farmers and workers were logical allies, the economic policies they supported, particularly inflation, offered nothing to labor. If this alliance existed, we would expect to see it reflected in the political process. It was not. The Populists failed to win the backing of workers and urban groups in 1892 and 1896.

Reader's Comments

The student has written a good essay that points out the basic conflict between an important element of Populist beliefs — inflation — and the economic interests of workers. He/she also makes the valid point that despite their attempt to win the support of workers, this was not successful given the results in the 1892 and 1896 elections.

The essay focuses a bit too much on the farmers' position and should have pointed to aspects of the American labor movement that support the thesis. Unlike the Populists, for example, organized labor didn't see factory owners as a hostile class. Also, while the Knights of Labor did advocate worker control of mines, factories, and railroads, which was similar to the Populists' call for government ownership of key industries, the American Federation of Labor strictly concerned itself with "bread and butter" issues — hours, wages, working conditions. The student might have pointed out that the Populists' support for immigration restriction, which the AFL backed, probably didn't go over well with the significant percentage of the labor force in the 1890s who were recent immigrants themselves.

Within its limits, the organization of the essay is fine. The point that the Populist platform contained planks that were contrary to the interests of workers should be included in the first paragraph as part of a stronger statement of the thesis.

Possible student score: 6

Part C

Question 5 Student Essay

During the 1950s and 1960s, the civil rights movement was the most important domestic issue in the United States. This period saw important victories for black Americans in their struggle for equality a century after the Civil War. Key actions by the Supreme Court, and legislation passed by Congress supported by strong presidential leadership both played a role.

A new era in the civil rights for black Americans began with the Supreme Court's decision in <u>Brown v. Board of Education of Topeka, Kansas</u> (1954). Here the Court overturned the more than a half century old "separate but equal" doctrine and ruled that segregated schools were inherently unequal. While the Court expected desegregation to go forward "with all deliberate speed," it did not. Segregated public schools continued to exist in both the South and the North for decades after the ruling. Still the decision was crucial because it gave confidence to the civil rights movement that it could count on the Court's support.

In the wake of the Montgomery, Alabama bus boycott, the Court also ruled segregation in public transportation was unconstitutional (1956). The combination of growing public awareness of and push to end segregation, and the actions of the Supreme Court probably encouraged Congress to pass the Civil Rights Act of 1957 and 1960. The legislation created the Civil Rights Commission and gave the Justice Department the power to go to court to protect the right of blacks to vote.

Under Johnson, two critical civil rights laws were enacted. The Civil Rights Act of 1964 banned discrimination in public accommodations, gave authority to the Justice Department to sue to end segregation in schools and other public facilities, and barred discrimination in employment on the basis of race, religion, sex, or national origins. The Supreme Court quickly declared the Act constitutional. In the following year, Congress, again at Johnson's insistence, passed the Voting Rights Act suspending literacy and other tests that were used primarily in the South to deny blacks the right to vote. The federal government also was to supervise elections where these tests had been used in the past. The new law led to a tremendous increase in black voter registration in the South.

Untangling the various forces at work to protect and expand the civil rights of blacks during the 1950s and 1960s is difficult. If we take out the role of those involved in the civil rights movement and the political leadership, a case can be made that the Supreme Court was the vital element in the 1950s while Congress was critical to advancing equality in the 1960s. Although it validated the civil rights legislation in the 1960s, the Court's activism at that time was focused in the area of civil liberties — the rights of criminal defendants and the separation of church and state (school prayer).

Reader's Comments

This student comes close to answering the question but just misses. The question asks for an analysis of the "relative importance" of the Supreme Court and Congress; the student's point made in the concluding paragraph that the Court was important in the 1950s while Congress was more important in the 1960s should have been made in the introduction as a thesis statement. Too much is left to the reader to decide about which side the student is supporting. The notion that the *Brown* decision created a climate in which Congress passed civil rights legislation suggests that the Court was the dominant factor.

The student shows a good command of most of the important civil rights legislation of the period. The essay fails to mention, however, the Twenty-Fourth Amendment to the Constitution (January 1964), which eliminated the poll tax for voting in federal elections. The poll tax was used to deny African-Americans the right to vote.

Possible student score: 6

Practice Test 2

Section I: Multiple-Choice Questions

Time: 55 Minutes

80 Questions

Directions: Select the best answer for the following questions or incomplete statements from the five choices provided. Indicate your answer by darkening the appropriate space on the answer sheet.

---

1. The Dred Scott decision held that a slave

   A. could sue for his freedom in the courts

   B. became free when transported to free territory

   C. was private property even in a free territory

   D. was a citizen when in free territory

   E. could not be transported out of a slave state

2. Open-range ranching came to an end due to

   A. overproduction of beef and declining prices

   B. federal support for irrigated agriculture

   C. the range wars between cattlemen and sheepherders

   D. fencing of the plains with barbed wire

   E. increase in cattle production in the Midwest and East

3. The vision of America as a country of yeoman farmers is most often associated with

   A. George Washington

   B. Alexander Hamilton

   C. Benjamin Franklin

   D. Thomas Jefferson

   E. Andrew Jackson

4. President Lyndon Johnson's reference to "guns and butter" meant that

   A. the domestic economy would not be affected by the Vietnam War

   B. the Vietnam War would require consumer sacrifice

   C. dairy producers would suffer economic recession

   D. the United States would alternate between fighting and peace settlement negotiations

   E. U.S. military goals would not be vulnerable to charges of weakness

GO ON TO THE NEXT PAGE

5. The first successful oil well was drilled in

A. Texas

B. Oklahoma

C. Pennsylvania

D. New Jersey

E. California

6. Henry Ford was able to reduce the price of automobiles significantly by

A. entering into price-fixing arrangements with steel companies

B. preventing his workers from joining unions

C. developing assembly-line production techniques

D. forming the automobile trust

E. getting Congress to support a national highway system

7. Which of the following New Deal agencies was NOT intended to provide jobs for the unemployed?

A. Civilian Conservation Corps

B. Works Progress Administration

C. National Recovery Administration

D. Civil Works Administration

E. Public Works Administration

8. Which of the following best describes the message of this cartoon?

A. A plea for keeping the Union together on the eve of the Civil War

B. An appeal to the colonies to unify against the threat from France

C. An appeal to slaveholding states against the Missouri Compromise

D. A call for Native American tribes to unite against white settlers

E. A plea to end sectional differences over tariff policy

9. The early nineteenth-century Native American leader who urged the Indian tribes in the Old Northwest Territory to unify to protect their lands was

   A. Chief Joseph

   B. Geronimo

   C. Tecumseh

   D. Powhatan

   E. King Philip

10. Which statement best describes the "Irreconcilables" during the debate over the Treaty of Versailles?

   A. They opposed the treaty because it failed to adequately protect national minorities in eastern Europe.

   B. They supported the treaty if certain changes were made on the reparations issue.

   C. They were opposed to American participation in the League of Nations on any terms.

   D. They were willing to accept the treaty if limitations were placed on U.S. participation in the League of Nations.

   E. They accepted the treaty as presented by Wilson but refused to make any changes.

11. Which of the following statements is NOT true about the Coercive Acts?

   A. They were directed against all of the colonies.

   B. They were called the Intolerable Acts by the colonists.

   C. They significantly strengthened colonial unity.

   D. They led to a boycott of British goods in the colonies.

   E. They were the British response to the Boston Tea Party.

12. The individual who best represented the Enlightenment in colonial America was

   A. Anne Hutchinson

   B. George Whitefield

   C. Alexander Hamilton

   D. William Bradford

   E. Benjamin Franklin

13. The principle that freedom of speech as guaranteed under the First Amendment is not absolute was stated in which early twentieth-century Supreme Court decision?

   A. *Marbury v. Madison*

   B. *Gibbons v. Ogden*

   C. *Brown v. Board of Education*

   D. *Schenck v. U.S.*

   E. *Miranda v. Arizona*

GO ON TO THE NEXT PAGE

Practice Test 2

14. The Civil Rights Act of 1866 was significant because

   I.   it meant that Congress rather than the President would determine Reconstruction policies

   II. it showed President Andrew Johnson's unwillingness to accept the Radical Republican approach to Reconstruction

   III. it was the first major piece of legislation that became law over a presidential veto

   IV. it guaranteed that former slaves would control the state legislatures in the South

   A.   I only

   B.   III only

   C.   I and III only

   D.   II and IV only

   E.   I, II, and III only

15. The American journalist William Allen White wrote that the United States was "tired of issues, sick at heart of ideals, and weary of being noble." This best describes the mood of the country in

   A.   1920

   B.   1932

   C.   1960

   D.   1968

   E.   1976

16. To Andrew Jackson, the spoils system

   A.   denied qualified persons the right to keep federal jobs

   B.   was needed in the absence of civil service laws

   C.   benefited the political process

   D.   was a political practice beyond his ability to control

   E.   kept him from appointing his friends to political office

17. The Virginia and Kentucky Resolutions argued that the right to determine the constitutionality of a law passed by Congress rested in

   A.   Congress

   B.   the states

   C.   the President

   D.   the Supreme Court

   E.   the vote of the people

18. Hamilton proposed a tariff soon after the launching of the United States government in order to

   A.   stop the export of raw materials to Great Britain

   B.   help develop manufacturing in the United States

   C.   help develop the American labor movement

   D.   punish Great Britain for postwar harassment of American shipping

   E.   support the creation of an American merchant marine

19. The Civil Rights Act of 1964

   A.   made de jure segregation illegal

   B.   made de facto segregation illegal

   C.   outlawed racial discrimination in all places of public accommodation

   D.   protected registration of black voters

   E.   ended segregation in private schools

20. According to Jay's Treaty

    A. the British agreed finally to evacuate the Northwest posts

    B. all prewar colonial debts were canceled

    C. American rights to the Mississippi River were secured

    D. a definite boundary between the United States and Canada was secured and extended to the Great Lakes region

    E. the British agreed not to take any more American sailors off merchant ships

21. The "Back to Africa" movement, which resulted in the creation of Liberia in 1822, found support in which twentieth-century group?

    A. National Association for the Advancement of Colored People

    B. Universal Negro Improvement Association

    C. Urban League

    D. Southern Christian Leadership Conference

    E. Congress of Racial Equality

22. In the seventeenth century, the Great Migration refers to the

    A. settlement of the Puritans in Massachusetts Bay

    B. trade in slaves between west Africa and the West Indies

    C. immigration of Irish to the colonies

    D. expansion of white settlement across the Appalachian Mountains

    E. settlement of French-speaking Canadians in Louisiana

23. All of the following statements about slavery and the Constitution are true EXCEPT

    A. There was some support for the abolition of slavery at the Constitutional Convention.

    B. An important compromise allowed slaves to be included in determining representation in Congress.

    C. The slave trade was immediately abolished.

    D. The Constitution included a fugitive-slave clause.

    E. The word "slavery" is never used in the Constitution.

24. "Forty acres and a mule" refers to

    A. the proposal to make freed slaves small-scale farmers

    B. the terms of the Homestead Act of 1862

    C. the allotment given to Native Americans under the Dawes Severalty Act

    D. the inducement given recent immigrants if they would settle outside of urban centers

    E. a typical homestead on the Great Plains in the 1870s

GO ON TO THE NEXT PAGE

25. "If the gold delegates dare to defend the gold standard as a good thing, we will fight them to the uppermost." Bryan's famous "cross of gold" speech called for

A. the unlimited coinage of silver

B. lower tariffs

C. a revival of greenback paper currency

D. renewed religious commitment for all Americans

E. federal and social welfare programs to deal with the Panic of 1893

U. S. POPULATION INCREASE 1800-1850

Population

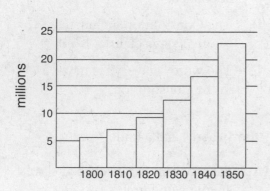

Population Per Square Mile

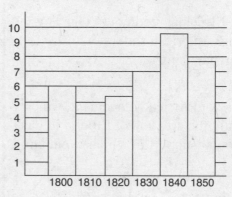

Source: U.S. Bureau of the Census, *Historical Statistics of the United States from Colonial Times to 1970.*

26. Which of the following events best explain the periodic declines in the population density of the United States in the first half of the nineteenth century?

  I. Railroad construction

  II. Louisiana Purchase

  III. Missouri Compromise

  IV. Mexican-American War

A. II only

B. IV only

C. I and III only

D. II and III only

E. II and IV only

27. Between 1920 and 1939, American foreign policy included all of the following EXCEPT

A. attempts to develop international agreements on disarmament

B. improved relations with Latin America

C. nonrecognition of territory acquired by force

D. concern over the war debt and reparations issue

E. active intervention to prevent aggression

28. By the end of his presidency, Ulysses Grant's popularity had declined substantially because of

A. the corruption evident in his administration

B. his harsh and brutal policies toward the South

C. his support for "greenbacker" monetary policies

D. his refusal to support the Radicals in Congress

E. revelations about his poor military leadership during the Civil War

29. Senator Stephen A. Douglas managed to engineer the Compromise of 1850 by

A. winning the endorsement of President Zachary Taylor for the Compromise

B. letting the southern Democrats dictate the terms of the Compromise

C. securing passage of the different parts of the Compromise as separate laws

D. threatening to remove political opponents from important congressional committees

E. a policy of conciliation for all factions

30. The "Insular Cases" decision of the Supreme Court declared that

A. the United States had the right to establish a Canal Zone in Panama

B. indigenous people in newly acquired colonies did not necessarily have the same rights as Americans

C. Puerto Rico and the Philippines could be lawfully annexed

D. newly acquired territories could eventually become states

E. annexation of the Hawaiian Islands had been unlawful

31. The British response to the American claim of "no taxation without representation" was that

A. colonial assemblies would be permitted to vote on all new taxes

B. monies raised through taxes would be used for internal improvements in the colonies

C. American approval was necessary for internal taxes

D. members of Parliament represented the interests of all people in the British Empire

E. Parliament agreed it had no authority to impose taxes on the colonies

GO ON TO THE NEXT PAGE

32. All of the following were part of American economic policy during the 1920s EXCEPT

    A. lower taxes on the wealthy

    B. high tariffs

    C. opposition to parity prices for farmers

    D. limits on regulation of business

    E. support of public-works projects

33. The individual associated with the development of the skyscraper was

    A. John A. Roebling

    B. Frederick Law Olmsted

    C. Louis H. Sullivan

    D. Edward Bellamy

    E. Thomas A. Edison

34. Which of the following events occurred LAST?

    A. The South Carolina Ordinance of Secession

    B. Abraham Lincoln's inauguration

    C. The surrender of Fort Sumter

    D. The secession of Virginia

    E. The secession of Alabama

35. The Seventeenth Amendment called for

    A. a personal income tax

    B. direct election of U.S. Senators

    C. woman suffrage

    D. moving up the date of presidential inaugurations

    E. raising the minimum-age requirement for U.S. Senators to thirty-five

36. The Ballinger-Pinchot controversy involved

    A. a diplomatic incident between the United States and France

    B. the regulation of the trusts

    C. child-labor laws

    D. conservation policy

    E. legislation to restrict immigration

37. In the Treaty of Ghent, which ended the War of 1812,

    A. most American demands were satisfied

    B. the Americans made substantial concessions to the British

    C. the issues that had led to war were finally resolved

    D. nothing was settled beyond a restoration of the prewar status quo

    E. Britain agreed to end the impressment of American seamen

38. Germany's notorious Zimmermann telegram .

    A. promised a temporary halt to submarine warfare

    B. proposed an alliance with Mexico if the United States declared war on Germany

    C. apologized for the sinking of the *Lusitania*

    D. warned the United States not to send merchant ships to belligerent nations

    E. rejected U.S. efforts for a truce in the fighting

39. Shays' Rebellion suggests that the most important problem facing the United States after the Revolution was

    A. the ongoing conflict with Native Americans

    B. the British refusal to recognize American claims to the Northwest Territory

    C. economic problems caused by debt and high taxes

    D. disputes over states' rights and the authority of the federal government

    E. the danger of an open slave revolt in the South

40. "Under our system of railroad ownership, an excessive competition exists for the business of all competing points, while the local business of the various competing lines is an absolute monopoly. This has naturally resulted in compelling the corporations to do through business at rates often ruinously unremunerative, which again has compelled those companies to recoup themselves for their losses and secure their profits by excessive charges on the local traffic."

    This passage explains which problem that farmers faced in the late nineteenth century?

    A. prices charged by grain-elevator operators

    B. agricultural overproduction

    C. high protective tariffs

    D. long vs. short hauls

    E. heavy debt

41. For the period from the end of Reconstruction to 1900, the position of the Supreme Court toward civil rights is best characterized as

    A. supporting the integration of African-Americans into society

    B. strictly interpreting the Constitution to broaden the rights of African-Americans

    C. establishing the constitutionality of segregation

    D. vigorously enforcing the terms of the Fourteenth and Fifteenth Amendments

    E. willing to end segregation in the South but not in the North

42. The so-called "Phony War" of 1939–40

    A. marked a period of time when nothing seemed to be happening

    B. was a nickname given to the Spanish Civil War

    C. was the undeclared war between Great Britain and Italy

    D. involved submarine warfare in the Atlantic between the United States and Germany

    E. ended with the attack on Pearl Harbor

GO ON TO THE NEXT PAGE

43. Jacob Coxey's 1894 march on Washington, D.C., called for

    A. tougher immigration restrictions

    B. a government takeover of the railroads

    C. an increase in the supply of paper money

    D. recognition of the legitimacy of labor unions

    E. generosity in granting pensions to Civil War veterans

44. Which of the following is in the correct chronological order?

    A. Articles of Confederation, Whiskey Rebellion, Constitutional Convention, Shays' Rebellion

    B. Shays' Rebellion, Articles of Confederation, Whiskey Rebellion, Constitutional Convention

    C. Articles of Confederation, Shays' Rebellion, Constitutional Convention, Whiskey Rebellion

    D. Whiskey Rebellion, Articles of Confederation, Constitutional Convention, Shays' Rebellion

    E. Constitutional Convention, Articles of Confederation, Shays' Rebellion, Whiskey Rebellion

Source: Library of Congress

45. The conditions shown in this photograph were captured in print by

    A. John dos Passos

    B. Ernest Hemingway

    C. John Steinbeck

    D. Frank Norris

    E. Eudora Welty

46. Land Ordinance of 1785 provided for

    A. a ban on the importation of slaves into the Northwest Territory

    B. a survey of the Northwest Territory and its division into townships

    C. the procedure by which new states would be admitted to the Union

    D. protection of Indians by prohibiting white settlement west of the Appalachians

    E. the establishment of a series of forts along the Mississippi

47. The official reason for the impeachment of President Andrew Johnson was his

    A. refusal to support ratification of the Fourteenth Amendment

    B. violation of the Tenure of Office Act

    C. veto of the First Reconstruction Act

    D. campaigning against Radical Republicans in the election of 1866

    E. belief that African-Americans were not equal to whites

48. The first federal law to restrict immigration, passed in 1882, was aimed at

    A. stopping Mexicans from crossing the border without first obtaining a visa

    B. excluding Chinese immigrants

    C. stopping immigration from eastern Europe

    D. restricting the number of people coming into the United States

    E. preventing smuggling of illegal aliens over the Canadian border

49. Wilson's Fourteen Points did NOT include the

    A. creation of an independent Czechoslovakia

    B. creation of an independent Poland

    C. return of Alsace-Lorraine to France

    D. creation of an international organization of nations

    E. creation of an international peacekeeping force

50. All of the following were advantages the North had over the South at the start of the Civil War EXCEPT

    A. a larger population

    B. better military leaders

    C. greater industrial production

    D. more railroad and canal networks

    E. a larger navy

GO ON TO THE NEXT PAGE

Practice Test 2

51. The trend taken by the Supreme Court under Chief Justice John Marshall was to

    A. strengthen state power at the expense of the federal government

    B. give more authority to state courts and state laws

    C. deny the national government authority concerning interstate commerce

    D. expand the federal government's powers

    E. deprive Native Americans of their ancestral land holdings

52. One of the consequences of the Great Awakening was

    A. a closer sense of unity between England and its colonies

    B. that the Church of England was adopted by the colonies as an officially established church

    C. the discussion of new ideas in religion

    D. a challenge to traditional beliefs

    E. a growing awareness of people in the colonies of their rights as Englishmen

Popular and Electoral Votes in Two Controversial Elections, 1876 and 1888

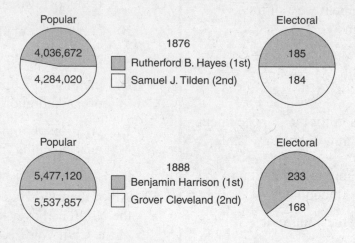

53. Based on the pie charts above, the presidential election of 1876 and 1888 were controversial because

    A. the elections were decided by the House of Representatives

    B. the electoral-vote winner lost in the popular vote

    C. less than fifty percent of the eligible voters cast ballots

    D. former slaves were an important factor in the outcome

    E. voter turnout was high compared to that of other elections after the Civil War

54. The "Critical Period" in American history refers to the

   A. decade between 1860 and Lincoln's election

   B. United States under the Articles of Confederation

   C. era of Jacksonian democracy

   D. New Deal

   E. rise of the United States to the status of world power from 1898 to 1920

55. During the presidency of Andrew Jackson, the issue that triggered the debate over states' rights was

   A. tariff policy

   B. expansion of slavery

   C. Indian removal

   D. internal improvements

   E. rechartering the Bank of the United States

56. Which of the following sources would NOT be useful in understanding the military campaigns of the Civil War?

   A. newspaper accounts

   B. diaries kept by soldiers

   C. photographs

   D. presidential speeches

   E. official unit histories

57. Which of the following statements regarding the Monroe Doctrine is true?

   A. The United States committed itself to provide military aid to countries in the Western Hemisphere that wanted to overthrow colonial rule.

   B. Throughout most of the nineteenth century, the effectiveness of the Monroe Doctrine depended on British naval supremacy.

   C. Monroe renewed George Washington's idea of not becoming involved in entangling foreign alliances.

   D. The Doctrine was rejected by the major European powers as a violation of international law.

   E. European acceptance of the Doctrine established the United States as a world power.

58. The disappearance of slavery in the North resulted from

   A. greater Northern devotion to American ideals

   B. economic competition from the South

   C. higher prices for slaves in the South

   D. the economic unprofitability of slavery in a region of small farms

   E. the Puritan tradition, which rejected slaveholding

GO ON TO THE NEXT PAGE

59. The injunction as a court order was often used in the late nineteenth and early twentieth century to

   A. break up trusts

   B. help farmers in danger of losing their farms

   C. stop strikebreaking

   D. prevent labor unions from striking

   E. protect blacks from civil rights abuses

60. During World War II, African-Americans in the military

   A. could serve only in the Army

   B. were integrated for the first time into white units

   C. served in leadership positions

   D. received training as airplane pilots

   E. were seldom given combat assignments

61. The Native American Group known as the "mound builders" is associated with

   A. the Anasazi

   B. the Sioux

   C. the Adena-Hopewell

   D. the Apache

   E. the Iroquois

62. All of the following are identified with the counterculture of the 1960s EXCEPT

   A. Woodstock

   B. Haight-Ashbury

   C. Flower Power

   D. James Dean

   E. the film *Easy Rider*

63. Richard Nixon's early success in politics was largely based on his

   A. support for civil rights legislation

   B. expertise in foreign policy, particularly China

   C. anticommunism

   D. backing of an expansion of the New Deal programs

   E. military service during World War II

64. The most likely cause of the increase in urban poverty in eighteenth-century America was that

   A. when people found it more difficult to acquire property, they went to the cities looking for work

   B. urban-dwelling people had more children than those living in rural areas

   C. rural jobs paid more than city jobs

   D. there was greater economic opportunity in rural areas

   E. the enclosure movement was brought over from England to displace colonial farmers

65. The main purpose of the Tennessee Valley Authority was to

A. create affordable housing in rural Appalachia

B. control floods and provide electric power to the region

C. demonstrate the benefits of socialism in a poverty-stricken area

D. win political support for the New Deal in traditionally Republican states

E. expand the jurisdiction of the Agricultural Adjustment Administration

66. The doctrine of popular sovereignty called for the question of permitting slaves in a new territory to be decided by the

A. House of Representatives

B. Supreme Court

C. people living in the territory

D. Compromise of 1850

E. Wilmot Proviso

67. Gabriel's rebellion, a Virginia slave revolt in 1800,

A. resulted in the destruction of most of Richmond

B. caused the deaths of more than a hundred whites

C. inspired slaves in other southern states to revolt

D. was planned but never took place

E. was exceptional for its time

68. The key issue in the 1978 Supreme Court decision in *Bakke* v. *Board of Regents* was

A. school desegregation

B. affirmative action

C. freedom of the press as applied to student newspapers

D. abortion

E. prayer in public schools

69. Which of the following events in the Cold War occurred most recently?

A. Hungarian uprising

B. Berlin airlift

C. U-2 incident

D. launching of Sputnik

E. Castro in power in Cuba

70. In the negotiations that led to the Treaty of Paris and formally ended the Revolution, the Americans

A. were helped by the French in formulating diplomatic strategy and objectives

B. settled for much less than they might have gotten through shrewd diplomacy

C. won many concessions through separate bargaining with the British

D. found the British obstinate on the issue of the Northwest outposts

E. failed to gain a clear claim to the lands west to the Mississippi River

GO ON TO THE NEXT PAGE

71. The first employees in the Lowell, Massachusetts, textile mills were

   A. slaves imported from the South

   B. young girls from New England farms

   C. farmers who could no longer support themselves through farming

   D. newly arrived immigrants from Europe

   E. people who could not find work in urban centers

72. The most important aspect of Jacksonian democracy was

   A. abolition of the property qualification

   B. granting of suffrage to free blacks

   C. permitting limited suffrage rights to women

   D. abolition of poll taxes

   E. creation of distinct political parties

73. The Annapolis Convention was called because

   A. merchants wanted a stronger navy to protect their shipping

   B. the Indians were effectively resisting the advance of settlers

   C. the Confederation Congress had proved incapable of dealing with commercial issues

   D. the British continued to challenge U.S. ships at sea

   E. of the debate over the status of free blacks

Questions 74–75 refer to the following map.

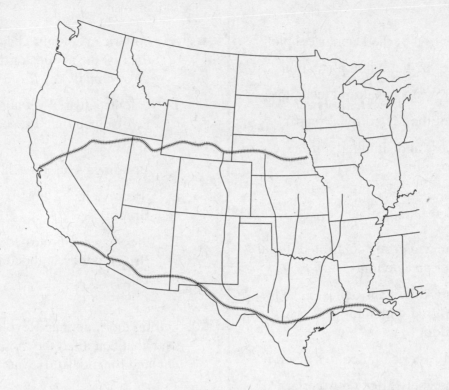

74. On the above map, the routes moving north from south Texas represent

- **A.** escape routes for slaves to the free territories

- **B.** advances made by Mexican troops during the war with the United States

- **C.** trails used for the "long drive" during the Cattle Kingdom

- **D.** patterns of migrant Mexican labor in the early twentieth century

- **E.** Native American resettlement in the "Indian Territory"

75. The railroad route linking New Orleans and Los Angeles shown on the map was made possible by

- **A.** the Mexican Cession

- **B.** the military defeat of the Apache Indians

- **C.** the success of the Union Pacific and Central Pacific railroads

- **D.** the Gadsden Purchase

- **E.** California's independence from Mexico

GO ON TO THE NEXT PAGE

76. Cotton production was made profitable by the

    A. invention of the Deere steel plow

    B. use of irrigation on plantations

    C. improved agricultural techniques

    D. use of the McCormick reaper

    E. success and simplicity of the cotton gin

77. Prohibition failed because

    A. organized crime controlled illegal liquor production

    B. many Americans believed the law interfered with their personal freedom

    C. rural America failed to support it

    D. it adversely affected American productivity

    E. the costs of enforcing it were too expensive

78. Dr. Martin Luther King, Jr., advocated the philosophy of

    A. economic equality

    B. Black Power

    C. accommodation

    D. nonviolence

    E. militant protest

79. As a consequence of the French and Indian War,

    A. American colonists began to distrust the actions of the British government

    B. colonists feared yet another involvement in a Franco-British conflict

    C. Britain gave up Florida to Spain

    D. Spain yielded Cuba to Great Britain

    E. the Shawnee protested against British policy in the Ohio River valley

80. During the American Revolution, the state that benefited the most from a demand for foodstuffs was

    A. Alabama

    B. Pennsylvania

    C. Connecticut

    D. Georgia

    E. Massachusetts

IF YOU FINISH BEFORE TIME IS CALLED, CHECK YOUR WORK ON THIS SECTION ONLY. DO NOT WORK ON ANY OTHER SECTION IN THE TEST.

Section II: Essay Questions

Part A

(Suggested writing time — 45 minutes)

Directions: Write an essay based on your analysis of Documents A–J as well as your knowledge of the period covered by the question. It is important for you to include information on the topic not provided by the documents.

1. The War of 1812, known mainly for its divisions among Federalists and Republicans over support of the war, resulted in a united nation confident of its abilities and optimistic about its future.

   Using the documents provided and your knowledge of the period from 1812 to 1824, assess the validity of this statement.

Document A

On the shore, dimly seen through the mists of the deep,
Where the foe's haughty host in dread silence reposes,
What is that which the breeze, o'er the towering steep,
As it fitfully blows, half conceals, half discloses?
Now it catches the gleam of the morning's first beam,
In full glory reflected, now shines in the stream.
'Tis the star-spangled banner. Oh! long may it wave
O'er the land of the free and the home of the brave!

Source: Francis Scott Key, "The Star-Spangled Banner," second verse, 1814.

Document B

Among the means of advancing the public interest the occasion is a proper one for recalling the attention of Congress to the great importance of establishing throughout our country roads and canals which can be executed under the national authority. No objects within the circle of political economy so richly repay the expense bestowed upon them; there are none the utility of which is more universally ascertained and acknowledged; none that do more honor to the governments whose wise and enlarged patriotism duly appreciated them. Nor is there any country which presents a field where nature invites more the art of man to complete her own work for his accommodation and benefit. These considerations are strengthened, moreover, by the political effect of these facilities for intercommunication in bringing and binding more closely together the various parts of our extended confederacy. Whilst the States individually, with a laudable enterprise and emulation, avail themselves of their local advantages by new roads, by navigable canals,

GO ON TO THE NEXT PAGE

and by improving the streams susceptible of navigation, the General Government is the more urged to similar undertakings, requiring a national jurisdiction and national means, by the prospect of thus systematically completing so inestimable a work; and it is a happy reflection that any defect of constitutional authority which may be encountered can be supplied in a mode which the Constitution itself has providently pointed out.

Source: President James Madison, Annual message to Congress, December 5, 1815.

Document C

What have we gained by the war? He [Clay] had shown we had lost nothing in rights, territory or honor; nothing for which we ought to have contended, according to the principles of gentlemen on the other side, or according to our own. Have we gained nothing by the war? Let any man look at the degraded condition of this country before the war — the scorn of the universe, the contempt of ourselves — and tell me, if we have gained nothing by the war? What is our present situation? Respectability and character abroad; security and confidence at home. If we have not obtained, in the opinion of some, the full measure of retribution, our character and constitution are placed on a solid basis never to be shaken.

Source: Report of a speech by Henry Clay to the House of Representatives, January 1816.

Document D

State	House of Representatives		Senate	
	For	*Against*	*For*	*Against*
New Hampshire	3	2	1	1
Vermont	3	1	1	0
Massachusetts	6	8	1	1
Rhode Island	0	2	0	0
Connecticut	0	7	0	2
New York	3	11	1	1
New Jersey	2	4	1	1
Delaware	0	1	0	2
Pennsylvania	16	2	2	0
Maryland	6	3	1	1
Virginia	14	5	2	0
North Carolina	6	3	2	0
South Carolina	8	0	2	0
Georgia	3	0	2	0
Ohio	1	0	0	1
Kentucky	5	0	1	1
Tennessee	3	0	2	0
TOTALS	79	49	19	13

CONGRESS VOTES FOR WAR AGAINST GREAT BRITAIN, 1812

Document E

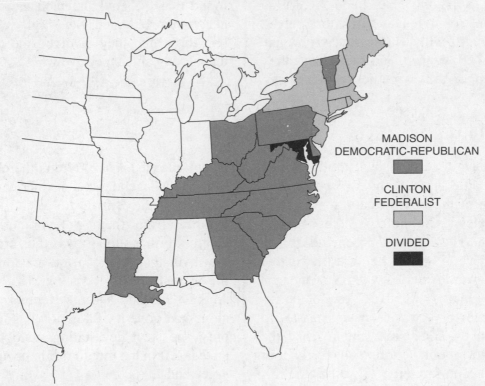

PRESIDENTIAL ELECTION RESULTS, 1812

MADISON
DEMOCRATIC-REPUBLICAN

CLINTON
FEDERALIST

DIVIDED

Document F

We will not mock the feelings of our readers at this moment by any diffuse comment on the exhilarating news the last eight-and-forty hours have announced to us. We will only say —

Americans! Rejoice!

For that, by the unsurpassed exploits of your army and navy, and the consummate wisdom of your statesmen, you have achieved an honorable peace with one of the most powerful nations on the globe, with whom you were at war —

Republicans, rejoice!

For that the men of your heart, those virtuous patriots whom you have cherished as the apple of your eye, have conducted you through a glorious contest, under every disadvantage, to an honorable peace with a powerful and arrogant enemy —

Federalists, rejoice!

For that your opposition has been unavailing in checking measures of your government; and that your Hartford Conventions, your plots and counterplots, have not arrested the march of the republic to the heights of fame and glory —

Rejoice, all men of whatever party ye be!

For that, while the effusion of blood is stayed, and the blessings of peace restored to our beloved land, your country is proudly exalted among the Nations of the Earth by her success in an honorable struggle, commenced in self-defense, and terminating in a recognition of justice of her cause.

Source: Daily National Intelligencer *(Washington, D.C.),* *February 16, 1815.*

GO ON TO THE NEXT PAGE

Document G

What the terms of peace are, we cannot tell. They will only be made known at Washington, by the dispatches themselves. But one thing I will venture to say now and before they are opened, and I will hazard my reputation upon the correctness of what I say, that when the terms are disclosed, it will be found that the government have not by this negotiation obtained one single avowed object for which they involved the country in this bloody and expensive war.

Source: New York Evening Post, *February 13, 1815.*

Document H

Critics have made much of the irony that since the battle was fought two weeks after the signing of the peace treaty, it was completely useless. Chronology here becomes important. The treaty, concluded on Christmas Eve 1814, was being wafted on the high seas toward America when New Orleans was fought, January 8, 1815. News of the exhilarating victory was sent posthaste to Washington by horseback, and reached the capital on or about February 4, nearly four weeks later. The tiny city, as well as the rest of America, burst into rejoicing. About ten days later, February 1815, the Treaty of Ghent reached Washington, thereby giving birth to the legend that the Americans, having humiliated the British at New Orleans, had extorted from them a favorable treaty at Ghent. Further support was thus provided for the myth that America had not only beaten the British in the War of 1812 but that Andrew Jackson and his Kentucky riflemen alone had done it. If a nation is going to win only one such devastating victory, a better taste is left in the mouth if it happens to come at the end.

Source: Thomas A. Bailey, Probing America's Past *(1973).*

Document I

Our moderation and conciliation have had no other effect than to encourage perseverance and to enlarge pretensions. We behold our seafaring citizens still the daily victims of lawless violence, committed on the great common and highway of nations, even within sight of the country which owes them protection. We behold our vessels, freighted with the products of our soil and industry, or returning with the honest proceeds of them, wrested from their lawful destinations, confiscated by prize courts no longer the organs of public law but the instruments of arbitrary edicts, and their unfortunate crews dispersed and lost, or forced or inveigled in British ports into British fleets, whilst arguments are employed in support of these aggressions which have no foundation but in a principle equally supporting a claim to regulate our external commerce in all cases whatsoever.

We hold, in fine, on the side of Great Britain a state of war against the United States, and on the side of the United States a state of peace toward Great Britain.

Source: President James Madison's war message to Congress, June 1, 1812.

Document J

The war has been productive of evil and good, but I think the good preponderates. Independent of loss of lives, and of the losses in property by individuals, the war has laid the foundation of permanent taxes and military establishments, which the Republicans had deemed unfavorable to the happiness and free institutions of the country. But under our former system we were becoming too selfish, too much attached exclusively to the acquisition of wealth, above all, too much confined in our political feelings to local and State objects. The war has renewed and reinstated the national feelings and character which the Revolution had given, and which were daily lessened. The people have now more general objects of attachment with which their pride and political opinions are connected. They are more Americans; they feel and act more as a nation; and I hope that the permanency of the Union is thereby better secured.

Source: Albert Gallatin to Matthew Lyon, May 7, 1816.

Part B

(Suggested writing time — 35 minutes, including a 5-minute planning period)

Directions: Choose ONE question from this part. Cite relevant historical evidence in support of your generalizations and present your arguments clearly and logically.

2. The French and Indian War, in its impact on the trans-Appalachian Indian tribes, the colonists, and the British government, proved the catalyst that brought on the American Revolution.

   Assess the validity of this statement.

3. Identify THREE of the following and evaluate the relative importance of each of the THREE in promoting the abolition of slavery.

   Frederick Douglass

   William Lloyd Garrison

   Angelina and Sarah Grimké

   Harriet Beecher Stowe

GO ON TO THE NEXT PAGE

Part C

(Suggested writing time — 35 minutes, including a 5-minute planning period)

Directions: Choose ONE question from this part. Cite relevant historical evidence in support of your generalizations and present your arguments clearly and logically.

4. Analyze the relative importance of the presidential and congressional phases of Reconstruction in determining the criteria for the readmission of the Southern states to the Union.

5. How lasting was the effect of World War II on women in American society?

IF YOU FINISH BEFORE TIME IS CALLED, CHECK YOUR WORK ON THIS SECTION ONLY. DO NOT WORK ON ANY OTHER SECTION IN THE TEST.

Answer Key For Practice Test 2

Section I: Multiple-Choice Questions

1. C	30. B
2. D	31. D
3. D	32. E
4. A	33. C
5. C	34. D
6. C	35. B
7. C	36. D
8. B	37. D
9. C	38. B
10. C	39. C
11. A	41. C
12. E	42. A
13. D	43. C
14. C	44. C
15. A	45. C
16. C	46. B
17. B	47. B
18. B	48. B
19. C	49. E
21. B	50. B
22. A	51. D
23. C	52. D
24. A	53. B
25. A	54. B
26. E	55. A
27. E	56. D
28. A	57. B
29. C	58. D

59. D	**71.** B
61. C	**72.** A
62. D	**73.** C
63. C	**74.** C
64. A	**75.** D
65. B	**76.** E
66. C	**77.** B
67. D	**78.** D
68. B	**79.** A
69. C	**80.** B
70. C	

Section II: Essay Questions

Student essays and analysis appear beginning on page 200.

Answers and Explanations for Practice Test 2

Section I: Multiple-Choice Questions

1. **C.** There were three main points in the Supreme Court's Dred Scott decision in 1857. A slave was not a citizen and therefore could not sue in federal courts; a slave remained private property even when in a free state; the Missouri Compromise had always been unconstitutional. Congress had already repealed the Compromise in the Kansas-Nebraska Act of 1854.

2. **D.** The invention of barbed wire in 1874 by Joseph Glidden is generally credited with ending the open range.

3. **D.** Jefferson, particularly in his *Notes on Virginia* (1785), emphasized that the basic purpose of commerce was to send American agricultural surpluses abroad.

4. **A.** Lyndon Johnson believed it was possible for the United States to fight the Vietnam War and still carry out his domestic programs. "Guns" and "butter" refer to military and domestic spending, respectively.

5. **C.** Edwin Drake drilled the first successful well in western Pennsylvania in 1859.

6. **C.** The introduction of mass-production, assembly-line techniques was critical. Ford liked to say that a customer could get a car in any color so long as it was black. Prices for Model T cars dropped from $850 to $290 between 1908 and 1924.

7. **C.** The NRA was intended primarily to stabilize business through fair competitive practice codes and to address such issues as minimum wages and child labor.

8. **B.** This cartoon was published by Benjamin Franklin at the time of the Albany Congress in 1754, and was a call for colonial unity against threats to English settlement west of the Appalachians. It is often called the first American political cartoon and is reproduced in many textbooks.

9. **C.** This question has two clues — early nineteenth century and "Old Northwest Territory" — that should help you eliminate all the incorrect choices: Chief Joseph was leader of the Nez Percé and Geronimo leader of the Apaches in the late nineteenth-century West; Powhatan led the Native American confederacy in Virginia at the time of the founding of Jamestown colony; King Philip (Metacomet) organized an uprising against New England colonies in 1676.

10. **C.** The key issue in the Senate ratification was U.S. participation in the League of Nations. While the "Reservationists" were willing to compromise with Wilson if he agreed to changes in the treaty that protected what they saw as American interests concerning the League, the "Irreconcilables" were completely opposed to the League. Reservationists were led by Henry Cabot Lodge.

11. **A.** The British response to the Boston Tea Party, the Coercive Acts, were intended to punish Boston. They included closing the Port of Boston until the tea was paid for. The Coercive Acts led to the First Continental Congress and the Continental Association that encouraged communities to form committees to enforce the boycott of British goods.

12. E. Franklin is the most obvious answer. Hamilton is not really considered a colonial figure. You should know that Hutchinson and Whitefield are associated with religious events, while Bradford was the leader of the Plymouth colony.

13. D. In *Schenck v. U.S.* (1919), Justice Oliver Wendell Holmes said that the First Amendment was subject to the "clear and present danger" test — someone cannot shout "fire!" in a crowded theater and claim free speech. *Marbury v. Madison* (1803) established judicial review; *Gibbons v. Ogden* (1824) dealt with federal control over interstate commerce; *Brown v. Board of Education* (1954) declared separate but equal schools unequal; *Miranda v. Arizona* (1966) pertained to protecting rights of the accused in which an individual must be told his/her rights at arrest.

14. C. The Civil Rights Act of 1866, which declared African-Americans citizens and denied states the power to limit their rights to hold property or testify in court, was passed over President Andrew Johnson's veto — the first successful override of major legislation. With the override, it showed that Congress had power to determine Reconstruction policy.

15. A. All of the dates given are presidential election years. While you might not be able to place White in time, you should realize that the quotation perfectly reflects the idea behind Warren Harding's 1920 campaign theme of "a return to normalcy."

16. C. Jackson believed that the spoils system, in which a victorious political party rewarded party supporters with government jobs, was a good way to maintain political party loyalty. Jobholders of the defeated political party were thrown out.

17. B. Jeffersonians, unhappy with Federalist domination, protested against such laws as the Alien and Sedition Acts (1798) by supporting the Virginia and Kentucky Resolutions (1798) which, though lacking the force of law, expressed their views.

18. B. A tariff would protect American manufacturing efforts, which in the 1790s could not have withstood competition from European manufacturers.

19. C. This landmark legislation prohibited discrimination in hotels, bus stations, and other places catering to public needs. The Voting Rights Act of 1965 was aimed at making it easier for blacks to register to vote.

20. A. This longstanding grievance was one of the few problems to be settled by the Jay Treaty which was generally unpopular among supporters of Jefferson. Its main accomplishment was British agreement finally to evacuate their soldiers from outposts in the Old Northwest region.

21. B. All the organizations listed were active in the cause of African-American civil rights. The Universal Negro Improvement Association, founded by Marcus Garvey in 1914, maintained that racial bias was so pervasive in the United States that the only hope for blacks was to return to Africa.

22. A. Between 1630 and 1642, some 18,000 Puritans settled in Massachusetts Bay and other parts of New England.

23. C. The Constitution stated that Congress could not prohibit the "migration or importation of such persons" prior to 1808. Despite the vague language, this referred to the international slave trade. The Constitution did include a provision for the return of runaway slaves, and the 3/5 Compromise determined how slaves would be counted for determining population.

24. **A.** Immediately after the Civil War, former slaves believed that they would get free land. Although there was some support among Radical Republicans for carving up the largest plantations for this purpose, the plan never was carried out.

25. **A.** Bryan orated against the gold standard and restriction on silver as monetary backing for the U.S. Treasury. His speech won him wide support and the Democratic nomination for President in 1896.

26. **E.** The two bar graphs show that while the population of the United States steadily increased between 1800 and 1850, population density declined twice: 1800–1810 and 1840–1850. These periods coincide with two events when the territory of the country was expanded: the Louisiana Purchase and the Mexican War, which resulted in acquisition of California and most of the Southwest through the Treaty of Guadalupe Hidalgo (1848).

27. **E.** The United States followed a policy of isolationism in world politics and made no active effort to oppose the aggressions of Germany, Italy, and Japan in the 1930s.

28. **A.** Though not himself involved, Grant (President from 1869 to 1877) was criticized for his poor judgment in appointing friends who acted dishonestly as government officials, such as in the Crédit Mobilier scandal in construction of the transcontinental railroad.

29. **C.** Although collectively known as the Compromise of 1850, it actually was composed of laws passed separately, including admission of California to the Union, creation of New Mexico Territory under popular sovereignty, and a new federal fugitive-slave law.

30. **B.** In effect, the Constitution did not follow the flag. The decision was consistent with the imperialist views of the United States in the first years of the twentieth century. These cases were decided in 1901.

31. **D.** The British response was the theory of virtual representation, which held that Parliament represented the interests of all Englishmen whether or not they elected the members of Parliament.

32. **E.** During the 1920s, government policy was decidedly probusiness. The conservative economic policies stressed lower taxes, higher tariffs, and reductions in federal spending. In an era of apparent prosperity there seemed little reason to support spending on public works.

33. **C.** Sullivan was a member of a group of Chicago architects that built skyscrapers in the 1880s–1910s period. He emphasized functional design. Roebling developed the steel cable suspension bridge, and Olmsted designed New York's Central Park.

34. **D.** This is a straightforward "when" question. South Carolina was the first state to secede (December 20, 1860) and did so before Lincoln's inauguration (March 4, 1861). Six deep South states, including Alabama, seceded before the surrender of Fort Sumter (April 13, 1861), and Virginia, along with North Carolina, Tennessee, and Arkansas, seceded after.

35. **B.** By the Seventeenth Amendment, the people of the states could vote directly for their Senators. Until 1913, Senators were chosen through the state legislatures.

36. **D.** The controversy concerned the use of federal coal lands in Alaska by private interests. Gifford Pinchot was head of the U.S. Forest Service, an ardent supporter of the conservation policies of Theodore Roosevelt; Richard Ballinger was Secretary of the Interior in the Taft administration.

37. D. The issues that brought both countries to war, primarily the question of impressment of sailors into the British navy, were not discussed in the treaty.

38. B. Americans were outraged at Germany's bald attempt to make an ally of revolutionary Mexico, a transparent effort to keep the United States out of the European war by holding out the promise of aiding in the recovery of lands lost almost seventy years earlier.

39. C. This question is asking about the causes of Shays' Rebellion — foreclosures of small farms due to debt and the refusal of the legislature to provide relief to small farmers.

40. D. The passage explains why railroads charged higher rates for short trips, usually within a state, than for longer trips between major cities. Several railroads operated between Chicago and New York, and intense competition meant lower rates; to make up these losses, railroads charged more on routes where they were the only carrier.

41. C. In two key decisions, *Civil Rights Cases* (1883) and *Plessy v. Ferguson* (1896), the Supreme Court approved segregation. The Court ruled the Civil Rights Act of 1875, which barred segregation in public facilities, unconstitutional and, in the Plessy case, announced the principle of "separate but equal" in schools.

42. A. The "Phony War" refers to the lull in the fighting after the German defeat of Poland in September 1939 until the invasion of Denmark and Norway in April 1940.

43. C. Coxey's "army" wanted an increase in the nation's money supply and a reform of federal monetary policy as ways of improving economic conditions of the nation during the Panic of 1893 period.

44. C. The correct chronological order is Articles of Confederation (1781), Shays' Rebellion (1786), Constitutional Convention (1787), Whiskey Rebellion (1794).

45. C. John Steinbeck's *The Grapes of Wrath* (1939) describes the migration of the Joad family from the Dust Bowl conditions in Oklahoma to the promised better life in California.

46. B. The Land Ordinance of 1785 provided for the survey of the Old Northwest Territory and established the rectangular pattern of settlement. The banning of the importation of slaves and the admission of new states were part of the Northwest Ordinance of 1787.

47. B. Andrew Johnson's dismissal of Secretary of War Edwin Stanton in 1868 violated the Tenure of Office Act, which required the President to obtain the approval of the Senate before removing an official appointed with the consent of the Senate.

48. B. This law placed a ten-year moratorium on Chinese immigration. Later laws excluded Chinese immigrants permanently. Chinese exclusion was not overruled until World War II when China was an ally of the United States and it proved embarrassing to have such a law on the books.

49. E. The Fourteen Points presented President Wilson's program for world peace. He did not, however, call for the creation of a military force to ensure that peace.

50. B. The North was burdened with mediocre generals at the beginning of the war. Lincoln worked through several, including McClellan, Burnside, and Hooker, before he promoted Grant to the top ranks.

51. D. Marshall believed in a strong national government to which state laws were subordinate, such as shown in the case of *McCullough v. Maryland,* which denied Maryland the right to tax the Bank of the United States.

52. D. The Great Awakening signaled a broadening of religious views and a sense that religion need not separate ordinary people from the elite. The movement became very popular in the early eighteenth century and resulted in a dramatic increase in church membership.

53. B. The pie charts compare only the popular and electoral vote margins. They provide no information on voter turnout or a breakdown of the vote by group. You should know from your reading that former slaves were largely disenfranchised, particularly in the South, and that neither election was decided by the House of Representatives. The percent of eligible voters was among the highest ever in a presidential election — 81.8% (1876) and 79.3% (1888).

54. B. The term was coined in 1787 by John Quincy Adams and has been used by historians to describe the period from 1781 to 1787 when the country was governed by the Articles of Confederation.

55. A. The key issue, particularly in the South, was high tariffs that both increased the price of manufactured goods and made it difficult to sell cotton abroad. Opposition to the Tariff of 1828 (the "Tariff of Abominations") and the Tariff of 1832 led to the nullification crisis.

56. D. While President Lincoln's speeches might touch on key battles, they would not be helpful in understanding the strategies on the battles themselves.

57. B. The Monroe Doctrine was largely ignored when it was issued in 1823. The only "teeth" the Doctrine had was that it coincided with British policy in Latin America, which both Monroe and his Secretary of State, John Quincy Adams, knew would stop any European nation. The Doctrine explicitly stated that the United States would not interfere with existing European colonies.

58. D. Northern slavery died out before the moral crusade against it because the North's economy did not require plantation slavery; hence there was no need for large numbers of slaves.

59. D. An injunction could so restrict the activities of a striking union as to make it impossible to win the strike. Judges friendly to employers would severely restrict picketing, for example, to the point where strikers couldn't gather near the front gates of the employer's premises, hold meetings, or even present their grievances.

60. D. African-Americans were trained as airplane pilots — at Tuskegee Institute, for example — and flew fighters and bombers during the war. They also served in the Navy as well as in the Army, though in segregated units and conditions.

61. C. The Adena-Hopewell of the Ohio River Valley were known for the burial mounds they left and elaborate earthen works.

62. D. James Dean became a cult figure in the 1950s in such films as *Rebel Without a Cause;* he was an "antihero" associated with the Beat Generation, not the counterculture of the 1960s.

63. C. Nixon's involvement in the Alger Hiss case as a member of the House Un-American Activities Committee in 1948 made him a nationally known figure. Anticommunism was the key to his election to the Senate in 1950 and his being selected as Eisenhower's vice-presidential candidate in 1952.

64. A. Large families made it difficult for younger sons to inherit farms or to save money to buy their own; they ended up in the cities looking for work and, lacking skills, had to accept low-paying jobs.

65. B. The Tennessee Valley Authority (1933) was a major attempt at regional planning that included federal multipurpose dams to generate electricity, to provide flood control, and to improve river navigation. Cheap power was expected to serve as a "yardstick" for rates charged by private utilities. Conservative critics charged that the TVA was an example of New Deal socialism.

66. C. The idea of popular sovereignty was to let the people living in a territory decide whether it should be a free or slave state. The most controversial example took place in Kansas where factions on both sides of the issue resorted to violence.

67. D. Heavy rains prevented the rebellion from being carried out, but its leaders were nevertheless severely punished. The most violent slave rebellion was the one led by Nat Turner in 1831 when several dozen whites were killed.

68. B. This case was brought by a white student denied admission to the medical school at the University of California, Davis, because of affirmative-action policies. The Court restricted the use of numerical quotas to achieve racial balance.

69. C. Remember that "most recently" is a tricky way of asking which event occurred last. The chronology is Berlin airlift (1948–1949), Hungarian uprising (1956), Sputnik (1957), Castro (1959), U-2 incident (1960).

70. C. Aware that France was actively aiding Spain in such objectives as attempting to capture the Rock of Gibraltar and that France favored restricting the new United States to the Appalachian Mountains as a western boundary, U.S. commissioners disobeyed their instructions from Congress and concluded a separate agreement with Great Britain that granted a territorial claim to the Mississippi River.

71. B. Farm girls were actively recruited by mill owners, who paid low wages. For their part, the girls saw such employment as temporary until they married and started families.

72. A. The only correct choice is **A** in that when states abolished property qualifications for voting, the number of men eligible to vote increased significantly between 1824 and 1832. Choices **B**, **C**, and **D** didn't occur as such until much later. Distinct political parties existed prior to the era of Jacksonian democracy.

73. C. The Articles of Confederation granted no authority to the central government to deal with questions of interstate commerce. Frustration over inability to negotiate over such questions as state boundaries that bordered on rivers led to calls for a meeting to resolve such issues, resulting in the Annapolis Convention, a prologue to the Constitutional Convention.

74. C. The "long drive" brought longhorn cattle from south and west Texas to the railheads in Missouri, Kansas, Nebraska, and Wyoming for shipment to the major markets in the East. The fact that the map shows the trails connecting with the main transcontinental railroad is significant.

75. D. The Gadsden Purchase (1853) not only completed the continental expansion of the United States but by acquiring the southernmost part of Arizona and New Mexico provided the crucial territory needed for a transcontinental railroad linking the South with the Pacific.

76. E. Eli Whitney's invention in 1793 of the cotton gin made it possible for seeds to be separated from the cotton boll by a simple machine process. Cotton production thus became cost-effective, and within a few years, cotton was the South's major export crop.

77. B. Although there was some initial success in solving problems of spouse and child abuse by drunken husbands and parents, the "Great Experiment" provoked opposition from people living in urban areas, from people whose cultural background saw nothing wrong in drinking alcoholic beverages, and from people who objected to being told how to live their lives by others.

78. D. King had studied the writings of Mohandas Gandhi, the leader of the independence movement in India who had used nonviolence as an effective tactic against British rule.

79. A. At the conclusion of the French and Indian War, the British Parliament, desperately in need of funds with which to operate its now far-flung empire, began to pass one revenue law after another that affected its colonies. American colonists resented these laws, believing that their help in fighting Britain's colonial wars was not appreciated and that the new taxes placed an unfair burden on them.

80. B. Pennsylvania was one of the colonies whose economic mainstay was the production of wheat and corn; as such, it supplied those colonies where agriculture was of lesser importance. Alabama was not a British colony.

Section II: Essay Questions

Part A

Student DBQ Essay

The War of 1812, also known as the Second War for Independence, gave the United States its final freedom from Great Britain. While it did bring about a strong sense of nationalism, it did not end the divisions in the country.

In his message to Congress in June 1812, Document I, President Madison strongly stated the reasons for a declaration of war against Great Britain — impressment of American sailors and the seize of American ships. But it is clear that the country was split over the issue. Document D, which shows the vote for the war in Congress, indicates that opposition was strong in the Middle Atlantic states and New England. These were the regions whose main source of income was through foreign trade that declined because of the crisis with Great Britain. Support was almost unanimous in the South and West.

The regional opposition continued during the war itself as the results of the election of 1812 demonstrate. New England and the Middle Atlantic states (with the important exception of Pennsylvania) went to the Federalist Clinton. The possibility of secession was very real at the Hartford Convention (1814) when representatives from New England wrote up a list of constitutional amendments that would have made it more difficult for the U.S. to go to war and in general to limit the power of the Federal government.

Immediately after the war, the split between Federalists and Republicans was still evident. In Document G, for example, the New York Evening Post, probably a Federalist newspaper, stated that the war was "bloody and expensive" and did not result in anything positive for the country. On the other hand, the Republican National Intelligencer (Document F), criticized the Federalists for their "plots and counterplots" and stated that their opposition still could not prevent an American victory.

Those who had supported the war all along, the War Hawk Henry Clay and Albert Gallatin, emphasized that the conflict meant that the U.S. was now respected in the world. The war brought the country together, and made Americans feel and act like a nation. (Documents C and J). The Republicans now believed in a stronger role for the Federal government and wanted to use this power to build on the national feelings created by the war's outcome. In Document B, President Madison outlined a plan for internal improvements by the Federal government. He pointed out that roads and canals were important in "bringing and binding more closely together the various parts of our extended confederacy."

The program of internal improvements was supported by Henry Clay. His "American System" not only included a national transportation network but high tariffs to protect American manufacturing. The Tariff of 1816, however, was opposed by New England and the South. Madison seemed to change the position he took in 1815 when he vetoed a bill two years later that would have provided money to the states for internal improvements. Here he followed the old Republican strict construction of the Constitution argument.

The victory over Great Britain in the War of 1812 did not result in a unified nation. The conflicts between Republicans and Federalists continued for a time after the war. The regional differences over economic policy continued as shown in the debate over the Tariff of 1816. Although the election of James Monroe brought in an "Era of Good Feelings," new problems that divided the country quickly arose. The most important of these was the slavery issue that resulted in the Missouri Compromise of 1820. The sectional differences over slavery made it impossible for the "permanency of the Union" to be preserved as Albert Gallatin hoped.

Reader's Comments

The student takes an interesting approach to this question by arguing that the War of 1812 did not bring about a unified country. This thesis, however, isn't fully developed in the rather weak introductory paragraph. The student could have pointed out more clearly that the documents supporting the counter position — Clay, Gallatin, and the *National Intelligencer* — reflect the views of the "winners." Did these in fact reflect the mood of the country?

The student brings in relevant outside information, the Hartford Convention and the American System, for example. Key facts, such as the Treaty of Ghent, are left out. Since the documents include Madison's war message and the statement from the *New York Evening Post,* the outcome of the war as expressed in the treaty is necessary to mention. Other outside information is mentioned only in passing. Given the thesis and the time frame of the question, both the Era of Good Feelings and slavery and the Missouri Compromise need to be discussed in the body of the essay, not just tacked on in the concluding paragraph.

Possible student score: 5

Part B

Question 2 Student Essay

The French and Indian War had a tremendous impact on the thirteen colonies as well as the Indians and on the British government. The colonists had fought no less than four wars for the British against the French and were feeling victorious. The Indians had chosen the wrong side and were the big losers after the French and Indian War. The British had finally defeated the French and now were in control of Canada.

The British also now controlled India and had a big empire, but running such a big empire required great responsibility, especially financial responsibility. Where would Great Britain get the money needed to run its empire? The answer was from the colonies. It is no coincidence that Parliament began to pass laws taxing the colonies so soon after the end of the French and Indian War. And quite naturally, the colonists soon resented these new tax laws. For much of the fighting in the wars the colonists had been on their own. British supplies were often inadequate, and British leadership was often incompetent, as had been the case with General Braddock.

Another thing the British tried to do was to keep the colonists and the Indians away from each other. After Pontiac's rebellion in 1763, the British issued a proclamation that tried to keep the colonists on the eastern side of the Appalachian Mountains. But many colonists were already crossing the mountains. Men who had served in the Army knew about the land in Kentucky that was good for farming. Some colonies such as Virginia and North Carolina had "sea to sea" grants that claimed territory all the way across the North American continent, even though no one knew what was out there. These colonies resented being told they could not move westward.

The colonies had not done well in trying to organize themselves during the French and Indian War. Benjamin Franklin had called for the Albany Plan of Union, but the colonies could not agree on common interests. By 1764, with Parliament planning new taxes and enforcing old tax laws, the colonies realized they all shared the same challenge of how to meet what they saw as unfair taxation.

The British, however, needed revenue to pay for the expenses of running the empire, and so Parliament started levying such taxes as taxes on sugar and stamps. The stamp tax especially angered the colonists because it was so unfair to them. The colonies protested against the tax so much that Parliament had to withdraw it. This victory brought the colonies together and brought them the unity that would be needed when Parliament tried again to keep them in line.

The French and Indian War was a catalyst that brought on the American Revolution in that it created a whole new set of problems for the British. Parliament's inability to solve those problems made a revolt of the colonists inevitable.

Reader's Comments

This essay has a general grasp of the issues but is vague on many of the specific details. Several openings lead nowhere instead of providing essential support for the general statements. The question calls for the impact of the French and Indian War on three groups. Little is discussed on the effect of the war on the Indians, and what is discussed is presented from the British and colonial side. It is not enough merely to mention such events as Pontiac's Rebellion; it is essential to tie them into the thesis. Why did Chief Pontiac rebel against the British shortly after the war ended? What did the end of the war mean for the Indians? These issues remain unanswered.

The essay also gets into the beginnings of the movement toward the American Revolution but does so without dealing with the essential question of whether the reasons for the movement toward independence were a cause in and of themselves or a consequence of the end of the French and Indian War. Again, there is a good outline of facts, but simply to agree with the statement is not enough. The student needs to provide greater documentation as to why the end of one war helped bring on another one.

Possible student score: 4

Part B

Question 3 Student Essay

William Lloyd Garrison, Frederick Douglass, and Harriet Beecher Stowe were all important contributors to the abolitionist movement in the years before the Civil War. Of the three, I believe that Harriet Beecher Stowe, the author of Uncle Tom's Cabin, had the greatest influence in promoting the end to slavery.

The rise of William Lloyd Garrison in the 1830s brought about an important change in the antislavery movement. In the pages of his newspaper the Liberator and through the American Anti-Slavery Society that he helped found, Garrison pushed the idea of the immediate emancipation of the slaves without compensation to the slaveholders. These developments certainly helped strengthen the abolitionist crusade. But Garrison was also responsible for the split in the movement. He strongly supported other reforms such as women's rights. In 1840, the Anti-Slavery Society broke into factions over the status of women.

Garrison believed that former slaves were the best spokesmen for the abolitionists. Certainly, one of the most famous was Frederick Douglass. He wrote his autobiography, Narrative of the Life of Frederick Douglass (1845), which became the most famous personal account of slavery. Douglass also founded an abolitionist newspaper. Although an important source for historians, it is hard to determine what effect Douglass' speeches and writings had on the antislavery movement in the 1840s and 1850s. His autobiography was one of many slave narratives and was probably only read by people who already supported the abolitionists.

Harriet Beecher Stowe's Uncle Tom's Cabin was published in 1852 in response to the Fugitive Slave Law that was part of the Compromise of 1850. Although it was not great literature, the novel was a strong indictment of slavery as an institution. Because it was a novel, the book reached a much wider audience than either the abolitionist newspapers or the pamphlets put out by the Anti-Slavery Society. As the question of the expansion of slavery became critical to the country during the 1850s, Uncle Tom's Cabin convinced many in the North of the evils of slavery. It is often recognized as providing the North with a moral justification for the Civil War.

Reader's Comments

The student provides good information on the three individuals selected. Although the Grimké sisters were not chosen, they could have been briefly mentioned in the context of the split in the American Anti-Slavery Society. The essay does tackle the "relative importance" part of the question but perhaps in too indirect a manner. From both the introduction and the body of the essay, it is clear that the student believes that Stowe was the most important of the three. The relative importance of Garrison and Douglass is less clear. There is the implication that Garrison "ranks" second because of the change he brought to the antislavery movement. If this is the case, a bit more should have been made of this and a brief statement provided on the nature of the movement before Garrison. Further, the same point the student made about

Douglass — that is, those who read him were probably already opposed to slavery — could have been made about Garrison. This lack of clarity in the essay could have been resolved in a concluding paragraph, which is really essential here.

Possible student score: 5

Part C

Question 4 Student Essay

Reconstruction fell into two distinct phases, both of which had to deal with the basic question of how the defeated Southern states were to be readmitted to the Union. In the first phase, President Andrew Johnson had to deal with creating a policy of Reconstruction for the South. President Lincoln had announced that he would restore the Southern states "with malice toward none, with charity for all." Lincoln said that the Southern states could be readmitted to the Union with only a minimum declaration of loyalty. His "10% Plan" would allow states to return to the Union if only ten percent of the registered voters in the election of 1860 pledged loyalty to the United States. But Lincoln was assassinated right after the end of the war, and Johnson, the new President, was no Abraham Lincoln.

The reason why the first phase is called the "presidential phase" is because from the time Lincoln was assassinated until Congress met in December 1865, Congress was not in session. This left policy-making for the South to the Executive Office. From April to December 1865, everyone waited for Johnson to formulate a plan for Southern Reconstruction. Johnson, however, did not seem to have much of a plan. He was a War Democrat who increasingly did not seem to be getting along with the Republicans who had supported him on the Union ticket in 1864. Johnson turned out to be someone who didn't care much for the former slaves. He didn't think the 13th Amendment was necessary, since the Emancipation Proclamation had freed so many slaves anyway. He also didn't call for punishing the Southern leaders.

When Congress met in December 1865, Northerners were shocked to find that many of the Southern senators and congressmen were the same people who had fought against them just a few months earlier. For example, Alexander Stephens, the former vice-president of the Confederacy, was now a senator from Georgia. Then Johnson started vetoing one Reconstruction bill after another. Radical Republicans began to look for a way to get Johnson out of the Presidency. They finally hit on an idea which was probably unconstitutional. This was the Tenure of Office Act which prevented the President from dismissing any Cabinet member without the consent of the Senate. Everyone knew that Johnson wanted Secretary of War Stanton out of the Cabinet. When Johnson fired Stanton, the Radical Republicans were then able to impeach Johnson. The trial vote was very close, and only one vote saved Johnson from conviction.

With Johnson's impeachment and trial, control of Reconstruction policy shifted to Congress. Under the control of Radical Republicans, Congress passed Reconstruction legislation dividing the South into military districts. The Southerners had to deal with carpetbaggers who went to the South to take federal jobs, with disenfranchisement, and with military rule. Not until 1877 were the last federal soldiers removed from Southern states.

Johnson called for a mild form of restoration in line with what Lincoln had planned. Congress passed laws which were much more punitive against the South. Had Johnson acted more responsible as President, and Congress more generously, then much of the bitterness of the Reconstruction period might have been avoided.

Reader's Comments

The biggest mistake this essay makes is in not paying enough attention to the question's calling for a conclusion on the relative importance of the two phases. Except for the final paragraph, what we have here is a brief summary of Reconstruction, first with Johnson as President and then with Congress. The congressional phase is treated very briefly and superficially. Very little hard information is given about the effect of Reconstruction on the people of the South, black or white, or the crucial question of readmission to the Union. The essay is very strong on Andrew Johnson, much weaker on Congress. This creates an imbalance of information on which to draw an informed conclusion. The final sentence of the essay indicates the possibility of a thesis the student might have followed in evaluating the two phases — all the more reason a student must consider what kind of question is being asked and plan an appropriate answer instead of immediately plunging into the essay, writing on everything about a topic in hopes that some of it will fit what the reader is looking for.

Possible student score: 4

Part C

Question 5 Student Essay

World War II had an immediate effect on women in American society, but how long that effect lasted is debatable. Perhaps the most famous symbol coming out of the war was "Rosie the Riveter." Unlike Nazi Germany which held to the idea that women's place was in the home, the United States significantly increased its war productivity by approving the hiring and training of women to work in a variety of wartime industries. Apart from the usual jobs that women held such as cafeteria workers and clerks, women were able to acquire job skills. Shipyards and aircraft plants needed workers trained in a wide variety of technical jobs. Manpower was short as America's young men went into the armed forces. Both unmarried and married women filled the void by taking these jobs.

By the end of the war women had made a clear contribution to the war effort. They had taken on jobs that before the war were unthinkable as far as men were concerned. With the end of the war, however, enormous social changes occurred. Returning veterans expected to get their old jobs back. The economy converted from wartime production to peacetime products. Women found themselves under increasing pressure to quit these jobs, return to the home, to get married and raise the family that had been postponed during the war years.

Many women protested against employer efforts to get them off the payroll. They had taken their jobs seriously and enjoyed the generous wages paid to them. Returning to the more traditional jobs of young women meant pay cuts and employment as sales clerks rather than technically skilled workers. But they lost out through seniority requirements, a traditional family structure in which the husband was the breadwinner of a one-income family, and the pressure to get married and start a family to make up for lost time (resulting in the famous "baby boom" of the late 1940s).

Minority women had obtained some brief advantages during the war years. Federal hiring policies did not want potential manpower denied through discrimination. African-American women found unprecedented opportunities in job training and employment. To a lesser degree, Mexican-American women also found a more open workplace. At the end of the war, however, these women lost their jobs and went back into more traditional roles.

Beyond the immediate postwar years, women even suffered a setback in their efforts at educational as well as economic equality. It is a stunning fact that more women held college degrees in the 1920s than in the 1950s. The emphasis in American society during the 1950s was for women to get married at a young age, usually shortly after high school, and stay in the home and devote themselves to domestic matters — raising children and keeping house. Unmarried women were considered somewhat out of the ordinary. Many women internalized this expectation through exposure to media images of housewives in TV commercials, the stereotype of women being incapable of learning to drive a car, and the restriction of women in the professions to careers as teachers, librarians, nurses, and secretaries.

So it was that World War II proved a disappointment in providing women with an opportunity to think and reach beyond stereotypical ideals. Not until the women's movement began in the 1960s did women begin to liberate themselves from the limitations placed upon them in the postwar period.

Reader's Comments

This is a well-argued essay that takes a clear position and presents evidence to support its thesis. More might have been said about women at different economic levels beyond the paragraph on minority women, and the student could possibly have discussed employment in the private sector as well as industries involved in war production. Tying in education to job opportunities broadened the discussion. The essay also shows appropriate courage in carrying the idea of the effect of the war into the 1950s to show the contrast between the roles of women during the war and in the Eisenhower era.

The final sentence brings an additional connection in noting that the women's movement had to pick up where the immediate wartime benefits had failed. The student wisely didn't turn the essay into a discourse on women's liberation, which would have created an imbalance in the essay and stretched the postwar period beyond reasonable limits. The comparison of college-educated women in the 1920s and the 1950s puts the student's nugget of information to good effect. Overall, the essay sticks to its basic thesis, doesn't go into tempting but extraneous areas, and does a good job of answering the question.

Possible student score: 9

Practice Test 3

Section I: Multiple-Choice Questions

Time: 55 Minutes

80 Questions

Directions: Select the best answer for the following questions or incomplete statements from the five choices provided. Indicate your answer by darkening the appropriate space on the answer sheet.

1. The first nationality excluded from immigrating to the United States was the

   A. Japanese

   B. Mexicans

   C. Chinese

   D. Haitians

   E. Ottoman Turks

2. The basic viewpoint of the U.S. Supreme Court in the 1920s was to

   A. uphold the antitrust laws

   B. favor the position of organized labor

   C. overturn progressive laws

   D. support government involvement in business

   E. refuse to consider cases involving labor disputes

3. The American antislavery movement split in 1840 largely over the issue of

   A. the participation of women

   B. gradual vs. immediate emancipation

   C. civil rights for free blacks in the North

   D. support for black abolitionists

   E. backing Martin Van Buren for President

4. The XYZ Affair resulted in

   A. the growth of pro-French sentiment in the United States

   B. a formal alliance between Great Britain and the United States

   C. an undeclared war between the United States and France

   D. embarrassment for President Adams

   E. a new alliance with France against Great Britain

GO ON TO THE NEXT PAGE

207

5. The best description of the political views of the delegates to the Constitutional Convention would be

A. anti-Federalist Jeffersonians

B. men who strongly supported states' rights

C. regionalists or sectionalists

D. men who held a national view of the country

E. total opposition to compromise

6. "The wisest among my race understand that the agitation of questions of social equality is the extremist folly, and that progress in the enjoyment of all the privileges that will come to us must be the result of severe and constant struggle rather than of artificial forcing."

This statement was most likely made by

A. Marcus Garvey

B. Booker T. Washington

C. W. E. B. Du Bois

D. Barbara Jordan

E. Malcolm X

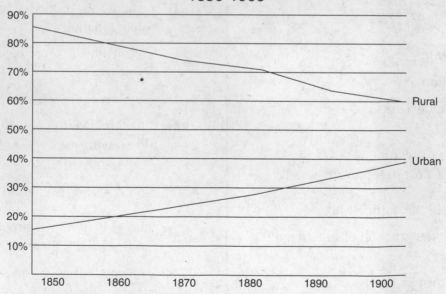

Percentages of Urban and Rural Population
1850-1900

Source: U.S. Bureau of the Census, *Historical Statistics of the United States from Colonial Times to 1970.*

7. The narrowing gap between rural and urban population in the second half of the nineteenth century is best explained by the

   A. migration of former slaves to Northern cities after the Civil War

   B. impact of immigration on the growth of cities

   C. closing of the frontier

   D. rapid industrialization of the country

   E. increasing mechanization of American agriculture

8. The major nations at the Washington Naval Conference in 1922 agreed to

   I. limit the number of ships in their navies

   II. support the U.S. Open Door Policy in China

   III. punish any nations violating the agreement

   IV. keep the status quo in the Pacific area

   A. I only

   B. II only

   C. I and III only

   D. I and IV only

   E. II, III, and IV only

9. The 1892 Populist platform did NOT include

   A. government operation of the railroads

   B. the initiative

   C. the referendum

   D. the subtreasury plan

   E. high tariffs

10. The earliest English colony was

    A. Maryland

    B. New York

    C. Massachusetts Bay

    D. Georgia

    E. Pennsylvania

11. When the Erie Canal was constructed

    A. industrial development suffered as farmers prospered

    B. New England manufacturers were forced into bankruptcy

    C. federal money helped speed construction

    D. New England farming declined

    E. local markets grew at the expense of a national economy

12. Which of the following describes the purpose of the Maine Law of 1851?

    A. banning the manufacture and sale of alcoholic beverages

    B. prohibiting the consumption of alcoholic beverages

    C. women's suffrage at the state level

    D. state-by-state slavery abolition laws

    E. women retaining legal rights to their property after marriage

GO ON TO THE NEXT PAGE

13. The Senate would probably have ratified the Versailles Treaty had President Wilson

    A. agreed to leave the American public out of the debate over the League of Nations

    B. been willing to compromise on the League of Nations issue

    C. insisted on the adoption of the Fourteen Points

    D. ignored the Reservationists

    E. renegotiated the League Covenant with the Big Four

14. The Louisiana Territory was ruled by nations in the following order:

    A. Spain, France, Mexico, United States

    B. Spain, France, Spain, United States

    C. France, Spain, United States

    D. Spain, France, United States

    E. France, Spain, France, United States

15. The slave states that remained in the Union included

    A. Missouri, Kentucky, and Virginia

    B. Delaware, Kentucky, and Tennessee

    C. North Carolina, Tennessee, and Arkansas

    D. Missouri, Kentucky, and Delaware

    E. South Carolina, Georgia, and Alabama

Source: Library of Congress.

16. This engraving is historically significant because it

    A. is a good example of American art in the colonial period

    B. reflects the attitude of Loyalists on the eve of the American Revolution

    C. was used by the British to justify the enactment of the Coercive Acts against Boston

    D. had propaganda value in rallying colonial support against Great Britain

    E. shows that the colonists in fact attacked the British troops first

17. The provisions of the Treaty of Guadalupe Hidalgo included all of these EXCEPT

    A. pay $15 million to Mexico

    B. set the Texas boundary at the Rio Grande

    C. yield California to the United States

    D. yield New Mexico to the United States

    E. yield the Mesilla Valley of Arizona to the United States

18. According to the Gentlemen's Agreement of 1908, Japan agreed to

    A. give Korea its independence

    B. respect the territorial integrity of China

    C. discourage its citizens from emigrating to the United States

    D. maintain the balance of naval forces in the Pacific

    E. allow American companies free access to Japanese markets

19. The purpose of the Open Door Policy was to

    A. open China to free trade

    B. guarantee Cuban independence

    C. give the United States a sphere of influence in Asia

    D. restrict the effect of dollar diplomacy

    E. justify military occupation of the Philippines

20. "Yesterday I came to Washington with a group of writers to protest the treatment given the bonus army in Washington. Coming to a President of my country to voice such a protest isn't a thing I like to do. With me it is like this: I am intensely interested in the lives of the common everyday people, laborers, mill hands, soldiers, stenographers, or whatever they may be. . . . I have been looking, watching, finding out what I could about American life."

The person most likely to have received this message was

    A. Herbert Hoover

    B. Franklin D. Roosevelt

    C. Pelham Glassford

    D. Douglas MacArthur

    E. J. Edgar Hoover

GO ON TO THE NEXT PAGE

Practice Test 3

21. The chief goal of African-Americans in the civil rights movement in the South in the 1960s was to

    A. end segregated education

    B. obtain the right for blacks to vote

    C. establish affirmative-action job programs

    D. secure ratification of the Twenty-Fourth Amendment outlawing the poll tax

    E. win control of southern state legislatures

22. Labor unions before the Civil War did not grow for all of these reasons EXCEPT

    A. women accepted low-paying factory jobs

    B. the existence of child labor

    C. employers provided adequate pension benefits

    D. immigrants were willing to work without union membership

    E. the possibility of upward mobility

23. Most of the people who went to California during the Gold Rush

    A. quickly returned to their homes back east

    B. went on to follow mining rushes in other areas

    C. returned with a fair profit for their efforts

    D. found barely enough gold to pay for the trip

    E. failed to find enough gold to pay their expenses

24. The Gilded Age received its nickname from the

    A. improvement in the average American's standard of living

    B. corruption, greed, and superficial appearance of wealth

    C. success of mineral strikes in California and the western territories

    D. growth of cities and their attractions

    E. monetary gold standard

25. Large numbers of Irish immigrants came to the United States in the 1840s because of the

    A. persecution of Irish Catholics

    B. civil war between North Ireland and Ireland

    C. massive failure of the potato crop

    D. British military aggression in Ireland

    E. lure of gold in California

26. Theodore Roosevelt's political offices before he became President were

    A. Governor of New York, Secretary of State in McKinley's Cabinet, Vice President

    B. Assistant Secretary of the Navy, Secretary of the Navy, Governor of New York

    C. Secretary of the Navy, Governor of New York, Vice President

    D. Governor of New York, Secretary of the Navy, Vice President

    E. Assistant Secretary of the Navy, Governor of New York, Vice President

27. For the historian, this document is most helpful for a study of

A. the economic development of Los Angeles after the Civil War

B. politics in Los Angeles during the second half of the nineteenth century

C. ethnic/immigrant groups in the city

D. municipal ownership of public utilities

E. Hispanic residential areas in Los Angeles

28. Twenty years after the adoption of the Constitution, Congress banned

A. the interstate sale of slaves

B. missionary work among slaves

C. slavery in territories acquired by the federal government

D. the importation of slaves to the United States

E. the sale of American-born slaves to slaveholding nations

29. "No matter how often you fail, keep on. But if you wish to get rich quickly, then bleed the public and talk patriotism. This may involve bribing public officials and dodging public burdens, the losing of your manhood and the soiling of your fingers, but that is the way most of the great fortunes are made in this country now."

This was most likely the view of

A. Horatio Alger

B. John Peter Altgeld

C. Andrew Carnegie

D. Henry Clay Frick

E. Russell Conwell

GO ON TO THE NEXT PAGE

30. Which of the following was NOT a factor in the American decision to declare war on Great Britain in 1812?

A. British Orders in Council

B. impressment of American sailors

C. War Hawk demands for taking Canada

D. boundary disputes between Vermont and Ontario

E. frontier conflicts between Americans and the British

31. The United States during World War II adopted all of the following strategies EXCEPT

A. unconditional surrender

B. victory in the European area first

C. an eventual second front by invading Europe

D. use of atomic bombs on Japan and Germany

E. support of de Gaulle's Free French forces

32. President Woodrow Wilson responded to the sinking of the *Lusitania* in 1915 by

A. demanding that the Germans stop using submarine warfare

B. ordering Americans not to be passengers on belligerent powers' ships

C. requiring exports to Europe to be sent only on American merchant ships

D. severing diplomatic relations with Germany

E. demanding an apology from Kaiser Wilhelm II

33. Reconstruction legislation passed by Congress included all of the following EXCEPT the

A. Tenure of Office Act

B. Civil Rights Act of 1866

C. Black Codes

D. First Reconstruction Act

E. Reconstruction Act of 1868

34. The "Crime of 1873" was

A. the blatant frauds exposed in the 1872 presidential election

B. the buying and selling of votes in attempts to defeat the Bland-Allison Silver Purchase Act

C. revelations of the Credit Mobilier railroad construction scandal

D. the decision by Congress to stop the coinage of silver

E. the refusal of Congress to remain on the gold standard

35. The amendments to the Constitution proposed by the Hartford Convention were intended to

A. limit the power of the federal government

B. increase the authority of the President at the expense of Congress

C. resolve the problems of slavery in the territories west of the Mississippi

D. bring about the immediate end to the War of 1812

E. make sure that Republicans controlled the Congress

36. The major issue in *Northern Securities Company v. U.S.* was

    A. the right of workers to join labor unions

    B. the antitrust laws

    C. limitations on child labor

    D. the constitutionality of the National Industrial Recovery Act

    E. the regulation of the railroads

37. Which is the correct order of chronology of these inventions?

    A. reaper, steamboat, telegraph, cotton gin

    B. cotton gin, steamboat, reaper, telegraph

    C. steamboat, cotton gin, telegraph, reaper

    D. cotton gin, reaper, steamboat, telegraph

    E. cotton gin, steamboat, telegraph, reaper

38. "While the Corps has something to do with spot benefits in a few isolated places, whether in sanitizing drinking water or building culverts, its work has, and can have, very little to do with the fundamental investments, reorganizations and reforms upon which the true and long-term economic development of backward countries depends."

This view takes a critical look at the

    A. Civilian Conservation Corps

    B. U.S. Marine Corps

    C. Peace Corps

    D. Job Corps

    E. Corps of Engineers

39. In the eighteenth century, the view of American whites generally about slavery was that it

    A. was wrong for religious and moral reasons

    B. should not be hereditary

    C. would soon fade as an economic practice

    D. affected white people in its political and social impact

    E. was a dangerous practice that could bring violence and race war

40. The Interstate Commerce Act included all of the following EXCEPT

    A. publication of railroad rate schedules

    B. creation of a commission to hear problems of shippers

    C. prohibition of railroad rebates

    D. declaration of short-haul differences as unlawful

    E. establishment of fixed rate schedules for railroads to charge shippers

GO ON TO THE NEXT PAGE

Practice Test 3

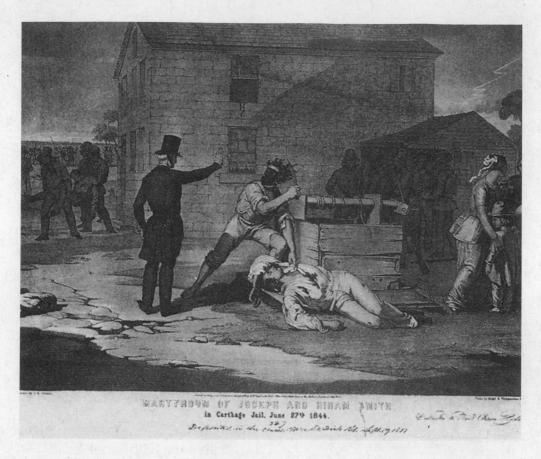

MARTYRDOM OF JOSEPH AND HIRAM SMITH
in Carthage Jail, June 27th 1844.

Source: Library of Congress.

41. This print depicts an important event in the history of

    A. the Abolitionist movement

    B. the Know-Nothing party

    C. the Mormons

    D. Bleeding Kansas

    E. the Second Great Awakening

42. The main spokesman for the cause of American socialism at the turn of the century was

    A. Jacob Riis

    B. Lincoln Steffens

    C. Eugene V. Debs

    D. Ignatius Donnelly

    E. Jacob Coxey

43. Horace Mann believed that

    A. education is a private matter and should not involve the state

    B. public education should be clearly separated from religious teaching

    C. public schools should be separate but equal between the black and white races

    D. families should have the right to choose between public and private schools

    E. business and industry should pay special taxes in support of public education

44. The nomination of Barry Goldwater for President in 1964 indicated that

A. a major party was willing to run a candidate from a small state

B. conservatism was a major force in the Republican party

C. there was strong support for an escalation of American involvement in Vietnam

D. the Republican party was ready to accept the Great Society programs

E. grass-roots organization was not effective in political campaigns

45. The Tariff of 1816 was notable as being the first tariff

A. that tried to protect the development of American industry

B. to raise revenue to pay federal government expenses

C. to be passed by Congress

D. to place a tax on imported foreign cotton

E. to shut out competitive foreign products

46. In the early years of Reconstruction, an important function of the Freedmen's Bureau was

A. the protection of the economic rights of former slaves

B. registering former slaves to vote

C. establishing schools for free blacks in the North

D. to encourage freed slaves to migrate to the North

E. the prosecution of plantation owners who had abused their slaves

47. Which of the following statements regarding the draft and the Union Army is true?

A. More than half of the men serving in the Union Army were draftees.

B. Congress passed the draft law at the beginning of the Civil War.

C. A potential draftee could hire a substitute or buy his way out of service.

D. There was widespread public support for the draft because of the patriotism generated by the war.

E. The minimum draft age was set at sixteen.

48. The post-World War II program of economic assistance to Western Europe was known as

A. the Alliance for Progress

B. NATO

C. UNICEF

D. the Marshall Plan

E. the Point Four Program

49. A major factor in the drastic decline of the Plains Indians in the nineteenth century was

A. their placement on reservations

B. the escalation of intertribal wars aided by modern weapons

C. the hunting of the buffalo to near extinction

D. the loss of military leadership when important chiefs were killed or imprisoned

E. their failure to live up to treaty obligations

GO ON TO THE NEXT PAGE

Practice Test 3

50. The purpose of the New England Confederation was to

    A. unite all the English colonies in a common bond

    B. organize colonial defense in New England

    C. ease Parliament's burden in administering colonial government

    D. prevent the smuggling of enumerated articles

    E. join with the Indians of the area to promote tolerance and coexistence

51. Under the Navigation Acts, the enumerated articles were

    A. goods that could be shipped to any country

    B. goods needed but not produced in England

    C. taxed more heavily than other products

    D. primarily produced in the West Indies

    E. regulated by Boards of Trade in the colonies

52. The consumer culture that emerged in the 1920s was largely due to

    A. the probusiness attitude of the federal government

    B. stock market speculation

    C. mass-production manufacturing techniques

    D. installment buying

    E. the emergence of the corporation

53. President Lyndon Johnson's Great Society programs

    A. won some important battles in health care and education

    B. demonstrated the importance of centralized administration in creating antipoverty programs

    C. had no effect whatsoever in solving problems of poverty and education

    D. actually resulted in poor people getting a worse education

    E. succeeded despite the expense of the Vietnam War

54. The Stamp Act Congress was significant because it

    A. demonstrated that the colonies were loyal to Parliament

    B. repealed the Stamp Act

    C. led directly to the First Continental Congress

    D. failed to persuade Parliament of colonial discontent

    E. marked an important step toward the unity of the colonies

55. Which of the following statements about the organization of the United Nations is accurate?

    A. The permanent members of the Security Council are the United States, the Soviet Union (Russia), France, and Great Britain.

    B. The General Assembly can override a veto by one of the permanent members of the Security Council.

    C. The Soviet Union originally had three votes in the General Assembly.

    D. The votes of two of the permanent members are needed to veto a measure in the Security Council.

    E. The Nationalist government in Taiwan represents China at the United Nations.

56. The book that is credited with raising the awareness of Americans of the threats to the environment is

    A. *Unsafe at Any Speed*

    B. *Silent Spring*

    C. *The Affluent Society*

    D. *The Shame of the Cities*

    E. *On the Road*

57. During the 1894 Pullman strike, President Grover Cleveland

    A. took the side of management in the dispute

    B. did nothing to stop the dispute

    C. took the side of labor in the dispute

    D. called on Congress to give the Interstate Commerce Commission enforcement powers

    E. invited management and labor representatives to the White House to settle the strike

58. Which of the following occurred most recently?

    A. Shays' Rebellion

    B. the ratification of the Articles of Confederation

    C. the publication of *The Federalist*

    D. the Constitutional Convention

    E. the Northwest Ordinance

59. The Supreme Court in *Worcester v. Georgia* (1832) declared that

    A. a citizen of one state could sue another state

    B. Indian tribes had no standing in federal courts

    C. Georgia could take over Indian lands within its borders

    D. Native Americans were entitled to U.S. citizenship

    E. Georgia law could not be enforced in the Cherokee Nation

GO ON TO THE NEXT PAGE

Practice Test 3

60. Henry Wallace ran as the Progressive candidate for President in 1948 because he

A. opposed Truman's policy on civil rights

B. saw himself as the true heir to the New Deal

C. favored a less hostile attitude toward the Soviet Union than Truman did

D. was defeated by Dewey in the Republican primaries

E. wanted to use the army to force the Soviet Union out of Eastern Europe

COLONIAL TRADE WITH ENGLAND, 1756–1759
(Value in pounds sterling)

	New England		New York		Pennsylvania	
	imports	exports	imports	exports	imports	exports
1756	384,371	47,359	250,425	24,073	200,169	20,095
1757	363,404	27,556	353,311	19,168	268,426	14,190
1758	465,694	30,204	356,555	14,260	260,953	21,383
1759	525,067	25,985	630,785	23,684	494,161	22,404

	Virginia/Maryland		Carolina	
	imports	exports	imports	exports
1756	337,759	200,169	181,780	222,915
1757	426,687	418,881	213,949	130,889
1758	438,471	454,362	181,002	150,511
1759	459,007	357,228	215,255	206,534

Source: U.S. Bureau of the Census. Historical Statistics of the United States from Colonial Times to 1970.

61. Based on the table above, the least valuable of England's American colonies in terms of exports was

A. New England

B. New York

C. Pennsylvania

D. Virginia and Maryland

E. Carolina

62. The purpose of the Kellogg-Briand Pact was to

A. enforce reparations payments from Germany

B. end the sale of weapons between nations

C. ban war as a method of dealing with international problems

D. enforce the battleship limitation provisions of the Washington Conference

E. establish perpetual friendship between the United States and France

63. The chief weapon used by Andrew Jackson in his dispute with the National Bank was

 A. his decision to print more paper money

 B. to deposit government money in state banks

 C. to give unqualified support to the Tariff of 1832

 D. the support of the Supreme Court in voiding the bank's charter

 E. paying government debts from tariff revenue only

64. The Battle of Midway resulted in

 A. the distinct possibility that Japan might invade the West Coast

 B. Japanese plans for another attack on Hawaii

 C. the loss of most of Japan's merchant marine

 D. a defeat for the Japanese and a brake on their control of the Pacific

 E. unsuccessful Japanese attempts to negotiate a conditional peace settlement

65. President Franklin Roosevelt's staff who helped shape the New Deal programs was known as the

 A. Ohio Gang

 B. Kitchen Cabinet

 C. Muckrakers

 D. Brain Trust

 E. Council of Economic Advisors

66. According to the Olive Branch Petition, the colonies

 A. were ready to declare their independence from Great Britain

 B. remained loyal to King George III

 C. demanded that British troops immediately leave the colonies

 D. agreed to raise a common army to defend themselves

 E. accepted the Stamp Act if they were allowed to elect members to Parliament

67. The issue of representation in Congress was resolved at the Constitutional Convention by the

 A. Virginia Plan

 B. 3/5 Compromise

 C. Great Compromise

 D. New Jersey Plan

 E. indirect election of senators

68. During the Civil War, African-Americans in the North

 A. were not allowed to join the Union Army

 B. fought in segregated regiments

 C. were allowed to join the Union Army but saw no combat

 D. were integrated into white regiments

 E. were permitted to select their own officers

GO ON TO THE NEXT PAGE

69. The correct chronological order of these efforts to combat the Great Depression is

A. Reconstruction Finance Corporation, Works Progress Administration, National Industrial Recovery Act, Securities and Exchange Commission, Fair Labor Standards Act

B. Securities and Exchange Commission, Reconstruction Finance Corporation, National Industrial Recovery Act, Fair Labor Standards Act, Works Progress Administration

C. Fair Labor Standards Act, Securities and Exchange Commission, Works Progress Administration, Reconstruction Finance Corporation, National Industrial Recovery Act

D. Works Progress Administration, Securities and Exchange Commission, Reconstruction Finance Corporation, National Industrial Recovery Act, Fair Labor Standards Act

E. Reconstruction Finance Corporation, National Industrial Recovery Act, Securities and Exchange Commission, Works Progress Administration, Fair Labor Standards Act

70. What action did President Eisenhower take to bring about school integration in Little Rock, Arkansas?

A. He urged Congress to pass civil rights legislation.

B. He issued an executive order mandating integration.

C. He began impeachment proceedings against Governor Orval Faubus.

D. He had the Justice Department file a suit in the federal courts.

E. He placed the Arkansas National Guard under federal command to carry out the desegregation plan.

71. Theodore Roosevelt's most controversial action involving Latin America was

A. building the Panama Canal

B. creating the Roosevelt Corollary to the Monroe Doctrine

C. mediating in the Venezuela/Great Britain boundary crisis

D. sending troops to Haiti

E. his opposition to the Platt Amendment

72. In the *Charles River Bridge* case, the Supreme Court declared that

A. government should regulate business for the good of society

B. states could regulate banks within their borders

C. vaguely worded clauses in charter grants could be decided in favor of the public interest

D. the strict constructionist interpretation was unconstitutional

E. interstate connections came under federal authority

73. The most significant consequence of the French and Indian War was that

   A. Spain received Florida as a prize of war

   B. England and the colonies began to distrust one another

   C. colonists feared being dragged into another European war

   D. there were British attacks against the tribes that had sided with the French

   E. French power in Canada was strengthened

Voter Participation in Presidential Elections, 1952–1988

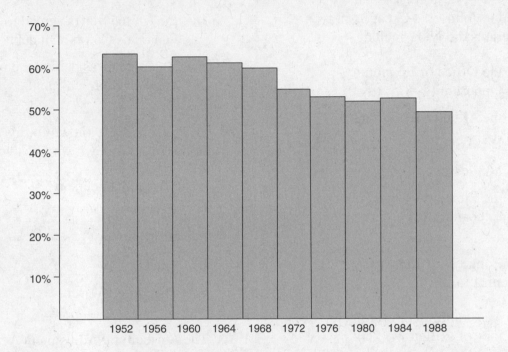

74. Besides the obvious decline in voter participation between 1952 and 1988, what other point can be made based on the above graph?

   A. In an election in which the President is running for a second term, voter participation declines.

   B. Voter participation increases in elections in which there is a strong third-party candidate.

   C. The sharpest drop in voter participation occurred in the election of 1972.

   D. 1988 was the first presidential election in which voter participation was less than fifty percent.

   E. Voter participation has never reached above sixty-five percent.

GO ON TO THE NEXT PAGE

75. The Declaration of Independence was based on the political philosophy of

    A. Edmund Burke

    B. Thomas Paine

    C. Thomas Hobbes

    D. John Locke

    E. Thomas Jefferson

76. Lyndon Johnson's Great Society programs did NOT include

    A. the Office of Economic Opportunity

    B. the Alliance for Progress

    C. Head Start

    D. Medicare

    E. the Elementary and Secondary Education Act

77. The Congress of Industrial Organizations

    A. was committed to protecting the jobs of skilled workers

    B. stressed organizing workers by industry rather than by craft

    C. remained a part of the American Federation of Labor

    D. did not sanction strikes to achieve workers' demands

    E. refused to accept African-Americans as members

78. According to the Hay-Buneau-Varilla Treaty,

    A. Panama agreed to let the United States build an isthmian canal on terms favorable to the United States

    B. France sold its canal company to the Panamanian government

    C. Colombia agreed to sell the Canal Zone for $25 million

    D. the United States agreed to assume Panama's Colombian debt

    E. Nicaragua was denied the right to build an isthmian canal

79. The novelist best known for his critique of life in small-town America was

    A. Maxwell Anderson

    B. Hart Crane

    C. William Faulkner

    D. Sinclair Lewis

    E. Theodore Dreiser

80. The Agricultural Adjustment Act was an attempt to deal with which chronic problem of American farmers?

    A. soil erosion

    B. high transporation charges

    C. overproduction

    D. declining labor supply

    E. inflation

IF YOU FINISH BEFORE TIME IS CALLED, CHECK YOUR WORK ON THIS SECTION ONLY. DO NOT WORK ON ANY OTHER SECTION IN THE TEST.

Section II: Essay Questions

Part A

(Suggested writing time — 45 minutes)

Directions: Write an essay based on your analysis of Documents A–G as well as your knowledge of the period covered by the question. It is important for you to include information on the topic not provided in the documents.

---

1. While President Franklin Roosevelt instituted a major shift in U.S.-Latin American relations, his Good Neighbor Policy was unable to survive in the atmosphere of the cold war.

   Using the documents provided and your knowledge of the period from 1933 through 1973, assess the validity of this statement.

Document A

Every observing person must by this time thoroughly understand that under the Roosevelt Administration the United States is as much opposed as any other government to interference with the freedom, sovereignty, or other internal affairs or processes of the governments of other nations. In addition to numerous acts and utterances in connection with the carrying out of these doctrines and policies, President Roosevelt, during recent weeks, gave out a public statement expressing his disposition to open negotiations with the Cuban Government for the purpose of dealing with the treaty which has existed since 1903. I feel safe in undertaking to say that under our support of the general principle of nonintervention, as has been suggested, no government need fear any intervention on the part of the United States under the Roosevelt Administration.

Source: Statement by Secretary of State Cordell Hull to the Seventh Pan-American Conference, December 19, 1933.

Document B

We have negotiated a Pan American convention embodying the principle of non-intervention. We have abandoned the Platt Amendment which gave us the right to intervene in the internal affairs of the Republic of Cuba. We have withdrawn American marines from Haiti. We have signed a new treaty which places our relations with Panama on a mutually satisfactory basis. We have undertaken a series of trade agreements with other American countries to our mutual commercial profit.

Source: Speech by President Franklin Roosevelt, August 14, 1936.

GO ON TO THE NEXT PAGE

Document C

By the end of the decade, Roosevelt had modified his method of handling Latin American affairs. The change nevertheless came slowly. Bolivia found that out in March 1937, when it annulled the oil concession held by Standard Oil and confiscated the company's property. The United States supported the firm in two ways. It brought pressure on other Latin American countries to prevent Bolivia from obtaining help in developing or selling its oil, and it refused to give Bolivia any economic aid.

Source: William Appleman Williams, The Tragedy of American Diplomacy *(1972).*

Document D

The reorganization and proper development of Mexico alone would afford an outlet for our capital and energies for some time to come. And while I think we should try in every way to maintain the friendship of our neighbors to the south, I think we should also make it clearly understood that no government in Mexico, Central America, and the Caribbean South American countries will be tolerated unless it is friendly to the United States, and that, if necessary, we are prepared to use force to obtain that object.

Source: Speech by General Robert E. Wood of the America First Committee, October 4, 1940.

Document E

The question may be raised as to what attitude this country would take if confronted with a break-down of law and order in any country of this hemisphere. Contemplating that contingency, the President has said: "It is only if and when the failure of orderly processes affects the other nations of the continent that it becomes their joint concern; and the point to stress is that in such an event it becomes the joint concern of a whole continent in which we are all neighbors."

Source: Speech by Laurence Duggan, Chief of the Division of American Republics, Department of State, April 2, 1938.

Document F

When Franklin Roosevelt became President he had for a long time taken a deep and constructive interest in inter-American affairs. He believed that in its own interest this country should put its relations with its American neighbors upon a new and completely different foundation. He believed primarily that it must abandon its long-standing policy of interference, and above all of military intervention. He was convinced that the juridical equality of all the American nations must be recognized in practice as well as in words. Furthermore, he was persuaded of the necessity for inter-American consultation whenever trouble within one republic threatened to become a source of danger to the others. This would ensure that mediation or any protective measure would be undertaken only by concerted action.

Source: Sumner Welles, The Time for Decision *(1944).*

Document G

The Government of the United States readily recognizes the right of any sovereign state to expropriate for public purposes. This view has been stated in a number of communications addressed to your Government during the past two years and in conversations had with you during that same period regarding the expropriation by your Government of the property belonging to American nationals.

On each occasion, however, it has been stated with equal emphasis that the right to expropriate property is coupled with and conditioned on the obligation to make adequate, effective and prompt compensation. This legality of an expropriation is in fact dependent upon the observance of this requirement.

Source: Secretary of State Cordell Hull to the Mexican Ambassador to the United States, April 3, 1940.

Part B

(Suggested time — 35 minutes, including a 5-minute planning period)

Directions: Choose ONE question from this part. Cite relevant historical evidence in support of your generalizations and present your arguments clearly and logically.

2. Analyze the ways in which THREE of the following helped shape the economy and social structure of the southern colonies in the seventeenth and eighteenth centuries.

   The environment

   The headright system

   Indentured servitude

   Slavery

3. "Any activity that throws woman into the attitude of a combatant, either for herself or others, lies outside her appropriate sphere." (Catharine Beecher, 1837)

   To what extent did women agree with this view in the decades before the Civil War?

GO ON TO THE NEXT PAGE

Part C

(Suggested time — 35 minutes, including a 5-minute planning period)

Directions: Choose ONE question from this part. Cite relevant historical evidence in support of your generalizations and present your arguments clearly and logically.

4. Identify THREE of the following and evaluate the relative importance of each of the THREE in promoting the growth of the conservation movement.

> The Sierra Club
>
> The Newlands Reclamation Act
>
> The Hetch Hetchy controversy
>
> The Pinchot-Ballinger controversy

5. Identify THREE of the following and analyze to what extent each of the THREE accurately reflected the accomplishments with which they were associated.

> The Return to Normalcy
>
> The Fair Deal
>
> The New Frontier
>
> The Great Society

IF YOU FINISH BEFORE TIME IS CALLED, CHECK YOUR WORK ON THIS SECTION ONLY. DO NOT WORK ON ANY OTHER SECTION IN THE TEST.

Answer Key for Practice Test 3

Section I: Multiple-Choice Questions

1.	C	29.	B
2.	C	30.	D
3.	A	31.	D
4.	C	32.	A
5.	D	33.	C
6.	B	34.	D
7.	D	35.	A
8.	D	36.	B
9.	E	37.	B
10.	C	38.	C
11.	D	39.	D
12.	A	41.	C
13.	B	42.	C
14.	E	43.	B
15.	D	44.	B
16.	D	45.	A
17.	E	46.	A
18.	C	47.	C
19.	A	48.	D
20.	A	49.	C
21.	B	50.	B
22.	C	51.	B
23.	E	52.	D
24.	B	53.	A
25.	C	54.	E
26.	E	55.	C
27.	C	56.	B
28.	D	57.	A

58. C	**70.** E
59. E	**71.** B
61. C	**72.** C
62. C	**73.** B
63. B	**74.** C
64. D	**75.** D
65. D	**76.** B
66. B	**77.** B
67. C	**78.** A
68. B	**79.** D
69. E	**80.** C

Section II: Essay Questions

Student essays and analysis appear beginning on page 238.

Answers and Explanations for Practice Test 3

Section I: Multiple-Choice Questions

1. **C.** Congress passed an exclusion act in 1882 barring Chinese for ten years. It was renewed in 1892 and then made indefinite. The policy was in effect until 1943.

2. **C.** The Supreme Court in the 1920s declared unconstitutional a federal child-labor law, a minimum-wage law for women, and restrictions on injunctions against labor. Examples include *Adkins v. Children's Hospital* (1923) and *Bailey v. Drexel Furniture Company* (1922).

3. **A.** At the annual meeting of the American Anti-Slavery Society in 1840, William Lloyd Garrison insisted on the right of women to participate equally with men in the organization. Those members who opposed this position split off and formed the American and Foreign Anti-Slavery Society. Sarah and Angelina Grimké rejected the idea that working for abolition of slavery was "unfeminine."

4. **C.** Anger at the attempts to make the American ambassadors pay a bribe before discussing the problem of French interference with American shipping led to U.S. and French warships firing on each other. A full war was averted when President John Adams refused to be stampeded into making such a commitment and a change in the revolutionary French government brought about a settlement of the dispute.

5. **D.** The delegates almost immediately demonstrated a concern for the creation of a Constitution in 1787 that would be national in its scope. The Virginia Plan, drafted by James Madison, reflected the idea of a truly national government and was the basis for the debate on the structure of the government provided for in the new Constitution.

6. **B.** In this 1901 statement, Booker T. Washington presented his views on accommodation to the dominant society and acceptance of the existing social inequality.

7. **D.** The rapid industrialization of the United States after the Civil War contributed to the population shift in several ways. Factories and mills located in urban areas acted as a magnet for workers, both American and the new immigrants. The mechanization of agriculture, which was part of industrialization, meant that fewer hands were needed on the farms. Farmers, displaced by machines, went to the cities to find work.

8. **D.** Britain, Japan, France, and the United States agreed to a status quo in the Pacific. They also agreed on a battleship and carrier ratio of 5–5–3 (United States and Britain each have five to every three of Japan's).

9. **E.** A high tariff was the position held by the Republican party. Populists, who were mainly farmers, wanted low tariffs or none at all on imported items they needed and used.

10. **C.** The colonies in this question were founded as follows: Massachusetts Bay (1630), Maryland (1634), New York (1664), Pennsylvania (1681), and Georgia (1732). New York was begun as New Amsterdam by the Dutch in 1624, but the question asks about *English* colonies, and the English took it over and renamed it in 1664.

11. **D.** New England farmers, whose soil wasn't particularly fertile to begin with, could not compete with western agricultural products transported to eastern cities through the canal.

12. **A.** The Maine Law was one of the earliest examples of a state's prohibiting the making and selling of liquor and reflected the growing importance of the temperance movement that emerged in the early nineteenth century.

13. **B.** The key word here is "compromise," which Wilson refused to do on the League of Nations issue. By refusing to compromise, Wilson *did* ignore the changes that the Reservationists wanted to make.

14. **E.** France claimed the Louisiana Territory until it ceded the area to Spain in 1763. Spain held it until 1800 when it was returned to France. France sold it to the United States in 1803 as part of the Louisiana Purchase.

15. **D.** The slave states that remained in the Union were Missouri, Kentucky, Maryland, and Delaware. West Virginia, which is usually included in this group, was admitted to the Union in 1863 with a provision in its constitution that its few slaves would be gradually emancipated.

16. **D.** The engraving was the work of Paul Revere, a leader of the Boston radicals. It was widely circulated and helped build support for the fight against Great Britain throughout the colonies.

17. **E.** The Mesilla Valley, the area south of the Gila River, was acquired from Mexico as part of the Gadsden Purchase in 1853.

18. **C.** In 1906, San Francisco required that Asian children — Chinese, Japanese, and Korean — attend segregated public schools. This requirement caused a major dispute with Japan. By the terms of the Gentlemen's Agreement, Japan agreed to limit immigration to the United States in exchange for an end to the segregation order.

19. **A.** The Open Door Policy was stated in a series of notes prepared by Secretary of State John Hay in 1899 and 1900. The policy urged that access to the markets in China be open to all nations and that countries respect the territorial integrity of China. The latter point reflected American concerns raised by the Boxer Rebellion.

20. **A.** The author of this message was trying to communicate with President Hoover after the Bonus Army was driven out of Washington, D.C., in July 1932. During the worst days of the Depression, the Bonus Army was demanding an early payment of the cash bonus to veterans of World War I.

21. **B.** In 1964, African-American civil rights workers began a major campaign to register black voters, an effort aided by passage of the federal Voting Rights Act of 1965.

22. **C.** This is a tricky (though not a trick) question. You are asked to eliminate all reasons labor failed to grow *except* for **C.** Employers didn't provide or rarely provided pension benefits to workers, and unions didn't at this time ask for them.

23. **E.** The Forty-Niners, and those who followed, for the most part failed to find mineral wealth in California. Most soon left the gold fields for other economic pursuits such as farming or urban employment.

24. **B.** The term "Gilded Age" came from the title of a novel by Mark Twain and Charles Dudley Warner satirizing the political corruption of post-Civil War America.

25. **C.** Beginning in 1845, the people of Ireland experienced famine as the result of the potato blight, ruining their basic food crop several years in succession.

26. **E.** Roosevelt served as Assistant Secretary of the Navy (1897–98), Governor of New York (1899–1900), and Vice-President (1901) before becoming President after McKinley was assassinated.

27. **C.** This page from the directory is interesting to historians because it indicates the cultural and self-help organizations ethnic/immigrant groups established in Los Angeles. Only the entire directory would allow the historian to map the neighborhoods in which Spanish-speaking residents lived, and the document indicates that the city's public utilities were in private hands.

28. **D.** As provided in the debates over the adoption of the Constitution, the importation of slaves from abroad was banned in 1808.

29. **B.** John Peter Altgeld made this bitter comment in 1895 following the ruin of his political career after he pardoned some of the men convicted of murder in the Haymarket bombing.

30. **D.** British Orders in Council exasperated American merchant shipping, which was neutral in Britain's war against France; British warships took (impressed) American sailors, accusing them of being British deserters; the War Hawks, led by Henry Clay, wanted Canadian territory; the British backed the Indians in unsettled frontier conditions.

31. **D.** Germany surrendered on May 8, 1945, before the atomic bomb was tested on July 16, 1945.

32. **A.** Germany agreed for a time to end its policy of unrestricted submarine warfare as a result of Wilson's complaint that innocent Americans went down with the *Lusitania* on May 7, 1915. It was the resumption of unrestricted submarine warfare by Germany in February 1917 that was an immediate cause of American entry into World War I.

33. **C.** Black Codes were passed in Southern states to exert control over the status of freed slaves. The Tenure of Office Act prohibited the President from removing officials without consent of the Senate; the 1866 Civil Rights Act made African-Americans U.S. citizens; the First Reconstruction Act (1867) divided the South into military districts; the 1868 Reconstruction Act declared that a majority of actual voters, not registered voters, was needed to ratify a state constitution.

34. **D.** The Coinage Act of 1873 omitted silver from the list of coins to be minted, to the outrage of western silver miners and farmers. The Treasury had maintained an artificially low ratio of silver to gold at sixteen to one. Silver miners refused to sell their silver to federal mints at this price, so Congress dropped the coining of silver dollars. Then new silver discoveries dropped the price of silver, but now the government wasn't buying it. Gold-standard advocates resisted returning to bimetalism because it would have caused inflation.

35. **A.** The proposed amendments of the Hartford Convention (1814) included requiring a two-thirds vote of Congress to declare war, restrict foreign trade, and admit new states and limiting the President to one term.

36. B. In this 1904 case, the Supreme Court ordered the dissolution of the first railroad holding company for violation of the Sherman Anti-Trust Act. It opened the way for other prosecutions of trusts and monopolies.

37. B. Cotton gin (Eli Whitney, 1793); steamboat (Robert Fulton, 1807); reaper (Cyrus McCormick, 1831); telegraph (Samuel F. B. Morse, 1844).

38. C. The journalist Eric Sevareid made this comment critical of the work of the Peace Corps in 1963. The key clue in the quotation is "backward countries," eliminating the CCC, Job Corps, and Corps of Engineers, which operated only in the United States.

39. D. In the eighteenth century, whites were less concerned with the moral and social effects of slavery on blacks than what it meant for themselves in a society that had pledged "all men are created equal."

40. E. The Interstate Commerce Commission lacked the power to fix rates. It could bring railroads into court only if it considered rates to be unreasonably high.

41. C. The print shows the murder of Joseph Smith, the founder of the Mormons, or Church of Jesus Christ of Latter-day Saints, and his brother Hiram. After Smith's death, Brigham Young became the leader of the Mormons and led them to their permanent settlement near the Great Salt Lake in Utah.

42. C. Eugene V. Debs (1855–1926) of Terre Haute, Indiana, led the American Railway Union in the 1894 Pullman strike; after its collapse, Debs declared himself "for socialism because I am for humanity." He ran for President on the Socialist ticket in 1904, 1908, 1912, and 1920.

43. B. Horace Mann (1796–1859) was firmly committed to public education and believed that religious indoctrination has no place in the public-school curriculum.

44. B. Goldwater represented the right wing of the Republican party, and his nomination reflected the success, not the failure, of a strong grass-roots organization.

45. A. This tariff marked a beginning in the effort to protect new American industries following the War of 1812. It was supported by Jeffersonian Republicans as well as Federalists.

46. A. In addition to providing both food and medical relief, the Freedmen's Bureau tried to regulate the new economic relations between former slaves and white landowners. This was done through formal labor contracts that specified wages and working conditions. The Bureau was active only in the states of the former Confederacy and encouraged African-Americans who had moved to the cities to return to farming.

47. C. The draft was enacted in March 1863 and applied to men between the ages of twenty and forty-five. A potential draftee could hire a substitute or pay $300 to have his service commuted. Perhaps because of the loopholes, opposition to the draft was widespread, leading, for example, to the infamous New York City draft riots of July 1863. Draftees and substitutes accounted for six percent of the Union forces.

48. D. The Marshall Plan was announced by Secretary of State George Marshall in June 1947. Although aid was offered to all the countries of war-torn Europe, neither the Soviet Union nor the Communist governments in Eastern Europe accepted.

49. **C.** For the Plains Indian culture, the buffalo provided far more than food. It also provided hides for tepees, blankets, and clothing; sinews for rope; bones for needles; and many other items.

50. **B.** The New England Confederation, founded in 1643, consisted of Massachusetts Bay, Plymouth, Connecticut, and New Haven. Rhode Island was not invited to join. Its purpose was to act in defense of its member colonies, most notably in King Philip's War in 1675–76.

51. **B.** Enumerated articles were products that could be shipped only to England or other English colonies and included tobacco, cotton, indigo, naval stores, and furs. These were goods that England needed but that it could not produce.

52. **D.** Installment buying allowed Americans to immediately purchase the host of consumer products that advertisers told them they needed. By the end of the 1920s, most cars, radios, and furniture were bought on the installment plan.

53. **A.** Successes included the Head Start program, the drop in infant mortality rates in minority communities, and a better economic condition for the elderly.

54. **E.** By bringing together representatives from nine of the colonies, the Stamp Act Congress (1765) was an important step toward colonial unity. The Congress petitioned Parliament for the repeal of the Stamp Act and claimed that Parliament had no right to impose taxes on the colonies.

55. **C.** As part of a compromise worked out during World War II, the Soviet Union was given three seats in the General Assembly — the USSR, Belorussia, and Ukraine. There have always been five permanent members of the Security Council — the United States, France, Great Britain, the Soviet Union, and China. China is now represented by the People's Republic of China. It takes the vote of only one permanent member of the Security Council to veto a measure.

56. **B.** Rachel Carson's *Silent Spring* (1962), which warned of the dangers of the pesticide DDT, is usually pointed to as the beginning of the environmental movement in the United States.

57. **A.** Cleveland sent federal soldiers to Chicago to safeguard delivery of the U.S. mail — an action that aided management and helped it to crush the strike.

58. **C.** Remember, "most recently" means last. The publication of *The Federalist,* which was intended to gather public support for the ratification of the Constitution, took place between October 1787 and July 1788.

59. **E.** In *Worcester v. Georgia* (1832), the Supreme Court ruled that the Cherokee Nation was a "distinct political community" in which Georgia law had no force. Although the decision was a victory for the Cherokees, President Andrew Jackson refused to enforce it. In another important case a year earlier, *Cherokee Nation* v. *Georgia,* the Court stated that while the Cherokees were not a foreign nation, and therefore did not have the right to bring suit, they did have an unquestioned right to their land.

60. **C.** Henry Wallace, former Secretary of Agriculture and Vice-President under Franklin Roosevelt, ran for President in 1948 because he supported a more liberal policy toward the Soviet Union. He represented the left wing of the Democratic party.

61. **C.** Based on mercantile theory, a colony was valuable to the mother country both as a source of raw materials and as a market for manufactured products. For the years given in the table, Pennsylvania shows least value of exports to England.

62. **C.** The Kellogg-Briand Pact, or Pact of Paris (1928), renounced war as an instrument of foreign policy. It included no method of implementation or enforcement. Although it was originally a treaty of friendship between the United States and France, dozens of other nations also signed it, including Germany, Italy, and Japan.

63. **B.** By depositing money in state "pet" banks, Jackson met federal expenses by drawing on Bank of the United States funds — in effect, draining the Bank of the United States of its funds.

64. **D.** The Battle of Midway in June 1942 has been considered a turning point in the Pacific war. The Japanese never regained the momentum lost by this defeat of their naval and air forces.

65. **D.** The Brain Trust included political scientist Raymond Moley, economists Rexford G. Tugwell and Adolf Berle, and Felix Frankfurter of the Harvard Law School.

66. **B.** Written by John Dickinson and issued by the Second Continental Congress in July 1775, the Olive Branch Petition stated that the colonies continued to be loyal to King George III.

67. **C.** The Great Compromise resolved the differences between the large and small states over representation by providing for equal representation in the Senate and representation based on population in the House of Representatives. The 3/5 Compromise, which decided how slaves would be counted for representation, is sometimes considered part of the Great Compromise.

68. **B.** Approximately 200,000 African-Americans served in the Union Army during the Civil War. They served in all-black units under the command of white officers, and over 30,000 lost their lives in combat.

69. **E.** Reconstruction Finance Corporation, 1932; National Industrial Recovery Act, 1933; Securities and Exchange Commission, 1934; Works Progress Administration, 1935; Fair Labor Standards Act, 1938.

70. **E.** President Eisenhower did not believe that desegregation could be brought about by government edict. When the Governor of Arkansas called out the National Guard to prevent the integration of Central High School in 1957, Eisenhower considered the action a direct challenge to federal authority. Integration was achieved when the President placed the Guard under federal control.

71. **B.** The Roosevelt Corollary stated that the United States would serve as the guardian of the Western Hemisphere — in effect, claiming the right to intervene in the internal affairs of Latin American nations.

72. **C.** The case was decided in favor of Warren Bridge, arguing that the original charter to Charles River Bridge did not confer a monopoly. Ambiguities in such contracts should be decided in favor of the public interest, as innovations should not be restricted under old charters.

73. **B.** Almost immediately after the French and Indian War, relations between England and the colonies became strained. One outcome of the war was a growing sense of American nationalism; the colonists began to think of themselves more as Americans than as Englishmen. England, of course, was faced with a huge debt and turned to the colonies to finance its empire.

74. **C.** The drop in voter participation in 1972 is the only other significant fact discernible from the graph. The presence of strong third-party candidates — George Wallace in 1968 — did not result in an increase in voter participation.

75. **D.** Thomas Jefferson, the author of the Declaration of Independence, effectively restated Locke's contract theory of government.

76. **B.** The Alliance for Progress program of economic assistance to Latin America was initiated under the Kennedy administration.

77. **B.** In contrast to the American Federation of Labor, the CIO believed that the best way to organize workers was on an industry-wide basis. The leaders were John L. Lewis of the United Mine Workers and the garment industry unions. These unions were expelled from the AFL because of their approach and formed the CIO in 1938.

78. **A.** In a controversial move, the United States abetted the Panamanian independence revolt against Colombia in 1903 and then signed a canal agreement that created a ten-mile-wide Canal Zone and gave the United States other economic and political advantages.

79. **D.** Lewis's novels *Main Street* and *Babbitt* are critiques of the blandness of small-town life in middle America.

80. **C.** The Agricultural Adjustment Act aimed at resolving the chronic problem of overproduction by paying farmers to withdraw land from cultivation. The law was declared unconstitutional by the Supreme Court.

Section II: Essay Questions

Part A

Student DBQ Essay

The Good Neighbor Policy was a sharp break with the previous American attitude toward Latin America, particularly from the end of the Spanish-American War to around 1920. Under President Franklin Roosevelt, U.S.-Latin American relations were based on non-intervention. The concern with Communist activities in the Western Hemisphere during the cold war, however, brought an end to this policy as shown by events in Guatemala (1954), Cuba (1961), and Chile (1973).

In the years following the war with Spain, the U.S. became the policeman for much of Latin America. Through the Platt Amendment (1901) the U.S. assumed the right to intervene in Cuba to preserve its independence. The so-called Roosevelt Corollary to the Monroe Doctrine (1904) broadened this authority and was used as the justification for sending American troops to Cuba, Haiti, the Dominican Republic, and Nicaragua. The U.S. also became involved militarily in the Mexican civil war between 1914 and 1917. Although we began to back away from an interventionist approach in Latin America during the late 1920s, the significant change came with Roosevelt.

Being a "good neighbor" meant that the U.S. would not interfere in the internal or external affairs of other countries. This position was clearly stated by Secretary of State Cordell Hull to the 7th Pan-American Conference in December 1933 (Document A), and the U.S. entered into several agreements during the 1930s with the other countries of the Western Hemisphere that reinforced this principle. The U.S. backed up its statements on non-intervention with actions. A new treaty with Cuba was negotiated that ended our right to intervene and American troops were withdrawn from Haiti and other nations in the Caribbean and Central America as President Roosevelt pointed out (Document B). The American response to the expropriation of the property of American oil companies in Mexico in 1938 is a good example of how major a break with the past the new policy was. Rather than sending in the troops, the U.S. demanded compensation for the companies (Document G). This serious issue between the U.S. and Mexico was eventually settled by arbitration.

A case could be made that the Good Neighbor Policy was not that dramatic a shift from earlier policies. First, intervention was not rejected completely. As both Roosevelt himself (Document E) and State Department official Sumner Welles pointed out (Document F), "a breakdown of law and order" in one country that affected other countries might result in some sort of joint action. It is possible that the U.S., because of its power and influence, might have been able to persuade other Latin American states to support armed intervention under certain circumstances. More important, as William Appleman Williams points out, the U.S. was still ready to use economic intervention as the case of Bolivia shows (Document C).

The onset of the cold war brought an end to the Good Neighbor Policy. The U.S. supported regimes that were strongly anti-Communist, and took action when pro-Communist or left-wing governments came to power. While American troops were not used, the U.S. provided covert support that led to the overthrow of the government of Guatemala in 1954. Again, the U.S. did not use its own military forces to invade Cuba but the Central Intelligence Agency was involved in the planning and training for the failed Bay of Pigs invasion by anti-Castro Cubans in 1961. In 1973, the CIA also supported the overthrow of the socialist government of Salvador Allende in Chile. The significance of these events in indicating a return to intervention, admittedly indirect, outweighs the evidence of a continuation of Roosevelt's policies — the creation of the Organization of American States and Kennedy's Alliance for Progress.

Reader's Comments

The student has written a good essay that provides enough outside information to satisfy the DBQ requirements. This question is interesting because it's rather obvious where the outside information fits in. The brief review of U.S. policy toward Latin America prior to the 1930s would have been strengthened, however, by reference to Dollar Diplomacy and the Clark Memorandum (1928). The latter rejected the idea that the Monroe Doctrine was intended to justify American intervention in the Western Hemisphere.

The student makes good use of the available documents. The point that the Good Neighbor Policy did not mean the complete abandonment of intervention is well taken; the distinction between military and economic intervention could have been more clearly made, however. The student should also have known that William Appleman Williams is a Revisionist historian of American foreign policy. The essay could have been made stronger if additional facts about the Good Neighbor Policy were included — for example, the importance of solidarity in the Western Hemisphere as the possibility of war in Europe became more likely.

Possible student score: 6

Part B

Question 2 Student Essay

In order for plantation agriculture to work, certain factors must exist. The southern colonies were particularly suited to plantation agriculture in the areas of environment and labor, much more so than the northern colonies. Patterns were set in the seventeenth and eighteenth centuries that clearly established plantation agriculture as the economic mainstay of the region.

The southern environment provided a long growing season and fertile soil for the cultivation of tobacco, rice, indigo, and, later, cotton. The only problem with these crops was that they required extensive labor, a commodity lacking in the southern colonies. The environment itself dictated the kinds of agricultural products to be grown as cash crops. Wheat and corn required little extensive labor; a farmer and his family could grow such crops with a reasonable effort. The South, on the other hand, needed many people to plant, maintain, and harvest their cash crops.

With the colonies offering an opportunity for a new start, it is understandable that colonists would be reluctant to remain in an employment situation that suggested some form of servitude. There are many stories of runaway apprentices who left their masters as soon as they were old enough to do so. For the South, planters might rely on indentured servants, a practice by which a person who could not afford passage across the Atlantic could come to the colonies. The typical indentured contract was seven years. During that time the servant was in effect a slave. The problem was that many indentured servants had no desire to remain in that position once they arrived in the colonies. It was extremely difficult for the holder of an indentured contract to trace the whereabouts of a runaway servant. These servants were mainly English and white, and if they got far enough away, could simply melt into the colonial population.

The South's answer was to import slaves from Africa. Slavery answered the labor question by providing a large work force to produce the cash crops grown by planters. At the same time, since slaves were African, running away was not much of an option, especially at a time when few people questioned the morality of slave ownership. By the nineteenth century, when those questions were raised, the South already had a pattern of almost 200 years of reliance on slavery as the foundation of its planter economy.

Reader's Comments

This is a weak essay. It is obvious that the student was unsure how to handle the question and really did not have the factual information to write a good answer. The theme of the interrelationship between environment and labor is valid but not developed. The student should have described the evolution of plantation agriculture, examined its impact on relations with the Native Americans — the demand for land led to conflicts — explained who indentured servants were and their status after their term of service ended, and gone into the transition from indentured servants to slaves brought from Africa as the principal labor force.

Possible student score: 2

Part B

Question 3 Student Essay

At first appearance the statement made by Catharine Beecher would seem to have little validity. Beecher clearly rejects the idea of women taking part in any reform or activity "outside her appropriate sphere." This viewpoint clashes superficially with the accomplishments of such women as Dorothea Dix and her crusade on behalf of the mentally ill, the Grimké sisters and others who became abolitionists, and the stand of the Seneca Falls Convention. In fact, textbooks often give the impression that outspoken women were the role models of their era, that women looked to the leadership of Elizabeth Cady Stanton, Susan B. Anthony, Amelia Bloomer, and others who stood up and spoke up for women's rights.

Beecher's argument may be much closer to the mainstream of women's thought for the era in which she wrote. There would really be very little reason for women to disagree with Beecher. In the 1830s, the time in which Beecher made her statement, women had few rights in the United States. Women could not vote, of course, but that was only the most obvious example of their second-class citizenship. They also could not own property in their own name in most states. If a woman inherited money, on her marriage the control of the fortune went to her husband. Divorce was rare, but when it took place the husband came out ahead, down to custody of the children and possession of the home.

The "appropriate sphere" for women was very limited. But this does not mean that Beecher herself opposed women holding views on slavery, mental health, or voting rights. She believed that if a woman became a combatant, her behavior was not appropriate. But there were other ways in which women could demonstrate their concern with the problems of society. Beecher's own sister was Harriet Beecher Stowe, the author of <u>Uncle Tom's Cabin</u>, and her brother, Henry Ward Beecher, was a prominent abolitionist. It would be difficult to believe that Catharine opposed her own family in taking moral positions unless the statement was written as sarcasm or hypocrisy. It all depends on what Catharine Beecher defined as woman's "appropriate sphere."

Reader's Comments

This essay offers a powerful beginning and middle while falling somewhat flat at the end. The endorsement of the validity of Beecher's statement is courageous, given the temptation to question it in the light of the much better known activity of such women as Susan B. Anthony and Dorothea Dix. The student correctly notes that just because these women are prominently featured in textbook history doesn't mean that in their own time they were especially influential or served as role models for most women. The essay shows a more realistic side of the role of women in the pre-Civil War era in stating their limited role and economic subjugation.

The student is less successful in describing the "appropriate sphere" in which women could function. The statement doesn't define "appropriate sphere," but the student doesn't fall into the trap of believing that Beecher meant that women's place was in the home. Neither, however, does the essay indicate in what ways women could engage in activity that didn't make them combatants. Citing the accomplishments of Beecher's famous siblings doesn't necessarily mean that sister Harriet's authorship of *Uncle Tom's Cabin* was done without having taken the "attitude of a combatant." One could argue that Stowe's book violates Catharine Beecher's definition of the appropriate sphere. Since no clear definition of that sphere is given, the essay is weakened by the conclusion. The student admits as much by confessing ignorance of what Beecher meant. The essay would be much stronger had the student tried to define the term.

Possible student score: 6

Part C

Question 4 Student Essay

In the first years of the twentieth century, the American people began to modify their earlier view of the resources of the nation as limitless. Under the leadership of President Theodore Roosevelt, the conservation movement made people aware of the importance of wise management of the forests and streams of America. The era, however, was not without its contestants and controversies. The Sierra Club was seen as an elitist organization by many people. The Newlands Reclamation Act failed to live up to expectations. Most controversial of all, the dispute between Gifford Pinchot and Secretary of the Interior Ballinger injected politics into the movement and helped split the Republican party.

The Sierra Club was formed in California around 1890 by John Muir. For many years it was an organization that was small in number but with political influence. When Theodore Roosevelt became President, he met with Muir and toured the redwood forests of California. The problem with the Sierra Club was that it seemed to be composed of wealthy people who had the image of trying to shut out average people from enjoying the environment. In the early 1900s few roads existed into the national parks and forests, for example, making a vacation trip to them both expensive and difficult. Muir wanted the wilderness to remain that way, but in doing so most people lacked the funds to visit places like Yosemite. Therefore, although the Sierra Club helped raise public consciousness about the environment, its actual contribution to the movement was limited and, given its elitist image, may even have been counterproductive.

In 1902 the Newlands Reclamation Act was passed, the idea being to reclaim marginal lands for agriculture through irrigation. This law had many supporters who argued that individual developers lacked the resources to build dams, irrigation ditches, and flood control projects. Only the federal government could afford to spend such money. The problem with the Newlands Act was that it was both radical and conservative at the same time, causing people from both ends of the political spectrum to oppose it. For example, farmers weren't happy with the idea of land coming under irrigation because it would create more farms, and therefore more farm surpluses, and falling prices. On the other hand, critics noted that the Act required farmers on reclamation land to repay the costs of the projects, and the monetary demands placed a burden on those farmers that had to be extended so they could repay the debts. The Reclamation Act was a good idea, but it tried to do too many things for too many people, and as a result did little for the cause of conservation.

Finally, the Pinchot-Ballinger controversy did not occur under the presidency of Theodore Roosevelt. William H. Taft was the President and he was caught in a dispute between Chief Forester Pinchot and Secretary of the Interior Ballinger over the question of whether certain lands could be leased for the mining of coal. Ballinger was legally correct in his approval of the leases for the mining of coal, but Pinchot bitterly criticized his decision. It got to the point that Taft had to make a decision, and since Pinchot was under Ballinger's authority, Taft fired Pinchot for insubordination.

The end result for the conservation movement is that these three factors have received considerable publicity in textbooks, but they actually did fairly little to promote the growth of conservation and in fact may also have contributed to an opposition movement that was not convinced of the motives behind supporters of the Sierra Club, the Newlands Act, or the defense of Pinchot.

Reader's Comments

Although the student gets around to evaluating the relative importance of the factors chosen, the introductory paragraph is not well thought out. The presidency of Theodore Roosevelt did not define the chronology of the early conservation movement, given the choices for selection. By focusing on Roosevelt, discussion of the Sierra Club is limited, and the student has to backtrack a little in noting that the Pinchot-Ballinger controversy took place after Roosevelt left the presidency. Why the Republican party was "split" is not explained. On the positive side, the student provides a fair amount of content in discussing each factor, and there are no serious or even minor factual errors. The conclusion is strongly stated, and the student demonstrates some courage in arguing that the factors did not do much to promote conservation. Whether the argument supports the conclusion, however, is another matter.

Possible student score: 5

Part C

Question 5 Student Essay

There is a measurable distance between promise and performance, and presidents who have created programs have found that critics will be only too willing to compare what the politicians hoped to accomplish with what was actually done. The Fair Deal, New Frontier, and Great Society offer examples of how presidents succeeded or failed in varying degrees in trying to make their programs accepted by Congress and the American people.

President Harry Truman probably had one of the roughest times putting his Fair Deal program into effect. The main reason for this was because many of his ideas were far too advanced for Congress or the voters to accept. After Roosevelt's death, Truman continued the New Deal programs, but he had his own agenda, especially in the area of civil rights and social welfare. He called his program the "Fair Deal" and hoped to expand government's role in providing for the health, well-being, and equality of all Americans. Southern Democrats strongly indicated they weren't ready for his civil rights views, modest as they were by the standards of a later era. Truman's main accomplishment in the arena of civil rights was to order the integration of the armed forces, an act he could do as commander-in-chief and without the consent of Congress. Legislation was another matter. The Fair Deal promised national health care, but the American Medical Association labeled it "socialized medicine." Truman's Fair Deal is admired for its intent, but the ideals it expressed had to wait for a generation that would be more accepting of such concepts as social equality.

That time seemed to come with John F. Kennedy's New Frontier program. Kennedy embodied youth and idealism, and many of his statements proved inspiring to young people. Unfortunately, Kennedy was elected president by so narrow a margin that he lacked a mandate to propose passage of controversial programs and laws. The successes of the New Frontier included the Peace Corps and, for a time, the Alliance for Progress. But the New Frontier encountered a deadlock in civil rights legislation, although many Americans sympathized with the movement that called for restoring voting rights to black

Americans. After the march on Washington in the summer of 1963, Kennedy seemed to be heading towards a stronger position on civil rights, but his assassination left his intentions to speculation.

It was the Great Society that most closely matched promise and performance, even if many of the Great Society programs did not endure. President Lyndon Johnson capitalized on the national grief over Kennedy's murder to propose important domestic programs, including the Job Corps, Head Start, and major civil rights laws, including voting acts that put teeth in the federal enforcement of laws protecting the rights of citizens to vote. Johnson might have been remembered as the greatest president of the 20th century, but his domestic Great Society programs were undermined by the costs of the Vietnam War.

In conclusion, all three of these programs demonstrate that unforeseen obstacles can undercut the most idealistic of presidential programs. Harry Truman misjudged the readiness of Americans to accept a government role in social concerns; Kennedy died before pursuing the most challenging ideals of the New Frontier; and Johnson lost his opportunity through his commitment to a controversial foreign policy.

Reader's Comments

This essay indicates that a student can do well in writing on a topic by first carefully reading what the question asks for. It does *not* ask for a "compare and contrast" or a relative evaluation of which program was most or least effective. It asks for an evaluation of each program's own accomplishment in relation to its promise. The student clearly follows this directive. In some areas, the programs are somewhat vaguely described, and there may be too much emphasis on civil rights platforms. The argument connecting the Great Society to national remorse over Kennedy's death is especially weak. But the structure on which the essay is built is solid, and the conclusion succinctly states a reasonable comprehension of the issues involved.

Possible student score: 8

Practice Test 4

Section I: Multiple-Choice Questions

Time: 55 Minutes

80 Questions

Directions: Select the best answer for the following questions or incomplete statements from the five choices provided. Indicate your answer by darkening the appropriate space on the answer sheet.

1. Which of the following statements about the alliance between the United States and the Soviet Union during World War II is true?

   A. The United States failed to recognize the contribution of the Soviet Union to the victory over Germany.

   B. The relationship was strained by the delays in opening up a second front in Europe.

   C. The United States fully supported the Soviet Union's security claims in Eastern Europe.

   D. Lend-lease was withheld from the Soviet Union until after the battle of Stalingrad.

   E. The Soviet Union supported free elections in Poland.

2. The practice of "impressment" involved

   A. seizure of purported British sailors from American merchant ships and pressing them into service with the British navy

   B. seizure of American sailors serving on French ships during the Napoleonic Wars

   C. French efforts to win the propaganda war against the British to gain American resources

   D. British use of Indian allies in the War of 1812

   E. French inducements to Americans to join the French navy

GO ON TO THE NEXT PAGE

3. The theory of mercantilism was

   A. strongly favored by Adam Smith in his book *The Wealth of Nations*

   B. a policy in which colonies existed for the benefit of the mother country, exchanging raw materials for manufactured products

   C. a colonial American policy favoring trade exclusively with England

   D. a way of avoiding widespread smuggling

   E. intended to encourage free trade among various European colonies in the Americas

4. "This conjunction of an immense military establishment and a large arms industry is new in the American experience. The total influence—economic, political, even spiritual—is felt in every city, every statehouse, every office of the federal government."

   This statement was made by

   A. President John Kennedy

   B. General Douglas MacArthur

   C. President Dwight Eisenhower

   D. President Franklin Roosevelt

   E. General George Patton

5. In the *Civil Rights Cases* (1883), the Supreme Court rejected the idea that

   A. public schools should be integrated

   B. all persons should have equal access to public accommodations

   C. African Americans were entitled to vote

   D. former slaves had a right to sue their masters for compensation

   E. the military academies should be open to African Americans

6. Supporters of states rights find constitutional support for the political position in

   A. the elastic clause

   B. the supremacy clause

   C. the Ninth Amendment

   D. the full faith and credit clause

   E. the Tenth Amendment

7. The Peace of Paris (1783) contained all of the following terms EXCEPT

   A. the evacuation of all British troops from American soil

   B. free navigation of the Mississippi River to New Orleans

   C. recognition of the independence of the United States

   D. extension of the boundary of the United States to the Mississippi River

   E. compensation of Loyalists for loss of their property

8. The 1917 Zimmermann telegram urging an alliance in war against the United States was sent by Germany to

   A. Japan

   B. Mexico

   C. Canada

   D. Russia

   E. Spain

9. The purpose of the 1887 Dawes Severalty Act was to provide Native Americans with

   A. independent tribal sovereignty

   B. communal tribal lands under federal jurisdiction

   C. individual family land allotments

   D. American citizenship and the right to vote in federal elections

   E. Economic aid in establishing industries on reservation land

10. Which of the following statements about education in the United States after the Civil War is true?

   A. Educational opportunities for women declined as more girls went into the labor force.

   B. The creation of land-grant colleges led to a significant expansion of higher education.

   C. African Americans were unable to attend college as a matter of law in the South.

   D. The influx of immigrants created a demand of bilingual education programs.

   E. Public school enrollment declined as the affluent turned to private schools.

11. The southern states of the Upper South area joined the Confederacy only when

   A. both sides had rejected the Crittenden Compromise

   B. Lincoln proclaimed the Lower South states in insurrection

   C. Lincoln took the oath of office as president

   D. The Confederacy moved its capital from Montgomery to Richmond

   E. Lincoln issued a preliminary proclamation of emancipation

12. During the 1960 election campaign, an important foreign policy issue was

   A. the military experience of Nixon and Kennedy

   B. U.S. relations with countries in the Middle East

   C. Nixon's willingness to open diplomatic relations with China

   D. Kennedy's claim there was a missile gap between the U.S. and the Soviet Union

   E. support for United Nations action in Korea

13. European wars in the late seventeenth and eighteenth centuries were known in the American colonies by the names of the rulers during the time of strife. A correct match of European war and its American version would be

   A. War of the Spanish Succession — King George's War

   B. War of the League of Augsburgh — King Louis's War

   C. War of the Spanish Succession — Queen Anne's War

   D. Seven Years' War — Queen Mary's War

   E. War of the Austrian Succession — King Charles's War

GO ON TO THE NEXT PAGE

14. The "Great Migration" refers to

    A.   the thousands of Puritans who settled in the Massachusetts Bay Colony

    B.   the Irish who came to the United States in the 1840s

    C.   the Pilgrims who established a Separatist colony in Plymouth

    D.   the Jews who fled persecution in Russian in the late nineteenth century

    E.   the movement of slaves from West Africa to the British colonies

15. The main purpose of France's North American empire was to

    A.   provide a refuge for French Huguenots from Catholic persecution

    B.   convert Native Americans to the Catholic faith

    C.   enlarge the fur trade activitiy with the Indians

    D.   block British expansion to the north and west

    E.   form an alliance with Spain to limit the area of British control

16. The Republican party's tactic of "waving the bloody shirt" referred to

    A.   reviving Civil War animosities and connecting Democrats to the Confederacy

    B.   praising Americans for their sacrifices in building a great nation

    C.   demanding the United States support the independence of Cuba

    D.   the violence of the labor movement in striking against the railroads

    E.   none of the above

17. Which of these women is NOT associated with the reform movements in the antebellum United States?

    A.   Sarah Grimke

    B.   Elizabeth Cady Stanton

    C.   Susan B. Anthony

    D.   Margaret Sanger

    E.   Sojourner Truth

18. The federal income tax, which was adopted in 1913 through the Sixteenth Amendment,

    A.   was regressive since it taxed all income at the same rate

    B.   was intended to redistribute wealth in the United States

    C.   regained revenue lost through tariff reduction

    D.   was not enforced until the late 1920s

    E.   was accepted in lieu of a national sales tax

19. The primary objective of the Marshall Plan was to

    A.   provide economic aid to Western Europe after World War II

    B.   create a military organization that could meet the threat from the Soviet Union

    C.   assist the countries of Eastern Europe to establish democratic governments

    D.   develop new weapons of mass destruction, including the hydrogen bomb

    E.   grant federal assistance to alleviate poverty in Appalachia

20. In the decades following World War II, there has been a massive migration of Americans to

    A. the "Sunbelt" states

    B. the New England states

    C. the Midwest

    D. the Pacific Northwest

    E. the South

21. President Jefferson called for naval action against the Barbary States because

    A. waging war was less costly than paying tribute

    B. most Americans would support such a political decision

    C. he wanted to divert attention from domestic political issues

    D. the United States had the active backing of France and Great Britain

    E. European nations had little faith in American words

22. "Your president may easily become a king. Your Senate so imperfectly constructed that your dearest rights may become sacrificed by what might be a small minority."

    This statement reflects the views of a

    A. Federalist

    B. Loyalist

    C. Democrat-Republican

    D. Antifederalist

    E. Whig

23. In the second half of the seventeenth century the economy of the Chesapeake region

    A. was characterized by small-scale subsistence farming

    B. rose dramatically with the increase in tobacco prices

    C. was linked to swings in the price of cotton

    D. depended largely on importation of food supplies from Europe

    E. created inequality in colonial society because tobacco prices were severely depressed

24. Which of the following was a consequence of the Glorious Revolution?

    A. Virginia became a royal colony.

    B. Georgia was established as a colony.

    C. The Dominion of New England was dissolved.

    D. France declared war on England.

    E. James reestablished his control over Parliament

25. Under the terms of the Treaty of Greenville,

    A. the Miami Confederation gave up its lands in Ohio

    B. the British agreed to give up their control of the fur trade in the Northwest Territory

    C. the Creeks and the Cherokees agreed to move west of the Mississippi

    D. Spain gave up its control of Florida to the United States

    E. boundary disputes between Canada and the United States were resolved

GO ON TO THE NEXT PAGE

26. Henry Ford believed that most Americans could own their own automobile if

   A. car companies advertised intensively

   B. mass production lowered the per unit cost to make cars affordable

   C. national car dealerships established a network to connect cars to potential customers

   D. they could be persuaded to pay their debts by installments

   E. factory owners raised the wages of workers

27. The term "Gilded Age" refers to

   A. America's military power in the post-Civil War years

   B. a time of political corruption and robber barons

   C. improvement in food preparation in the late nineteenth century

   D. new discoveries of gold in the West

   E. none of the above

28. The creation of a segregated society in the South after the Civil War was the result of

   A. federal laws enacted by Congress during Reconstruction

   B. executive orders issued by President Andrew Johnson

   C. legislation enacted by the Southern states

   D. law suits filed by such groups as the Ku Klux Klan

   E. state court decisions after Reconstruction

29. President Hoover's main strategy in dealing with the Great Depression was to

   A. reduce the tariff

   B. cut the federal income tax

   C. create federal relief agencies to help people in need

   D. encourage private voluntary relief agencies to assist the unemployed

   E. none of the above

30. Which book is credited with creating the consumer protection movement?

   A. *Silent Spring*

   B. *The Crabgrass Frontier*

   C. *Man in a Gray Flannel Suit*

   D. *Unsafe at Any Speed*

   E. *The Population Bomb*

31. Which of the following statements about the election of 1876 is NOT true?

   A. Rutherford B. Hayes had a one vote margin in the Electoral College.

   B. Samuel Tilden won the popular vote by a clear majority.

   C. The election was ultimately decided by the House of Representatives.

   D. Democrats were in control of the South with the exception of South Carolina, Florida, and Louisiana.

   E. Congress created a special commission to resolve disputed votes in the South.

32. Washington's response to the Whiskey Rebellion showed that

   A. he was determined to enforce federal laws

   B. he wanted Americans to drink more

   C. he did not support Hamilton's economic program

   D. he encouraged farmers in western Pennsylvania to resist the excise tax

   E. he did not believe in the Bill of Rights

33. Indictment by a grand jury, protection against double jeopardy and self-incrimination are provided for in the Bill of Rights in the

   A. First Amendment

   B. Third Amendment

   C. Fifth Amendment

   D. Sixth Amendment

   E. Eighth Amendment

34. Which of the following was the most important event of 1969?

   A. Student demonstrators were killed at Kent State University.

   B. Martin Luther King, Jr. was assassinated in Memphis, Tennessee.

   C. American astronauts landed on the moon.

   D. The Tet Offensive was launched in South Vietnam.

   E. The Watergate break-in took place in Washington, D.C.

35. The Civil War amendments to the Constitution provided for all of the following EXCEPT

   A. the abolition of slavery

   B. the extension of the right to vote to African Americans

   C. the granting of citizenship to African Americans

   D. that all persons were entitled to the equal protection under the law

   E. the readmission of the states of the Confederacy to the Union

36. Andrew Johnson escaped removal from the presidency

   A. as a result of public anger at the methods used to try to force him out of office

   B. because the Senate failed to convict him

   C. when the Supreme Court declared the impeachment charges were unconstitutional

   D. when neither house in Congress could muster a majority vote

   E. none of the above

GO ON TO THE NEXT PAGE

37. In 1867 Secretary of State William H. Seward engineered the purchase of Alaska from Russia

    A. partly in appreciation of Russian support for the Union in the Civil War

    B. because of potential wealth from gold deposits there

    C. as a strategic line of defense for American interests in the Pacific

    D. to end Russian persecution of native peoples there

    E. as a region for exiling southern diehards

38. The first suburbs developed in the late nineteenth century because of

    A. the fear of the rising urban crime rate

    B. the rising cost of real estate in the central city

    C. a housing shortage due to the influx of immigrants

    D. the desire of middle class residents to live in the "country"

    E. the development of mass transit made longer commutes possible

39. Dissatisfied progressives within the Republican party prior to 1912 were known as

    A. Insurgents

    B. Radicals

    C. Muckrakers

    D. Wobblies

    E. none of the above

40. Who of the following was associated with the Harlem Renaissance?

    A. Louis Armstrong

    B. Claude McKay

    C. W. E. B. DuBois

    D. Malcom X

    E. Booker T. Washington

41. Plantation owners might encourage slaves to marry because

    A. married slaves were less likely to runaway

    B. married slaves made better household servants

    C. married slaves were worth more as a couple

    D. slaves marriages were encouraged in many Southern states

    E. the Anglican Church supported slave marriages

42. All of the following statements accurately reflect American economic policy during the 1920s EXCEPT

    A. Tax policy benefited wealthy Americans.

    B. Tariff rates were increased to protect American industry.

    C. Regulatory enforcement, including anti-trust laws, was lax.

    D. Government spending was cut to balance the budget.

    E. Agriculture prospered with federal price supports.

43. A major factor in the eventual victory of Britain over France in their wars in North America was

    A. French abandonment of strategic outposts

    B. British commitment to permanent settlement

    C. the failure of the French to win Indian alliances

    D. British willingness to abandon outposts that could not be defended

    E. British control over Atlantic sea routes

44. The major purpose of the Gadsden Purchase was to

    A. prevent an invasion by Mexico in an attempt to recover its lost territory

    B. expand slave territory into southern Arizona

    C. provide a southern route for a proposed transcontinental railroad

    D. buy Baja California and secure total control of the Colorado River

    E. none of the above

45. The most important result of Bacon's Rebellion was that

    A. wealthy planters in the Tidewater lost political power

    B. small farmers in Virginia were given the right to vote

    C. Native Americans were driven out of the Southern colonies

    D. planters turned to slaves as the chief source of cheap labor

    E. indentured servants got the length of their labor contracts reduced

46. The Venezuelan crisis of 1895 involved the United States in a dispute with

    A. France

    B. Brazil

    C. Germany

    D. Great Britain

    E. Portugal

47. All of the following are true about American labor in the late nineteenth century EXCEPT

    A. The most successful unions focused on higher wages and the eight hour day.

    B. No attempt was made to organize unskilled workers.

    C. Strikes were often put down by local police, state militia, and federal troops.

    D. Federal laws, such as the Sherman Antitrust Act, were used against unions.

    E. Unions supported legislation to restrict immigration fearing competition for jobs.

48. Which of the following does NOT support the idea that civil liberties is the first casualty of war?

    A. Executive Order 9066

    B. Espionage and Sedition Acts

    C. Lincoln's policy toward habeas corpus

    D. Creel Committee

    E. *Ex Parte Milligan*

GO ON TO THE NEXT PAGE

49. Which of the following statements best reflects a valid assessment of the Kennedy administration?

   A. Kennedy was considerably more successful in the foreign policy arena than handling domestic issues.

   B. The administration was responsible for most of the accomplishments of the civil rights movement in the 1960s.

   C. Kennedy strengthened the presidency by his ability to get legislation through Congress.

   D. Kennedy created problems for his administration by his legislative and diplomatic inexperience.

   E. Most of the accomplishments of the Kennedy administration are due solely to the advisers he had around him.

50. Hamilton's economic program included all of the following EXCEPT

   A. an excise tax

   B. federal assumption of state debt

   C. protective tariffs

   D. a national bank

   E. creation of the Treasury Department

51. Minstrel shows, which became popular before the Civil War,

   A. poked fun at all minority groups in the country, particularly Irish immigrants

   B. were put on by African Americans before both black and white audiences

   C. created a stereotype of African Americans, providing a racial justification for slavery

   D. were banned in the South because they presented a positive portrait of African-American life outside of slavery

   E. declined in popularity once slavery was abolished

52. The Alien and Sedition Acts of 1798 were

   A. never enforced by federal marshals

   B. supported by most Americans

   C. eventually declared unconstitutional by the Supreme Court

   D. intended by the Federalists to weaken Jefferson's Republican party

   E. none of the above

53. Which of the following statements about the population the New England colonies in the seventeenth century is true?

   A. Immigration was not a factor in population growth.

   B. The birthrate was low because women were in short supply.

   C. It was rare for children to know their grandparents.

   D. Settlers typically came in family groups.

   E. Germans made up a significant percentage of the population.

54. All of the following were ways in which England tried to strengthen the Navigation Acts EXCEPT

    A. Governors took an oath to enforce the laws.

    B. English customs officials were sent to the colonies to inspect ships for smuggled goods.

    C. The Board of Trade and Plantations was created.

    D. Admiralty courts with judges appointed by the crown tried smuggling cases.

    E. Fewer goods were included in the enumerated articles.

55. American foreign policy during the 1920s

    A. focused on the growing threat from Japan and Germany

    B. was strictly isolationist after the failure to ratify the Treaty of Versailles

    C. was committed to controlling the spread of Communist influence around the world

    D. was actively involved with Europe and Asia on such issues as disarmament and reparations

    E. concentrated on maintaining American supremacy in the Western Hemisphere

56. Modern investigations have revealed that the explosion and sinking of the U.S.S. *Maine* in Havana Harbor was caused by

    A. a Spanish mine planted on the outside of the ship

    B. a device placed on the ship by Cuban revolutionaries

    C. the age and decrepit state of the battleship

    D. an accident inside the ship

    E. Spanish militants eager for a war with the United States

57. The Populists committed political suicide in 1896 when they

    A. focused on the adoption of the gold standard as their main goal

    B. concentrated on coinage of silver money as a way to solve their economic problems

    C. supported William McKinley for president

    D. rejected the advice of William Jennings Bryan to advocate silver coinage

    E. none of the above

58. Despite Woodrow Wilson's record of liberal accomplishment, his "blind spot" was his endorsement of

    A. segregation of federal employees

    B. harassment of socialists during World War I

    C. antisemitism among the upper class

    D. British colonialism in Africa

    E. none of the above

GO ON TO THE NEXT PAGE

59. President Nixon's New Federalism was intended to

A. create a balance between the responsibilities of the federal government and the states

B. limit the power of Washington, and shift power to the states

C. make sure the states enforced all federal environmental laws

D. increase the power of the president at the expense of the Congress

E. give Congress additional authority over setting national goals in education

60. The massive migration of Irish to the United States was prompted by the

A. civil war in Ireland

B. Protestant persecution of Irish Catholics

C. Famine in Ireland when the potato crop failed

D. Desire of Irishmen to fight in the war against Mexico

E. British declaration of war against Ireland in 1845

61. The term "pet banks" referred to

A. foreign banks chosen by Andrew Jackson to receive deposits of federal money

B. state banks receiving preferential treatment from the Bank of the United States

C. state banks chosen by Jackson to receive deposits of federal money

D. branches of the Bank of the United States in states hostile to Jackson

E. state banks established in states hostile to Jackson

62. The British response to the American claim of "no taxation without representation" was

A. to allow the colonial legislatures to vote on taxes approved by Parliament

B. to give authority to the Continental Congress to tax the colonies

C. to claim that Parliament recognized colonial concerns by virtual representation

D. to agree not to impose internal taxes in the future

E. to use the revenue generated by internal taxes to support schools in the colonies

63. Which of the following Supreme Court decisions strengthened the constitutional protection against self-incrimination?

A. *Gideon v. Wainwright*

B. *Board of Regents v. Bakke*

C. *Miranda v. Arizona*

D. *Mapp v. Ohio*

E. *Shaw v. Reno*

64. The mechanical reaper dramatically affected American agriculture by

    A. creating more jobs for farmers

    B. mechanizing cotton production in the South

    C. encouraging farmers to grow more corn

    D. saving time and labor in wheat harvesting

    E. helping farmers plow prairie lands

65. In the 1877 case of *Munn v. Illinois*, the Supreme Court stated

    A. railroad regulation by states was constitutional

    B. state railroad regulation was unconstitutional

    C. railroad rate regulation should be left to federal courts

    D. only Congress could regulate railroads

    E. railroads had the right to set their own rates regardless of destination

66. The difficulty in managing an empire was clearly demonstrated after the Spanish-American War by

    A. the cost of administering colonies in the Caribbean and the Pacific

    B. the need to intervene militarily in Central America frequently

    C. the strong domestic opposition the U.S. colonial policy

    D. the protracted fighting to put down the Philippine Insurrection

    E. the opposition of the European powers to growing U.S. influence

67. All of the following were arguments used to support restrictions on immigration in the late nineteenth and early twentieth century EXCEPT

    A. Immigrants were radicals and would subvert the country

    B. Because they worked for less, immigrants took jobs away from Americans

    C. Immigrants refused to abandon their old world culture, and would not assimilate

    D. Immigrants were poor and became a drain on the resources of the society

    E. Most immigrants were women of questionable character and morality

68. Under the Neutrality Act of 1939, the United States

    A. prohibited Americans from traveling on ships of countries at war

    B. could not make loans or extend credit to belligerents

    C. could not sell armaments to either side in a civil war

    D. could sell military equipment to belligerents on a cash-and-carry basis

    E. prohibited Germany from trading with countries in the Western Hemisphere

GO ON TO THE NEXT PAGE

69. Which of the following statements about the integration of public schools is true?

   A. Integration was accomplished quicker in the North than in the South.

   B. The timetable for integration was spelled out in *Brown v. Board of Education.*

   C. Busing to achieve integration in the North was a controversial program.

   D. The Supreme Court did not support busing to achieve integration.

   E. The *Brown* decision only applied to schools in Kansas.

70. The Missouri Compromise of 1820

   A. was the brainchild of Henry Clay

   B. admitted Missouri to the Union as a slave state

   C. admitted Maine to the Union as a free state

   D. drew a boundary line separating slave and free states

   E. all of the above

71. The Era of Good Feelings was

   A. the period after the War of 1812 when the Republican party dominated American politics

   B. the period after the end of Reconstruction when the animosity of the Civil War began to fade

   C. the period immediately after the French and Indian War when the Great Britain and the American colonies were on good terms

   D. the period after World War I and before the Depression when the country was prosperous

   E. the period just before and after the Mexican War when Americans were satisfied with the results of Manifest Destiny

72. Parliament repealed the Stamp Act and the Townshend duties because

   A. Parliament feared the colonies would revolt against the government

   B. the colonies agreed to create their own tax structure

   C. anticipated revenues proved lower than expected

   D. colonial boycotts harmed British business

   E. Edmund Burke argued that the colonists should tax themselves

73. The theory of nullification, which declared that the states could declare a federal law null and void, is found in

   A. Article IV of the Constitution

   B. the Federalist Papers

   C. the Kentucky and Virginia Resolutions

   D. the Tenth Amendment

   E. Jefferson's First Inaugural Address

74. Which of the following acronyms was associated with the Cold War?

   A. WIN

   B. ERA

   C. MAD

   D. CIO

   E. OPA

75. The presidential election of 1828 demonstrated that

   A. first-term presidents usually are reelected

   B. political parties could be strongly sectional in their political allegiance

   C. relaxation of state eligibility requirements for voting could produce a dramatic increase in the popular vote

   D. a "southern" president would rarely be elected

   E. supporters of the common people would have difficulty getting elected because of the electoral college structure

76. The main purpose of the Ku Klux Klan in the South during and after the Reconstruction era was to

   A. persecute African Americans

   B. established a stratified social structure in southern communities

   C. keep law and order in an era of political chaos

   D. prevent Republicans from holding state and local offices in the South

   E. all of the above

77. The 1903 Platt Amendment, written by the United States for inclusion in the Cuban Constitution

   A. required Cuba to have a democratic government

   B. joined Cuba and the United States in a pledge of eternal friendship

   C. awarded the United States trading advantages with Cuba

   D. granted the United States the right to intervene in Cuban domestic affairs

   E. all of the above

78. Albert Fall, secretary of the interior under President Harding

   A. strongly favored conservation of natural resources

   B. was the first cabinet-level officer to go to prison

   C. believed Indians should be assimilated into the dominant society

   D. was one of the few reliable cabinet officers appointed by Harding

   E. rejected bribes offered by prominent oil producers

79. Bruce Barton's book *The Man Nobody Knows*, a best-seller of the 1920s, claimed that the founder of modern business methods was

    A. Attila the Hun

    B. Jesus Christ

    C. Christopher Columbus

    D. Charlemagne

    E. George Washington

80. Early in his term, Richard Nixon faced stagflation which meant that

    A. stock prices were falling and interest rates were rising

    B. both inflation and unemployment were high

    C. the saving rate was low and job creation was high

    D. home prices were depressed but employment was high

    E. the budget deficit was growing while revenue increased

IF YOU FINISH BEFORE TIME IS CALLED, CHECK YOUR WORK ON THIS SECTION ONLY. DO NOT WORK ON ANY OTHER SECTION IN THE TEST.

Section II: Essay Questions

Part A

(Suggested writing time—45 minutes)

Directions: Write an essay based on your analysis of Documents A–I as well as your knowledge of the period covered by the question. It is important for you to include information on the topic not provided for by the documents.

1. During the period of the American Revolution and the early years of the Republic, political expediency rather than principle determined the fate of slavery as a national institution. Do you agree or disagree with this statement. Support your position.

Document A

Slavery in the States according the First Federal Census		
State	*Number of Slaves*	*Number of Slaveholding Families*
Connecticut	2,648	1,563
Delaware	8, 887	-
Georgia	29,264	-
Kentucky	12,430	-
Maine	0	-
Maryland	103,036	12,226
Massachusetts	0	-
New Hampshire	157	123
New Jersey	11,423	-
New York	21,193	7,796
North Carolina	100,783	14,973
Pennyslvania	3,707	1,858
Rhode Island	958	461
South Carolina	107,094	8,859
Vermont	0	-
Virgina	-	292,627

Source: Cenus of 1790; http//fisher.lib.virgina.edu/egi-local/cenusbin/census/cen.pl

Document B

Governor Randolf. [W]here is the part that has a tendency to the abolition of slavery?

Is it the clause which says, that "the migration or importation of such persons as any of the states now existing, shall think proper to admit, shall not be prohibited by congress prior to the year 1808?" This is an exception from the power regulating commerce, and the restriction is only to continue till 1808. Then congress can, by the exercise of that power, prevent future importations; but does it affect the existing state of slavery? Were it right to here mention what passed in convention on occasion, I might tell you that the southern states, even South Carolina herself, conceived this property to be secure by these words. I believe, whatever we may think here, that there was not a member of the Virginia delegation who had the smallest suspicion of the abolition of slavery.

Source: Debate on the Ratification of the Constitution at the Virginia Convention, June 21, 1788.

Document C

Be it enacted, and it is hereby enacted, by the representatives of the freeman of the commonwealth of Pennsylvania, in general assembly met, and by the authority of the same, that all persons, as well as Negroes and Mulattos as others, who shall be born within this state from and after the passing of this act, shall not be deemed and considered as servants for life, or slaves, and that all servitude for life, or slavery of children, in consequence of the slavery of their mothers, in the case of all children born within this state, from and after the passing of this act as aforesaid, shall be, and hereby is utterly taken away, extinguished, and for ever abolished.

Source: Pennsylvania Act for the Gradual Abolition of Slavery, March 1, 1780.

Document D

We will neither ourselves import, nor purchase any slave, or slaves imported by any person, after the first day of November next, either from the West Indies or from any other place.

Source: Virginia Non-Importation Agreement, August 1, 1774.

Document E

Resolved, That after the year 1800 of the Christian era, there shall be neither slavery nor involuntary servitude in any of the states described in the resolve of Congress of the 23rd day of April, 1784 [Report of the Government for the Western Territory], otherwise than in punishment for crimes whereof the party shall have been personally guilty. And that this regulation shall be an article of compact, and remain a fundamental principle of the constitutions between the thirteen original states, and each of the states described in said resolve of Congress of the 23rd day of April, 1784; . . . Provided always, that upon the escape of any person into any of the states described in the said resolve of Congress of the 23rd day of April, 1784, from who labor or service is lawfully claimed in any one of the thirteen original states, such fugitive many be lawfully reclaimed and carried back to the person claiming his labor or service . . . .

Source; Resolution to the Committee of the Congress re Exclusion of Involuntary Servitude in the States Described in the Resolve to Congress of the 23rd day of April, 1784.

Document F

Under the present confederation, the States may admit the importation of slaves as long as they please; but by this article, after the year 1808, the Congress will have power to prohibit such importation, notwithstanding the disposition of any State to the contrary. I consider this as laying the foundation for banishing slavery out of this country; and though the period is more distant than I could wish, yet it will produce the same kind, gradual change which was pursued in Pennsylvania. . . . It was all that could be obtained.

I am sorry it was no more; but from this I think there is reason to hope that yet a few years, and it will be prohibited altogether.

Source: Statement by James Wilson at the Pennyslvania Convention to Ratify the Constitution, December 3, 1787.

Document G

I can only say that there is not a man living who wishes more sincerely than I do, to see a plan adopted for the abolition of it [slavery], but there is only one proper and effectual mode by which it can be accomplished, that that is by Legislative authority . . . But when slaves who are happy and contented with their present masters, are tampered with and seduced to leave them; when masters are taken unawares by these practices; when a conduct of this sort begets discontent on one side and resentment on the other . . . it introduces more evil than it can cure.

Source: Letter from George Washington to Robert Morris, April 12, 1786.

GO ON TO THE NEXT PAGE

Document H

Without enquiring into the practicability or the most proper means of establishing a Settlement of freed blacks on the Coast of Africa, it may be remarked as one motive to the benevolent experiment that if such as asylum was provided, it might prove a great encouragement to manumission in the Southern parts of the U.S. and even afford the best hope yet presented of putting an end to the slavery in which not less that 600,000 unhappy negroes are now involved.

Source: James Madison, Memorandum on a Colony in Africa for Manumitted Slaves, October 20, 1789.

Document I

It ought to be considered as a great point gained in favor of humanity, that a period of twenty years may terminate forever, within these States, a traffic which has so long and so loudly upbraided the barbarism of modern policy; that within that period, it will receive a considerable discouragement from the federal government, and may be totally abolished, by a concurrence of the few States which continue the unnatural traffic, in the prohibitory example which has been given by so great a majority of the Union.

Happy would it be for the unfortunate Africans, if an equal prospect lay before them of being redeemed from the oppressions of their European brethren!

Source: James Madison, The Federalist Papers, No. 42, January 22, 1788.

Part B

(Suggested writing time—35 minutes, including a 5-minute planing period)

Directions: Choose ONE question from this part. Cite relevant historical evidence in support of your generalizations and present your arguments clearly and logically.

---

2. Discuss the impact of THREE of the following on American foreign policy at the end of the 18th century:

   Citizen Genet

   Jay's Treaty

   Pickney's Treaty

   Washington's Farewell Address

3. After his visit to the United States in 1831-1832, the Frenchmen Alexis de Tocqueville wrote that there was ". . . no country in the whole world in which the Christian religion retains a greater influence over the souls of men than in America."

   Assess the validity of this statement.

Part C

(Suggested writing time—35 minutes, including a 5-minute planing period)

Directions: Choose ONE question from this part. Cite relevant historical evidence in support of your generalizations and present your arguments clearly and logically.

4. Compare Teddy Roosevelt's New Nationalism and Wilson's New Freedom. Did Wilson effectively implement the New Freedom as president?

5. 1954, 1965, 1968, and 1970 were critical turning points in American involvement in South East Asia. Explain why THREE of these years were significant.

IF YOU FINISH BEFORE TIME IS CALLED, CHECK YOUR WORK ON THIS SECTION ONLY. DO NOT WORK ON ANY OTHER SECTION IN THE TEST.

Answer Key for Practice Test 4

Section I: Multiple-Choice Questions

1. B		30. D	
2. A		31. C	
3. B		32. A	
4. C		33. C	
5. B		34. C	
6. E		35. E	
7. B		36. B	
8. B		37. A	
9. C		38. E	
10. B		39. A	
11. A		40. B	
12. D		41. A	
13. C		42. E	
14. A		43. B	
15. D		44. C	
16. A		45. D	
17. D		46. D	
18. C		47. B	
19. A		48. D	
20. A		49. A	
21. A		50. E	
22. D		51. C	
23. E		52. D	
24. C		53. D	
25. A		54. E	
26. B		55. D	
27. B		56. D	
28. C		57. B	
29. D		58. A	

59. B	**70.** E
60. C	**71.** A
61. C	**72.** D
62. C	**73.** C
63. C	**74.** C
64. D	**75.** C
65. B	**76.** A
66. A	**77.** D
67. E	**78.** B
68. D	**79.** B
69. C	**80.** B

Section II: Essay Questions

Student essays and analysis appear beginning on page 274.

Answers and Explanations for Practice Test 4

Section I: Multiple-Choice Questions

1. B. Stalin demanded a second front, i.e, an invasion of Western Europe, almost as soon as Germany attacked the Soviet Union in June 1941. The repeated postponements of the cross-Channel invasion until June 1944 did strain the wartime alliance.

2. A. Desperate for sailors to man their warships during the Napoleonic Wars, British vessels stopped American ships on the pretext of searching for British deserters, and often took American sailors who allegedly fit that description.

3. B. The mother country theoretically benefited from being the exclusive supplier of manufactured goods to its colonies. Colonists, however, resented high prices, and resorted to smuggling. Spain, England, and France endorsed mercantilism and passed laws to enforce the policy, but colonial officials often accepted bribes to ignore the enforcement.

4. C. This is from President Eisenhower's 1961 Farewell Address to the nation in which he warned about the dangers of the "military-industrial complex."

5. B. The Supreme Court ruled on a series of cases involving the Civil Rights Act of 1875 and found that the federal government had no jurisdiction to protect social rights as opposed to civil rights.

6. E. The Tenth Amendment was included to counterbalance the strong federal government established under the Constitution, and provides that powers not delegated to the United States or denied to the states, are reserved to the states or the people.

7. **B.** Since traffic down the Mississippi River was controlled by Spain at the time, free navigation was not in the power of Great Britain to grant to the United States.

8. **B.** In the midst of a major revolution, Mexico had tense relations with the United States, especially concerning the U.S. occupation of Vera Cruz. Germany's proposal, revealed by the British to the United States, played a major part in Wilson's decision to declare war on Germany.

9. **C.** Intended as a means of assimilating Native Americans into the dominant society by allotting farms to individual families, the Dawes Act negatively affected tribes by failing to provide for their posterity, subverting their cultural heritage, and opening tribal land to white speculators and settlers.

10. **B.** The creation of land-grant colleges, including six black colleges in the South, by the Morrill Act of 1862 clearly did expand education. It was also during this period that women's colleges—Vassar (1861) and Smith (1871)—were founded.

11. **A.** After the Confederates fired on Fort Sumter on April 12, 1861, Lincoln proclaimed a state of insurrection. The Upper South, including Virginia, North Carolina, Arkansas, and Tennessee, then joined the Confederacy.

12. **D.** Kennedy used the allegation that the Soviet Union had more intercontinental ballistic missiles than the United States to bolster his image as a cold warrior.

13. **C.** The War of the Spanish Succession (1702–1713), fought between England and France over English concerns that Louis XIV would control Spain through his half-French grandson Philip V, was fought during the reign of Queen Anne.

14. **A.** Between 1629 and 1635, more than 20,000 Puritans, including entire families, left England for the Massachusetts Bay Colony.

15. **D.** At its height the French empire controlled the Mississippi Valley, the Great Lakes, and eastern Canada. Great Britain saw this as an effort to curtail its own expansion in North America.

16. **A.** Republicans after the Civil War attempted to blame the Democratic party for starting it. Although the charge was untrue, Republicans managed to create an image that linked Democrats to the Confederacy. Another slogan the Republicans used was "Vote as you shot."

17. **D.** Margaret Sanger was the leader of the movement to win acceptance for birth control in the early 20th century.

18. **C.** Democrats favored a low tariff to enable working-class consumers to afford imported products. The progressive income tax made up for low tariffs. Since the 1930s, however, the growth of government programs and bureaucracy has made the income tax a source of controversy among Americans who seek reduced government spending and tax relief.

19. **A.** The Marshall Plan was a massive program of economic aid to rebuild the economies of Western Europe after World War II. The U.S. was prepared to help the Soviet Union and the countries under its control in Eastern Europe, but the aid was refused.

20. **A.** Population has increased significantly in California, Arizona, Nevada, Texas, and Florida, whereas it has declined or failed to grow in the Upper Midwest and New England states.

21. **A.** Given the yearly cost in tribute payments, insults to the American flag, and no indication that such treatment would not continue, President Jefferson supported action against the Barbary States.

22. **D.** The statement was made by Patrick Henry at the Virginia Convention (1788) to ratify the Constitution and sums up key Antifederalist concerns.

23. **E.** A plunge in tobacco prices began in 1660 and lasted a half century. Planters made up for their losses through rents, lending money, and raising cattle for export. Poor whites suffered poverty and exploitation.

24. **C.** The Dominion of New England included New York, New Jersey, and various New England colonies. Its creation in 1686 by James II reflected his desire to exercise greater control over the colonies. When the king was deposed by the Glorious Revolution in 1688 that colonies that had been part of the Dominion received separate charters.

25. **A.** The Treaty of Greenville (1795) ended for about twenty years the conflict over land in the Ohio Valley between American settlers and Native Americans.

26. **B.** The more cars Ford built, the lower the per-unit cost, and Ford passed this savings on to consumers by charging lower prices for his vehicles.

27. **B.** Taken from the title of a novel written by Mark Twain and Charles Dudley Warner, the "Gilded Age" denoted an era of government corruption centering on the administration of President Ulysses S. Grant. Also during this time, lack of business regulation enabled aggressive entrepreneurs to gain wealth through unethical and controversial tactics such as stock manipulation and monopolies.

28. **C.** While certainly advanced by the Supreme Court decisions in the *Civil Rights Cases* (1883) and *Plessy v. Ferguson* (1896), segregation was the result of laws passed by the state legislatures in the South to separate the blacks and whites in everything from schools to public places. The legislation is collectively known as Jim Crow laws.

29. **D.** Hoover created the President's Emergency Committee for Employment (PECE) to act as a clearing house for local volunteer agencies offering suggestions for employment. The PECE did little to ease the unemployment crisis.

30. **D.** Ralph Nader's *Unsafe at Any Speed* (1965) was specifically an attack on the safety of the Chevrolet Corvair, and generally on the lack of concern of the automobile industry with safety, reliability, and fuel economy.

31. **C.** The electoral commission set up by Congress awarded the electoral votes of Louisiana, Florida, and South Carolina to Hayes. Since that gave him a majority in the Electoral College (185/184), there was not constitutional reason for the election to go to the House.

32. **A.** When farmers in western Pennsylvania refused to pay the excise tax on whiskey and rioted against tax officials in July 1794, Washington ordered the militias of several states to move against the rebels.

33. **C.** You should be familiar with the idea of "taking the Fifth," which is the constitutional protection against self-incrimination.

34. C. The moon landing is the only event among the possible choices that took place in 1969. The King assassination and Tet Offensive occurred in 1968, while the shootings at Kent State were in 1970 and Watergate happened in 1972.

35. E. The Civil War amendments—Thirteenth (1865), Fourteenth (1868), and Fifteenth (1870)—dealt with the status of newly freed slaves. Although the amendments played a role in the readmission process, they did not provide for readmission.

36. B. Conviction required a two-thirds vote of the Senate. The Senate was one vote short of conviction.

37. A. During the Civil War, Russia demonstrated friendship towards the Union, sent Russian ships on a good-will mission to the United States, and praised the Emancipation Proclamation which followed on Tsar Alexander II's freeing of the serfs.

38. E. Improvements in transportation, ranging from steam locomotives to electric subway systems, allowed middle class and even the poor to live miles from work.

39. A. The Insurgents included Republicans from midwestern states who favored progressive legislation regarding federal expenditures, the labor movement, and reform of the political process.

40. B. The Harlem Renaissance was a flowering of African-American literature and art during the 1920s. If you don't know that Claude McKay was one of the leading black poets of the time, you should get the right answer through the process of elimination.

41. A. The ever-present threat of selling a slave's wife or children was an effective way of maintaining control over slaves.

42. E. Agriculture was the one sector of the economy that did not share in the prosperity of the 1920s. The conservative philosophy of Secretary of the Treasury Andrew Mellon left no room for federal aid to American farmers.

43. B. Between 1689 and 1763, four major wars were fought between Britain and France. During that time British settlement and population increased enormously, whereas France never was able to attract French settlers in significant numbers to Canada.

44. C. The population in California, grown to over 200,000 in just two years as a consequence of the Gold Rush, wanted a fast and efficient connection to the east. The southern route would bypass the difficulty of crossing the Sierra Nevada Range.

45. D. Since former indentured servants played a prominent role in the rebellion, Tidewater planters decided that slave labor would prove more reliable and less dangerous.

46. D. When Great Britain and Venezuela disputed the boundary between Venezuela and British Guiana, the United States held the view that the Monroe Doctrine empowered it to deal with European nations. Great Britain accepted the principle; a few years later an international tribunal settled the dispute.

47. B. The Knights of Labor reached out to all workers, including unskilled, African Americans, and women.

48. D. The Creel Committee, also known as the Committee on Public Information, certainly contributed to the anti-German hysteria in the United States during World War I but did not in fact reflect the limitations on civil liberties the other choices did.

49. A. Kennedy found it difficult to get his domestic program through Congress, but, following the Bay of Pigs invasion, had a number of foreign policy accomplishments, including handling the Cuban missile crisis and the Nuclear Test Ban Treaty.

50. E. Hamilton actually served as George Washington's secretary of the treasury. The position had originally been called the Superintendent of Finances under the Continental Congress.

51. C. Minstrel shows had white performers in black face, who portrayed African Americans as lazy and stupid.

52. D. The Federalist-dominated Congress enacted laws, which included extending the naturalization period for citizenship to fourteen years and making criticism of the federal government a libelous offense, aimed at Republican critics of the Adams administration.

53. D. In contrast to Virginia where the early colonists were single men, New England was settled by family groups. From the beginning, the Pilgrims and Puritans came with their wives and children.

54. E. Between 1660 and 1704, the goods designated as enumerated articles by the British actually expanded to include rice, pitch, tar, turpentine, and masts.

55. D. The Senate's rejection of the Treaty of Versailles did not signal an American retreat into isolationism. The United States was actively involved in reaching arms control agreements with Japan and other major powers as well as in the attempt to find a solution to the twin problems of war debts and reparations.

56. D. The explosion that sank the *Maine* occurred within the ship. Stories of Cuban revolutionaries and Spanish militants are conjectural.

57. B. The Populist party abandoned a broad platform of reform objectives to support Bryan's position on remonetizing silver. They nominated Democrat Bryan as their own candidate; when Bryan lost to McKinley, the Populists were left without a platform, candidate, or silver.

58. A. Originally from Virginia, Wilson accepted segregation in American society.

59. B. The key method of shifting power to the states was revenue sharing, which provided grants to state and local government without federal strings attached.

60. C. Irish peasants relied on the potato crop as a basic supply of food. They raised wheat to pay for the rent. When a blight destroyed the crop in a succession of years, the Irish could eat the wheat and lose their land, or starve in order to stay on it. A million Irish people starved to death; a million emigrated.

61. C. Jackson's hatred of the Bank of the United States, and its use by his enemies as an election issue in 1832, resulted in his veto of the Bank's charter renewal. He then bled the Bank of its deposits by placing federal money in state-chartered banks and making withdrawals of operating funds from the Bank of the United States.

62. C. The colonists considered and rejected the idea that the colonial legislatures could approve internal taxes, and the Continental Congress was not even created. The British concept of virtual representation pointed out that there were citizens in Great Britain that did not have the right to vote for members of Parliament, but that Parliament did represent their interests as well.

63. C. In *Miranda v. Arizona* the Supreme Court held that a person who is arrested must be informed by the police of his constitutional right to remain silent and the consequences of not remaining silent. The decision provided for the famous Miranda warning.

64. D. Cyrus McCormick's mechanical reaper reduced the number of men needed for wheat harvests from fifty in a work crew to two, creating a surprlus labor force that would find employment in factory work.

65. B. The Supreme Court argued that since railroads crossed state lines, states could not regulate interstate commerce.

66. A. The Spanish-American War in its action phase lasted about three months, ended in less than a year, and won recognition of the United States as a world power. The U.S. also acquired the Philippines, Guam, and Puerto Rico from Spain.

67. E. Although the movement to restrict immigration did raise the issue of white slavery, the fact is that most immigrants were not women. The other claims listed in the choices were key arguments raised by groups such as the Immigration Restriction League.

68. D. The Neutrality Act of 1939 reflected the changing attitudes toward events in Europe after the outbreak of the war in September 1939. The cash-and-carry provisions were intended to assist Great Britain. The ban on travel and loans and the extension of the arms embargo to civil wars were elements of the neutrality legislation passed between 1935 and 1937.

69. C. Although the Supreme Court called for integration under the *Brown* decision "with all deliberate speed," it never provided a timetable or examined methods of achieving its goal. When the question of ending segregation based on housing patterns rose in the Northern states, busing students from one school to another was a logical but highly disruptive approach.

70. E. The compromise set a precedent in the admission of states to the Union, one free balanced by one slave state, that lasted until 1850.

71. A. The Era of Good Feelings began with the defeat of the Federalists in the election of 1816 that begin a short-lived period of the Republican party when national sentiment seemed strong. Nationalism was expressed in Henry Clay's American system and the decisions of the Supreme Court under John Marshall that strengthened the power of the federal government.

72. D. In retaliation against the Stamp Act and Townshend duties, colonists successfully organized a boycott that compelled British merchants to urge Parliament to revoke the tax laws.

73. C. In 1798, both the Kentucky and Virginia legislatures passed resolutions nullifying the Alien and Sedition Acts that had been passed by the Federalist controlled Congress. They based action on the claim that when a law broke the compact made between the states and the federal government that law could be declared null and void.

74. C. MAD is an acronym for mutually assured destruction, a concept of nuclear deterrence during the Cold War. It was based on the premise that neither the United States nor the Soviet Union would use nuclear weapons because each could destroy the other many times over.

75. C. In the 1820s, state constitutions were amended to remove property requirements for voters. As a result, the 1828 popular vote was triple that of 1824.

76. A. The KKK intimidated, threatened, and committed violence against blacks in an effort to make them a permanently subservient population.

77. D. The Platt Amendment denied full independence to Cuba, prewar promises notwithstanding. The United States retained the right to intervene in Cuban domestic issues, including political unrest or policies deemed contrary to U.S. interests.

78. B. Fall was convicted of taking a bribe in what became known as the Teapot Dome scandal.

79. B. Barton said that Jesus "sold" the Christian faith in a manner that strongly resembled the success of advertising agencies to convince consumers to buy products.

80. B. The term "stagflation" was a combination of the idea of a stagnant economy, indicated by rising unemployment rates, and inflation or rapidly rising prices. It was an unusual economic situation that the Nixon administration found difficult to deal with.

Section II: Essay Questions

Part A

Student DBQ Essay

Many of the founding fathers—Southerners like Madison, Jefferson, and Washington included—were opposed to slavery on moral grounds. Despite the notions of freedom and equality that the American Revolution emphasized, the new country accepted slavery, even if somewhat reluctantly, because of the political realities of the time.

While the leaders of Virginia agreed not to import or purchase slaves from the West Indies or Africa (Document D), the 1774 Non-Importation Agreement was intended as a blow against British economic interests not an attack against slavery. In evaluating the attitude toward slavery at this time, it is more important to point out that the Declaration of Independence as originally drafted by Thomas Jefferson included an attack against King George III for spreading slavery to the Western Hemisphere. This language was dropped from the Declaration of Independence as adopted by the Continental Congress because of the opposition of Georgia and South Carolina. Although Blacks were allowed to serve in the Continental Army, this was permitted only after the British promised freedom to slaves who joined the Loyalist cause. When the states had the opportunity to take action on slavery, only Vermont abolished slavery completely; Pennsylvania's 1780 law, although clearly a positive step, was a half measure (Document C).

After the revolution, there is ample evidence that both the leaders of the new nation and Congress wanted to do something about slavery. George Washington personally wanted the abolition of the slavery, but felt this could only be accomplished through legislative action (Document G). Madison, apparently, put less faith in Congress doing something than in returning freed slaves to Africa. He suggests that the establishment of an African colony would encourage slave-owners to free their slaves.

The resolution before Congress in 1784 that would have prohibited slavery in the western lands (Document E) was eventually incorporated into the Northwest Ordinance of 1787. While limiting the spread of slavery was one thing, the drafting of the Constitution and the debates over ratification showed that doing more was politically impossible.

Even though slavery per se is not mentioned in the Constitution, the issue was central to the debate. The so-called Three-Fifths Compromise counted slaves as three-fifths of a person for purposes of determining representation in the Congress. Congress was prohibited from making any law against the slave trade until 1808, and a provision was included for the return of runaway slaves. That the slave trade was allowed to continue was a controversial point. Opponents of slavery like James Wilson of Pennsylvania and Madison of Virginia tried to put the best face on the provision by arguing that it might eventually lead to the abolition of slavery; they assumed that Congress would end the importation of slaves in 1808. Governor Randolph, on the other hand, tried to persuade the delegates to the Virginia ratifying convention that no one believed the limitation on the slave trade to be a threat to slavery as an institution (Document B). The most telling point, however, was made by Wilson. He recognizes that the language was a necessary compromise. "It was all that could be obtained." (Document F) The slaveholding states, probably Georgia and South Carolina, would not have gone along with immediate end to the slave trade. Their opposition would have been enough to scuttle the Constitutional Convention. Political expediency ruled.

Reader's Comments

This essay provides an excellent model of how to balance a content narrative with the documentation needed to support it. The position taken by the student is clearly stated at the beginning and end of the essay. Nowhere in the essay does the student succumb to the temptation of using the documents as a "laundry list"; the student uses the documents, not the other way around. Note also that the student quotes only minimally from the documents, spending the writing time to better advantage by placing the documents in support of the narrative. Judicious selection of documents helped make a strong argument for the essay's thesis. Considerable "outside" information makes the essay stronger and its tone convincingly authoritative.

Possible student score: 9

Part B

Question 2 Student Essay

Jay's Treaty (1795), Pickney's Treaty (1795), and Washington's Farewell Address (1796) pertain to the relations between the United States and the major European powers, particularly Great Britain, France, and Spain. While the treaties dealt with specific foreign policy questions, the Farewell Address attempted to outline where the long term interests of the new nation lay in the world arena.

Despite the terms of the Treaty of Paris, British troops continued to be stationed in the Northwest Territory. To this longstanding point of contention, two new issues surfaced in the wake of the war between Great Britain and France: British seizure of American ships trading with French colonies in the Caribbean and the impressment of American sailors on the pretext that they were in fact British citizens. While the British were concerned that the United States would side with France in the European war, this possibility did not make Britain willing resolve all the problems between the two countries. Through Jay's Treaty, named after Chief Justice John Jay who negotiated the agreement, the British finally agreed to withdraw its troops from American soil (by 1796) and granted the United States limited rights to trade with the British West Indies. The British refused to budge on the definition of neutral rights or end impressment. Although there was considerable opposition to the treaty (the Senate ratified it by one vote), the fact is that the treaty gave the United States undisputed control over the Northwest Territory.

The British evacuation combined with the Treaty of Greenville (1795), through which Native American tribes conceded lands north of the Ohio River, opened the region up to American settlement.

Pickney's Treaty also ended a dispute that had simmered since the end of the American Revolution. The Treaty of Paris recognized the Mississippi River as the western boundary of the United States and gave the United States the right to navigate the river to its source, i.e., the port of New Orleans. The Spanish, who controlled the Louisiana territory, repeatedly had challenged these American claims. The attempt to resolve the issues in 1785 through the Jay-Gardoqui Treaty ended in failure. In 1795, with Spain about to switch its allegiance from Great Britain to France, time was right for an agreement. Pickney's Treaty (formally known as the Treaty of San Lorenzo) established the thirty-first parallel as the boundary between Spanish Florida and the Southwest Territory of the United States, gave Americans full access to the Mississippi River, and allowed for the deposit of goods in New Orleans. The agreement was seen as a major diplomatic coup for the United States.

In a very real sense, Washington's Farewell Address set the tone of American foreign policy for the next century. Contrary to popular belief, Washington did not outline a strictly isolationist approach to world affairs. He warned Americans about the danger of "permanent alliances" and had in mind here the treaty with France signed during the American Revolution and still technically in effect. Washington had no problem with "temporary alliances" with other countries that might be necessary or beneficial to the United States in specific circumstances. More important than the distinction he drew between permanent and temporary alliances was his emphasis that the interests of the United States and the interests of European countries were fundamentally different. The idea that we see embodied in the Monroe Doctrine that the United States would not interfere in European affairs and that the European countries should not interfere in American (Western Hemisphere) affairs can be traced back to the Farewell Address.

Reader's Comments

This student clearly did the studying necessary to recall and understand the treaties and the Farewell Address and their meaning for American foreign policy. The essay flows effortlessly from one topic to the next, with attention to details that make the essay informative and authoritative. The concluding paragraph demonstrates a mature understanding of the significance of the Farewell Address. What is lacking here is a concluding statement bringing together the three choices in a comment about their impact on American foreign policy.

Possible student score: 8

Part B

Question 3 Student Essay

It is almost impossible to determine the validity of de Tocqueville's assertion about the religiosity of the American people. His statement was an impression based on limited observation; he did not conduct a scientific poll of Americans' religious beliefs; he did not do a comprehensive study of the number of Christian denominations in the country, and the level of church attendance in each or the degree to which members financially supported churches. What we can say is that de Tocqueville was writing at a time when the country was experiencing the tail end of the religious revival known as the Second Great Awakening.

The Second Great Awakening began along the frontier in the late 18th century, and then moved to the east by the 1830s. Among the most fertile areas for camp meetings and revivals organized by preachers like Charles Finney was western New York State. His emotional brand of Christianity that emphasized the individual road to salvation found considerable support in a part of the country that was undergoing significant social and economic change with the beginnings of the Industrial Revolution. There were so many "fire and brimstone" sermons given in western New York that the region became known as the "burned over district."

The Second Great Awakening contributed to the growth of evangelical Christian denominations, particularly the Methodists and Baptists, in the decades before the Civil War. New religious groups also emerged. The Unitarians, for example, emphasized the "head" over the "heart," i.e., the importance of reason versus emotion in religion. The "burned over districts" also supplied supporters of small sects such as the Shakers, and was the birthplace of the Church of Jesus Christ of the Latter Day Saints, better known as the Mormons. The Mormons were founded by Joseph Smith in Palmyra, New York in 1830. They migrated to Ohio and then to Illinois, where violence and persecution because of their religious beliefs forced them to trek west and establish a settlement near the Great Salt Lake in Utah in 1847.

Reader's Comments

This essay has a very strong introduction that begins a convincing argument placing de Tocqueville's statement in the context of its time, the period of the so-called Second Great Awakening. The student wisely stays clear of de Tocqueville the observer, noting that the statement was impressionistic at best and has no empirical evidence to support it. Instead, the student focuses on why de Tocqueville said it.

The paragraphs following provide an accurate summary of the religious fervor of the period. Unfortunately, the student forgets to bring de Tocqueville back at the conclusion of the essay. Given the religious excitement of the time, just how observant was de Tocqueville in making his statement, and was it valid after all?

Possible student score: 7

Part C

Question 4 Student Essay

In the election of 1912, former president Teddy Roosevelt, running as the candidate of the Progressive Party after loosing the Republican nomination to William Howard Taft, and the Democratic candidate Woodrow Wilson campaigned on different programs to address the issues facing the country. Roosevelt called his program, which he had first outlined in 1910, the New Nationalism while Wilson backed what he called the New Freedom.

The New Nationalism accepted both big government and big business. Roosevelt argued that busting up the trusts was less a priority than regulating business in the public interest. A strong federal government was necessary to control business but also to protect the interests of those who could not protect themselves—workers, women, and children. The Progressive party platform called for the 8-hour day, an end to child labor, and giving women the right to vote. The New Freedom was based on the premise that it was not enough to regulate monopolies — they had to be eliminated completely. Wilson criticized Roosevelt often during the campaign for his willingness to tolerate the trusts.

While he may have believed that a strong central government was necessary in the short term to restore competition in the business world, Wilson did not believe it was a permanent feature of American life. Indeed, he felt that many of the social issues that Roosevelt expected the Federal government to address were best left to the states and cities.

With the Republican vote split between Roosevelt and Taft, Wilson easily won the presidency in 1912 and quickly implemented key parts of the New Freedom program—tariffs were significantly reduced as a means of increasing competition, a new banking system was created, the Federal Reserve, to limit the influence of large Wall Street banks over interest rates and the country's money supply, and uncompetitive business practices were outlawed through the Clayton Anti-Trust Act. The Clayton Act along with the creation of the Federal Trade Commission did little to eliminate the trusts, and were more clearly attempts at regulation. Wilson's priorities also seemed to change as he moved into his second term.

While Wilson's second term was dominated by World War I and the fight over ratification of the Treaty of Versailles, important pieces of domestic legislation were passed with the president's support that were more in line with the New Nationalism than the New Freedom. These included low interest federal loans to farmers, the establishment of the 8-hour day for railroad workers across the country, and the Keating-Owen Child Labor Act that prohibited goods made by children under the age of 14 from being sold in interstate commerce. The new laws suggested had come to accept a larger role for the federal government than he had advocated during the campaign, recognizing as Roosevelt had that big government had become a fact of American political life.

Reader's Comments

This essay provides some excellent comparisons and contrasts between the New Nationalism and the New Freedom. It would have been strengthened considerably had the student clearly stated a thesis concerning the programs. The first paragraph merely identifies what is already given in the question. The essay does pick up steam in the remainder of the narrative, providing a clear understanding of what the two programs were and how they differed. The essay finishes with a very strong conclusion noting that not only did Wilson implement his program, he borrowed from Roosevelt in acknowledging the larger role of the federal government. The stylistic and grammatical errors are minimal enough not to detract from the essay.

Possible student score: 8

Part C

Question 5 Student Essay

With the authority of the Gulf of Tonkin Resolution (August 1964) and justified by attacks on American military personnel, the Johnson administration began the build up of combat troops in Vietnam in March 1965. In addition to ground troops, an extensive bombing campaign known as Operation Rolling Thunder got underway. By the end of the year, there were close to 200,000 American troops in South Vietnam, and the troop level rose to almost 400,000 by 1966, 1965 marked a critical turning point in the war because the decision was made by the administration to "Americanize" the conflict in Southeast Asia.

1968 is a crucial year in the history of the Vietnam conflict for several reasons.

The North Vietnamese and the Viet Cong were able to launch major actions throughout the South in what became known as the Tet Offensive. American military commanders had been convinced that North Vietnam was on the verge of defeat before Tet. More important, the offensive convinced many Americans, including those in the media who had long supported the war, that the conflict in Vietnam was unwinnable. This noticeable shift in public opinion combined with the stronger than expected showing by Senator Eugene McCarthy in the New Hampshire primary convinced President Johnson not to run for a full second term. Johnson announced a limited halt to the bombing against North Vietnam and direct negotiations to end the war began in Paris in May 1968.

Vocal opposition to the war intensified and turned violent at the Democratic convention in 1968. The war was an important factor in the election of Richard Nixon.

By 1970, Nixon's "secret plan" to end the war—which was to withdraw American ground troops and turn more and more of the fighting over to the South Vietnamese army—had significantly reduced U.S. involvement. Ironically, Nixon also expanded the war. He announced that American troops have moved into Cambodia to attack North Vietnamese bases. Nixon's announcement of the move into Cambodia led directly to the most deadly confrontation of the anti-war movement when several demonstrators were killed by National Guard troops at Kent State University. The war continued to drag on for another three years.

Reader's Comments

The student has an unusual command of the specific details in the events of 1965, 1968, and 1970. However, less attention is paid to the question of why these years were significant as "critical turning points in American involvement in Southeast Asia." The challenge for the student is to see the events in the broader context of the question, and to use that context as a thesis to justify the significance of those years. The last sentence of the first paragraph would serve better as a thesis statement for 1965. Instead, the reader must read through supportive details before getting to the main point. The idea is to capture the reader's attention with a strong topic statement, then follow with the supporting information.

The second paragraph offers a stronger assessment since it begins with a promise to give the reasons why the year 1968 is significant. The final paragraph, however, basically summarizes the year's events without really stating why 1970 would be more critical than 1971 or 1972. The essay doesn't really end—it just leaves the war "to drag on for another three years." The essay contains a high level of accurate content, but this is offset by a lack of focus on explaining the significance of the years.

Possible student score: 6

Final Preparation

Before the Exam

1. Begin your final preparation about a month before the exam. Start with taking one of the sample tests in this study guide to identify either subjects or time periods that you need to review in more detail.

2. Devote the week before the exam to reviewing the information in this study guide on the format and analysis of exam areas; review your notes one more time.

3. Relax the evening before the exam, and get a good night's sleep. Trying to cram a year's worth of reading and studying into one night is a waste of time.

Taking the Exam

4. Give yourself plenty of time to get to the test location early.

5. Remember to bring all the materials you need for the exam — admission ticket, identification, two Number 2 pencils with good erasers, and two good-quality, medium-tip ballpoint pens with blue or black ink.

6. Listen carefully to the instructions of the proctor, and follow the directions in the test booklets.

7. On the multiple-choice section, make sure to read each of the questions carefully and completely; underline or make notes to clarify the questions.

8. Avoid wild guessing. If you don't know the answer, clearly mark it so that you can come back to it later.

9. Use the fifteen-minute reading period to make notes on the DBQ and documents, outline your answer, and review the standard essays.

10. Write your essays to inform, not to impress the reader; pay attention to organizing the essays as tightly as possible.

11. Don't panic if you draw a complete blank as soon as you open the test booklet. Take a deep breath, and the panic will pass.